CLUSTER COMPUTING

CLUSTER COMPUTING

RAJKUMAR BUYYA AND CLEMENS SZYPERSKI
(EDITORS)

Nova Science Publishers, Inc.
Huntington, New York

Senior Editors: Susan Boriotti and Donna Dennis
Office Manager: Annette Hellinger
Graphics: Wanda Serrano and Dorothy Marczak
Information Editor: Tatiana Shohov
Book Production: Cathy DeGregory, Matthew Kozlowski, Jonathan Rose, Jennifer Vogt and Lynette Van Helden
Circulation: Ave Maria Gonzalez and Andre Tillman

Library of Congress Cataloging-in-Publication Data
available upon request

ISBN 1-59033-113-3

227 Main Street, Suite 100
Huntington, New York 11743
Tele. 631-424-6682 Fax 631-425-5933
e-mail: Novascience@earthlink.net
Web Site: http://www.nexusworld.com/nova

Printed in the United States of America

CONTENTS

PREFACE

The history of computing has always also been a history of hunting for higher performance. Until recently it was accepted that to go beyond the current sweet spot in terms of performance per money of available machines, it was required to invest. In fact, to invest enormously. While dedicated high end machines still have their place, and probably always will, the construction of special machines close to the top and that of clusters of less dramatic machines co-evolved to something quite comparable. As a result, engineering sparks could bridge the gab and we now find high-performance system area and even local area networks that derive from the backbone communication infrastructure of massively parallel supercomputers.

Being faced with the possibility to assemble ones own supercomputer out of off-the-shelf components, such as high-end PCs, changed the performance scene markedly. The hardware substrate for modest to impressive supercomputing equipment is now suddenly ubiquitously available. As a result, not surprisingly, the parallel computing are attracted a boost of attention. Also not surprisingly, there is a desire to reduce the traditional reliance on a select few who intimately understood the inner workings of the latest generation supercomputers to really make them fly. Finally, there is often a need to share the computing infrastructure between virtual supercomputers and the more mundane everyday use of the `borrowed' workstations. Methodology and software infrastructure need to be almost reinvented to properly address all the new challenges – but without losing what has been learnt in the past.

This book suggests that there are a lot of activities on the way indeed. As a result, the editors had great difficulty selecting papers out of the overwhelmingly large number of submissions. The selected articles both demonstrate diversity and quality of this still relatively young field.

Rajkumar Buyya
School of Computer Science and Software Engineering
Monash University

Clemens Szyperski
School of Computing Science
Queensland University of Technology

EXPERIENCES WITH WINDOWS NT AS A CLUSTER COMPUTING PLATFORM FOR PARALLEL COMPUTING.

MARKUS FISCHER * AND JACK DONGARRA †

Abstract. The increasing number of clusters built by commercial, off the shelf hardware shows a new trend in scientific computing. Within this movement is the propagation towards Windows NT as an operating system on PCs. The UNIX environment and Windows NT differ in terms of administrative issues as well as programming techniques. In this paper, we describe the modification of PVM (Parallel Virtual Machine) to enable interoperation with WIN32 (Windows NT 4/5 and Windows 95/98). PVM provides the functionality to harness the computing power of an WIN32 cluster environment. Our migration from UNIX to the WIN32 architecture not only shows where porting existing software is easy and where more generic modules have to be designed, but also the limitations.

Key words. Heterogeneity, Message Passing, Cluster Computing, Networking, Windows NT

1. Introduction. Cluster computing on networks of workstations has been thoroughly researched on various UNIX-type architectures in the recent years. However, the familiar environment is about to change. Clusters built from commercial, off the shelf systems running Linux or Windows NT are joining the platform of scientific computing and are considered to be a new trend in supercomputing. In addition to the inexpense of the hardware, its compatibility is a major advantage.

A major change can also be seen in the performance of commodity interconnects. New network technologies like Myrinet [1] or Scalable Coherent Interface (SCI) [2] that connect single units to large scaling clusters offer communication latency and throughput previously known only on high-end, massively parallel systems.

PVM (Parallel Virtual Machine) has been available for the WIN32 (Windows NT 4/5 and Windows 95/98) platform for approximately two years [3]. During that time, the inverse relationship between price and performance of Intel based architectures has grown significantly. Thus, it is not surprising to see an increased interest in clustering WIN32 machines using PVM as the distributed communication interface. Our statistics show that the download numbers of the WIN32 version from Netlib account for one third of the total PVM downloads. Windows NT is even being considered as an up-and-coming front-end standard. However, the WIN32 environment is not as practical for a cluster approach as one might think. This is especially the case when the system is taken right out of the box. For example, a typical configuration of an Windows

*University of California, San Diego, CA 92093

†Mathematical Science Section, Oak Ridge National Laboratory, Oak Ridge, TN 37831

NT cluster including one Windows NT Server and multiple Windows NT Workstations allows multiple users to work on a set of machines, but resources are limited to the machine a user is actually physically present. Only the installation of additional software which is partly provided by Microsoft (e.g: Resource Kit, Developer Kit) but mainly available as shareware tools, extend the properties to a time shared system. Other popular projects like HPVM [5] even require to use expensive commercial software like Platform Computing's LSF [6] to be able to handle a cluster consisting of up to 256 Windows NT workstations. While LSF is providing scheduling mechanisms and process placement, additional software is available which allows the visualization and interaction with a remote desktop. While these features are standards on UNIX flavored systems, some of these modifications lower security standards to Windows NT. With the lack of a network file system and the demonstrated resource limitations, the handling of a larger Windows NT cluster can be seen as unsatisfactory.

This is already a fact in a homogeneous WIN32 environment, but a heterogeneous scenario including UNIX based systems even worsens the situation. Here software packages like Samba allow file exchange between UNIX and Windows NT, but interoperability between both architectures is still unstandardized. Basically the huge number of non standard installation types is responsible for a large amount of time spent in user support. A big difference can also be seen in completing a product under laboratory conditions and a successful installation on different sites.

By providing PVM on Windows based machines, it has been our approach to ship a software package, that allows the clustering of Windows and UNIX machines. Although the information policy and the description of available interface calls does not ease development progress, we finally succeeded in offering a message passing environment, which does not rely on any other shareware tool. As a matter of fact, any user can install, start and use PVM with a default Windows NT cluster installation. Only the configuration of a service that ships with our software requires administrative privileges. This service adds a remote shell daemon to WIN32 machines to enable remote computations. So far this feature has been available as a limited shareware tool only.

PVM was the first non commercial message passing interface on top of Windows NT starting with PVM version 3.3.11 in May 1996. At this time WPVM [7] from the University of Coimbra, Portugal was also available. This product however was in a very unstable condition and most people even did not get it running at all.

Currently, several commercial MPI versions also work on Windows NT (see [8]). In addition, Calypso [9] is another possible solution for providing a parallel processing environment on Windows NT networks. Calypso, however, can only run within a homogeneous Windows NT environment. PVM, on the other hand, runs in a heterogeneous environment across multiple platforms, which allows a virtual machine to consist of a variety of systems ranging from laptop's to Supercomputers. Besides different message passing implementation details, all projects have thus far originated from the UNIX environment and have not had to cope with Windows NT as a new environment. Our experience shows, that such a migration can not be expected to be straight forward. Changing only the system calls does not work and several issues related to network computing have to be addressed. These issues include the following:

- security
- the installation of additional services/daemons
- interprocess communication, external data exchange
- dynamic process control for local or remote systems
- various Windows installation types and configurations

The subject of this paper is to evaluate the approach and feasibility of cluster computing on Windows NT.

The paper is organized as follows. First we will give an overview of the PVM system followed by the description of our implementation. This will lead to a more general discussion about migrating from UNIX to WIN32. Finally, after providing a small guide to our software package, we conclude our experience.

2. The PVM System. PVM (Parallel Virtual Machine) is a popular message passing interface. It is an integrated set of software tools and libraries that emulate a general-purpose, flexible, heterogeneous, and concurrent computing framework on interconnected computers of varied architectures. The overall objective of the PVM system is to enable such a collection of computers to be used cooperatively for concurrent or parallel computation.

2.1. Available Architectures and Network Layers. PVM is available for **40+** different architectures combining Unix workstations, shared memory machines, and MPP's to one single parallel virtual machine. The WIN32 architecture was added to PVM in Version 3.4 after developing a compatible version to its predecessor. WIN32 is becoming popular and more important from day to day. This can also be seen in the amount of available hardware platforms. Following Intel and Alpha, SGI will support an Windows NT platform for their systems as well. Even though commercial processors achieve the same performance as processors on supercomputers at lower costs [10], the trend on local systems is the migration to SMP machines. In fact, the scheduling mechanism within Windows NT is being optimized for eight processors in the next version. Multithreaded programming can then make use of the potential resources but can not perform distributed computing. Windows applications have existed for several years and the benefits that come with using PVM are obvious. Using existing equipment and operating systems, PVM's application could be used to

- solve large industry problems like parallelized combinatorical optimization algorithms (Job Scheduling, Cutting Stock, DNA Analysis) in your office
- utilize computers in High Schools for teaching purposes.
- combine built-in and compiler optimized functions with parallel processing power.
- route scientific data to standard front ends with special hardware (3D Graphic cards)

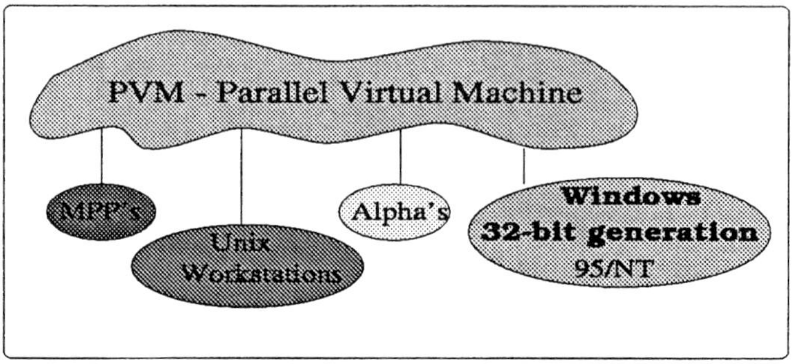

FIG. 2.1. *The PVM Model*

PVM's most powerful feature is that it provides the message passing interface that makes an application believe its running on a single machine. Another advantage within the dynamic concept is that PVM is easily extendible to take advantage of other network architectures that are providing lower latency and higher bandwidth than conventional interconnects. Most of them ship with a TCP/IP layer but TCP implementations have been shown to be inefficient on many platforms [4]. UNIX extensions for PVM exist on Parastation [11] and Scalable Coherent Interface (SCI) [12] to take advantage of the underlying network. PVM-SCI is also available on Windows NT and based on our WIN32 implementation.

A port of PVM on top of Easynet and BIP [13] is planned as well. Basically, a trend can be seen in eliminating the protocol stack when communicating with remote processes. The new network layers have in common that they offer mechanisms for bypassing the OS kernel, where convential protocols (using sockets for example) spend significant time. Such mechanisms reduce latency to 6-10 μ and increase bandwidth to 60 MB/s at the user level.

2.2. Facing the WIN32 Implementation of PVM. Although Windows 95/98 and Windows NT 4.0/5.0 are members of the WIN32 architecture, restrictions apply to the number of available WIN32 API calls for Windows 95/98. While Windows 95/98 is designed to provide downgrade compatibility, Windows NT is considered a real multi-user, multi-tasking operating system. As a matter of fact, only Windows NT offers SMP capability. A further step towards a WIN32 operating system is the separate process / address space in Windows NT. This results in better performance and fault tolerance, whereas processes under Windows 95/98 only run in a virtual DOS machine.

In prior versions of Windows, direct access to the hardware was possible, which caused undesired shutdowns when conflicts arose. Windows NT is more stable since function calls are passed to device drivers that access the hardware. This difference is kept transparent to the programmer. Although Windows NT does not offer much multi user support by default an interface exist to impersonate different users. In this context, *impersonation* means the validation of new processes under a different account. As opposed to UNIX, this is not an easy task. For example, Windows 95/98 allows only one user to be logged in at one time. Therefore, it does not provide a function which lets the system differentiate access privileges, thus every process actually has administrative privileges. In general, one can say that WIN32 provides API calls that only work on one of the operating systems. Basically, Windows 95/98 only provides a subset of available WIN32 API calls.

Besides stability and performance issues, the lack of any security under Windows 95/98 even worsens the situation. Under Windows NT, security can be set to a variety of objects. Objects in this sense can be the file system, named pipes, mutexes, shared memory segments and so on.

For this reason, the PVM code itself switches to the operating system being executed on.

One general major drawback with WIN32 is unavailable remote process creation. Unlike UNIX, basic services are missing in the standard WIN32 implementations. In this case, PVM's feature not to distinguish between operating systems during runtime causes problems when creating the virtual machine. For remote startup, the PVM package provides a BSD compliant remote shell service for Windows 95/98 and Windows NT that allows process startups from remote hosts. However, a username and the matching password have to be provided when this service is configured, since both parameters are required by the WIN32 API to log on a different user. In this context, one might say that Windows NT is not providing a friendly environment for distributed computation. While primitive exist to pass authenticated handles to other hosts within an NT cluster, this concept fails when programs are executed in an heterogeneous environment including UNIX for example.

PVM's Process Control. Like the original PVM, this version uses the concept of daemon processes for the setup of the virtual machine. The main functions of these daemons are to start or delete new tasks, to route messages between tasks, and to establish direct connections for better performance [14]. Different from the UNIX version is the need for a separate *hoster* process, which is responsible for starting up slave daemons on other hosts. Invisible to the user, the host process is started automatically and runs as a task of the virtual machine. Since PVM is designed to run accross multiple platforms, a common startup mechanism is required. Originating from UNIX the *rsh call* fires up remote daemons. Since PVM does not differentiate between hosts and architectures, a rsh call is also placed to add WIN32 hosts. To overcome the security problems involved with the installation of an rsh daemon, it is also possible to perform a manual startup. Fig. 2.2 gives an overview of the startup of pvmd clients. It also portrays the processes involved when creating a virtual machine.

The Communication Layer. Messages between processes are exchanged using Windows WinSockets, which offer TCP and UDP on top of the IP layer. The specification is close to the BSD standard, however it is not possible to handle sockets as file or stream descriptors. It differs also from the standard by initializing and closing a socket structure, where the version of the socket layer must be specified. However, WinSockets allow communication across the WIN32

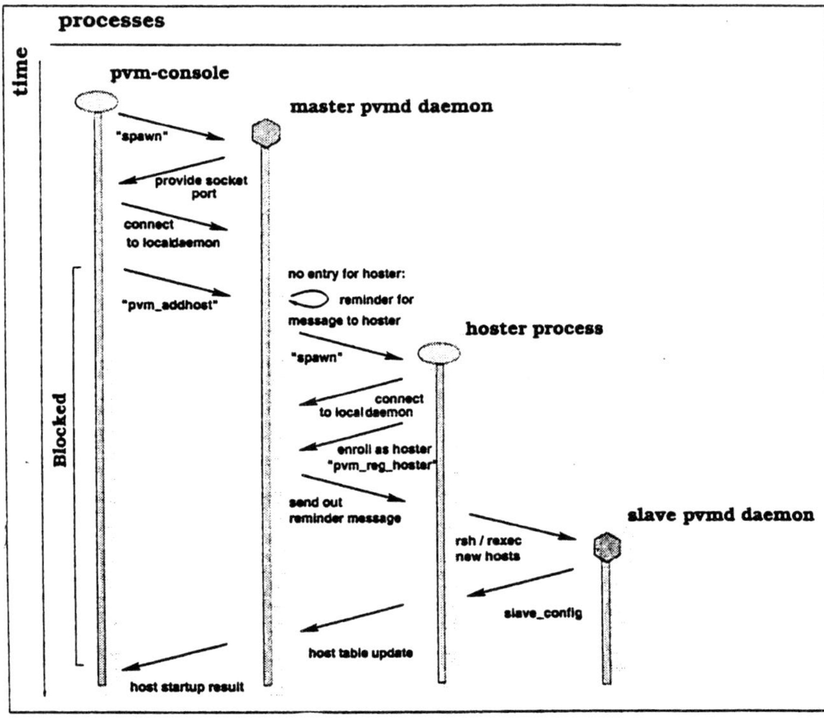

FIG. 2.2. *PVM Startup Protocol*

architecture and a faster TCP connection can be established as well. Using a heterogeneous system with different architectures requires encoding and decoding of messages if messages are sent to a different platform. The WIN32 version offers its own XDR en- / decoding possibilities. Like the existing PVM, message buffers can be created in three different manners; PvmDataInPlace (fastest method, only pointer to the message data is stored and packed for message transfer without encoding), PvmDataRaw (a copy of the data is made and sent out without encoding), PvmDataDefault (a encoded copy is sent out).

Messages sent between one architecture type should use PvmDataRaw or, even better, PvmDataInPlace, if possible. XDR en- /decoding is expensive and slows down performance (dependent on CPU power).

Security Aspects. As mentioned earlier, WIN32 offers sufficient security only for Windows NT. Security can be set to objects, where objects range from sockets, processes, files, or pipes. Access is restricted to objects by a personal Security Identifier (SID), which stores granted privileges. In PVM, an important security aspect is a secure file system so that users can deny access to their files. Thus security is only given on Windows NT and furthermore only, when NTFS is available on the system. Using Windows 95/98 (FAT32), data can be

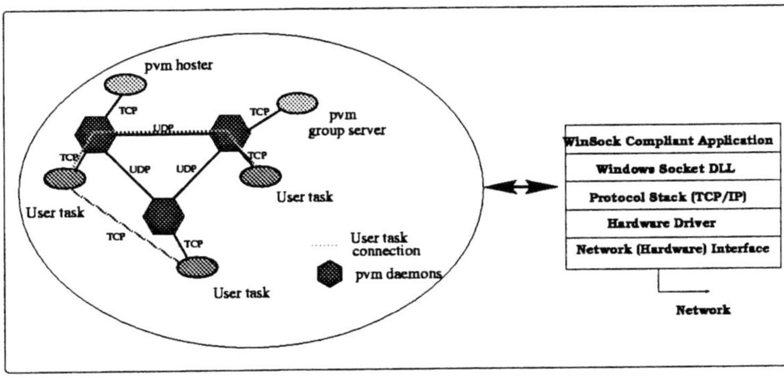

FIG. 2.3. *Communication and Layout of PVM*

accessed by everyone in *read-* as well as in *write mode.* In PVM a process that would like to enroll into the virtual machine reads a socket address out of the `%PVM_TMP%\pvmd.username` file. Since this file is readable for every process, different users can get access to the pvmd daemon. It is therefore recommended, for security reasons, to run Windows NT with at least one partition under NTFS as the operating system.

3. Using WIN32 as a Platform for Cluster Computing. When originating from the UNIX environment, a developer's first option is to look at the Windows NT POSIX subsystem. However, this subsystem only supports POSIX 1003.1, which was the only POSIX version standardized when Windows NT was created. Since then, there has been little demand for extending this subsystem because most applications have been converted to WIN32. The 1003.1 system is of limited interest for fully featured applications because it does not include many capabilities (such as those in 1003.2, network support, etc.). Full featured applications that run under the Windows NT POSIX subsystem do not have access to Windows NT features available to Win32 applications, such as memory-mapped files, networking, and graphics. Applications such as VI, LS, and GREP are the main targets for the Windows NT POSIX subsystem.

The second option UNIX programmers normally consider is using third-party, UNIX-like libraries to let their UNIX code compile as a WIN32 executable. Several commercial (and at least one public domain) libraries do this. This is an option for some applications. The advantage of these porting libraries is that they minimize the initial porting effort. The main disadvantage for a competitive software product is that a native WIN32 port of an application will generally be faster and will inevitably have more functionality. It can be awkward for the application to step outside of its UNIX shell if it needs to make WIN32 calls to get more power from Windows NT. Furthermore announced operating systems like the Windows 2000 series will execute existing WIN32 programs by default but third party packages may not work immediately and their policy often requires the purchase of an upgrade.

The third option is porting UNIX applications directly to Win32. Using ANSI C/C++ libraries and commercial C compiler libraries, many of the traditional system calls that UNIX applications rely on are available in Win32 applications.

3.1. Different Views of NT Clusters. Parallel computing on systems running a UNIX-like operating system brought along the ease of accessing different machines remotely. Access in this case means sharing computing resources as well as data storage (using NFS for example). However, WIN32 is more like a client server architecture in terms of file distribution, except it does not offer remote activities at all. This sharing concept leads to three installation types of PVM.

First is a *single node* type where PVM is installed on each drive of potential hosts. This requires entries to the registry as well as file storage on several hosts. The single node type, however, is not easy to maintain, since remote access is difficult. A registry entry for PVM_ROOT would look like PVM_ROOT=`c:\pvm\pvm3.4` for example. Second is a *server* type where PVM is installed on one sharable drive. This means that the executables must also be accessible from remote machines. This is fairly easy since WIN32 provides this *sharing* mechanism. Note that such access is granted to the file system only, not to computing resources. With this server type, a client type can be set up such that clients point their registry entries to the file location on the server. During startup, files would be transferred via the network. This type reflects the NFS installation known from UNIX. Clients would then have a PVM_ROOT entry of PVM_ROOT=`\\servername\c\pvm\pvm3.4`. Finally, a multiple Server type has to be used when distributed applications are in different domains and a trust relationship is not set up for security reasons.

3.2. Extending current programming methods to more dynamic modules. Besides configuration management, the WIN32 architecture differs from UNIX-like environments in various ways when using it as a programming platform. Programming not only affects the call of different API's, but the modification of program layout is affected as well, since most of the known POSIX functions are not provided. Within the PVM on WIN32 project, first steps are made in porting an existing software package. This allows distributed computation to a different environment, which further allows us to work on a more general specification of interfaces to an open, extendible environment. Portability is especially essential for HARNESS, our next, even more flexible, environment [16].

When choosing Windows NT as a cluster computing platform our experience shows that changing the system calls will not work in a safe way. Basically, the following modules have to be redesigned or ported from UNIX:

WIN32 API Calls vs ANSI C. The work involved in porting code is a question of how operating system-specific the existing application is. Basically, WIN32 provides a C Runtime library which covers most of existing application's code. But several functions or features are not available in WIN32 or have a different interface. Advanced programming using signals, for example, is not available under WIN32. Here, methods would have to be developed to use structured exception handling (SEH). Furthermore, different API's have to be called for accessing or creating files if security is available. File descriptors are another factor for breaking up existing code. Under UNIX file descriptors are used for stdin, stdout, files, sockets and so on.

When programming for Windows NT, a developer will actually find a way to open a socket and treat it as a file descriptor.

However, this is not working for Windows 9X and some actions on the socket will cause this transformed socket to shut down under Windows NT as well. Another situation is given when using file descriptors on console based applications. A `select()` call on input from the console and sockets has to be split up using different methods under WIN32.

There are several other WIN32 API calls that are new when coming from the UNIX site. Most of them are closely related to the operating system (like writing services, developing device drivers, creating several flavors of pipes) but they also deal with the versatile ways of configuring a machine. Depending on the purpose of a cluster (public pool, dedicated computing platform), one could lower security while restricting the environment to allow word processing only. Since there are many issues about migration existing code from UNIX to WIN32 that cannot be generalized, web sites or databases will help most in finding an individual solution (see [15] for example).

Security Issues and Privileges

. Security in PVM is based on a secure file system. Convenient commands like `chmod()` are not available under WIN32. Whereas UNIX provides three classes of privileges (root, groups and user), WIN32 provides a variety of different privileges. Using a security model, such privileges can be assigned to handle objects. In this context, security can be set for file handling while restricting access to other users, even administrators. In this way, the security model in WIN32 is much better than in UNIX, however it is more difficult to program.

The Installation of Services/Daemons

. PVM uses *rsh* for starting up slave hosts. Since the PVM model is transparent to various architectures, it does not differ between architectures on startup either. Since WIN32 does not offer remote computation, a rshd compliant service had to be developed. The programming of a service is versatile task. On the one hand a service can be seen as a regular process, on the other hand it has to follow specific steps to enroll as a service. This also involves a handling section for incoming requests from the operating system, for example, to request whether the service is still active, but also to halt the service. Furthermore there is not much documentation available in writing a service. It actually makes a big difference if the service is in a debugging phase or has been installed. The reason is that the usage of advanced API's requires special privileges, which are not set to any user by default. During our research, we were surprised that, even with administrative privileges, impersonating a process is not an easy task (a UNIX developer may think of the `setuid()` call for this case). As a matter of fact a combination of three privileges finally granted access to the required API call. On the one hand this increases security but on the other hand this property questions the number of incoming requests for support for a shipping product. Fortunately, a service which runs under the SYSTEM account holds every privilege by default. This way no special privilege has to be set up for a user during installation and the program has been tested thoroughly. However, during the development phase the programmer's machine has to be modified.

Moreover, it is still unsatisfying, that a user has to provide its password so that a service will be able to put a request in a user's context. For a heterogeneous scenario this is definitely a required fact. The latest research however shows, that within a Windows NT environment these policies are different, assumed the user has logged on to the domain. In this case the user received an access token from the machine he is working on. This access token can be passed to other machines when using an object where this access token can be set to. Then a service can actually duplicate this access token and place a new process in this context. For this reason, our service has been extended to handle both possibilities.

Distributed Computing in a Windows Production Environment

. Assumed that a distributed application is running on a Windows cluster, a bizarre situation can occur when people working on a machine decide to log off. In this case Windows 95/98/NT decides to kill all running applications, no matter if they have been running before or are running under a different user context. The only solution for this case is to place remote processes in a service context. The major drawback is that for this group of people a privilege has to modified to be allowed to log on as service. Although this is not a security issue, it requires additional administration and a reconfiguration of the OS after a successful installation is again error prone. Fortunately the placement into a service context can be build transparent into the PVM library and the process control coming with the PVM daemon is responsible for cleaning up application tasks.

IPC and Network

. WIN32 offers several mechanisms for IPC. In addition to anonymous pipes, it provides named pipes, which offer security even across the network. Named pipes, however, only work under NT. Other mechanisms are Mailslots or shared memory, which is based on the file interface yet kept in memory. These functions are not portable from UNIX but can be encapsulated in a module. Using sockets to communicate via the network requires additional startup, but as our experience shows, a fault tolerant wrapper is also needed around the send routines. While still up and running under WIN32, some sockets shutdown under UNIX. Besides this feature, WinSockets behave like expected and allow interoperability with UNIX without further complications.

Dynamic Process Control for Local or Remote Systems

. A major disadvantage is the lack of the `fork()` command. Several advanced UNIX programs use this call for convenient mechanisms. Some programs, however, follow the setting of new environment variables with an execute command.

WIN32 offers several options to create a new task, but the `CreateProcess()` is most usable, since it enables setup of environment variables as well as special startup parameters (e.g., for debugging purposes). It is also the only command which has the same behavior under both Windows 9X and Windows NT.

Besides migration issues, WIN32 lacks standardization, which increases the amount of support time. WIN32 is a highly commercial platform that has a variety of software developers and vendors in tow, which is causing the most problems when entering the new area.

3.3. Non - compatibility within WIN32

. Our experience in migration reveals not only the need for dynamic modules in a plug-in like manner, but that the modules also have to cope with different compilers. Code running under Visual C++ might fail when recompiled with Watcom, for example. Even worse, libraries from different vendors can be used for linking. Therefore, we provide multiple compiler brands since a limitation to only one compiler would force users to purchase the provided product. Providing only the source files with a generic makefile that includes several compiler switches, as our experience shows, will result in a flood of help messages because NT offers too many methods of installation. But even after a successful compilation, the software may not work. Administrators may find their own method of installation and put too tight of security on a system, which might not even allow the storage of temporary data for installation.

4. Using PVM. The hassle in providing basic information about how to set environment variables under WIN32 and the restrictions mentioned above resulted in providing a guided installation. Our product is using Installshield which is a Back, Next, and Browse-clickable tour to install PVM without any problems. Users can choose between a local, remote, or server installation. This installation is subdivided again in a *Typical, Common* or *Administrative* type where the latter one also allows the rshd configuration. Furthermore, different compiler libraries are provided and the registry is modified to start PVM with ease. For recompiling our examples, makefiles are modified during installation, so that the user is ready to go after clicking the *Finish* button.

4.1. Setting Up a Virtual Machine. The PVM console can be used as a convenient way to interact with the pvmd. This process can be used to add other hosts to the virtual machine. It will pass a hostfile to the master daemon if provided, as well as allow manual add's. It will also reset the parallel virtual machine if tasks hang.

Finally, the PVM console provides the possibility of a proper shutdown. Tasks can be started within the console and the 'ps -a' command gives information about running tasks on every machine in the VM.

4.2. Creating and Debugging a PVM Application. Sequential code can be parallelized using PVM's message passing interface. The algorithm has to be changed so that processes can divide up work and gather the solution. These functions can be found in the PVM library.

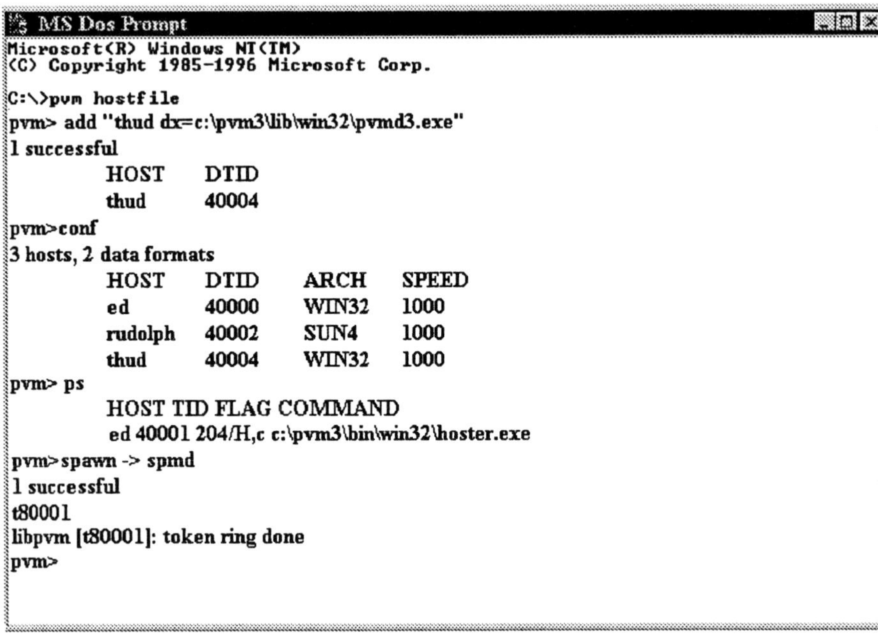

FIG. 4.1. *PVM Session*

A linking with `$(PVM_ROOT)`/lib/`$(PVM_ARCH)`/libpvm3.lib is necessary. When group functionality is needed, the application also has to link with `$(PVM_ROOT)`/lib /`$(PVM_ARCH)`/libgpvm3.lib.

Fortran applications will also run in WIN32. They have to be linked with `$(PVM_ROOT)`/libfpvm/`$(PVM_ARCH)`/libfpvm3.lib. Note that this is the first Fortran interface in a WIN32 message passing interface. Current WIN32 MPI implementations still do not support the Fortran interface.

Debugging is also possible in the WIN32 version. The common way in PVM is to start a new task with the PvmTaskDebug flag. Under UNIX, the task is then started under a debugger. Different from the existing Unix version, the new task is started on the local or remote machine but waits for the connection of debugger. Users then have to start their debugger manually on the local machine and then choose the option for local or remote process attachment.

5. Conclusion. As tests have shown, the PVM package on top of Windows NT brings reliable parallel computing possibilities. Crashed applications do not interfere with the operating system and users do not have to to be afraid of causing unwanted shutdowns. It is also possible to have multiple, communicating processes running on one machine as well as share one host for multiple virtual machines. Users can take their existing PVM application and run it on the new architecture. There is no need for long lasting modifications since the PVM programming paradigm is mimicked by the PVM library.

Basically, the number of extensions to new interconnects and the number of downloads occurring with WIN32 shows the popularity of PVM as a research platform. Especially the service, being a very important part of our software package, has been an ongoing research project for approximately 15 months. While a shareware tool was needed earlier, we now offer a solid and complete solution to start cluster computing under Windows 95/98/NT without the installation of any other tool or third party software package.

To summarize the experience made in porting existing code from UNIX to Windows one can say that it is not possible to provide a general solution, which addresses all possible development situations. However, facing PVM's dynamic properties we had to deal with most problems we can think of. For sure several months have to be spent in research before porting code takes place. Progress during this time is not necessarily evident, but experiences are made in getting a look and feel on the new environment in that way that problems can be at least addressed to the appropriate forums. Another big step is then to actually start developing programs in this versatile environment.

PVM for UNIX and WIN32 environments and the services for WIN32 are freely available at netlib [17].

REFERENCES

[1] Myricom. Myrinet link and routing specification, 1995. http://www.myri.com/myricom/document.html

[2] IEEE Std for Scalable Coherent Interface (SCI). Inst. of Electrical and Electronical Eng., Inc., New York, NY 10017, IEEE std 1596-1992,1993.

[3] M. Fischer and J. Dongarra. *PVM comes into every office.*, CCC 97 Atlanta, USA 1997.

[4] J. Kay and J. Pasquale. *Profiling and reducing processing overheads in tcp/ip.* IEEE/ACM Transactions on Networking, December 1996.

[5] http://www-csag.cs.uiuc.edu/projects/clusters.html

[6] http://www.platform.com

[7] University of Portugal, Coumbria.

[8] M. Baker, G. Fox. *MPI on NT: A preliminary evaluation of the available systems* In Workshop PC-NOW, IPPS/SPDP98, Orlando, USA, 1998.

[9] http://calypso.eas.asu.edu/calypso/default.htm

[10] Alfred Aburto *PDS: The Performance Database Server* November 26, 1995, Naval Ocean Systems Center, San Diego http://performance.netlib.org/performance/html/PDStop.html

[11] J.M. Blum, T.M. Warschko, W.F. Tichy. *PULC: ParaStation User-Level Communication. Design and Overview*, IPPS Orlando March 98.

[12] Markus Fischer, Jens Simon. *Embedding SCI into PVM. Proc. of EuroPVM/MPI '97*, Cracow, Poland, pp. 183-191,1997.

[13] L. Prylli and B. Tourancheau. Bip: a new protocol designed for high performance networking on myrinet. In Workshop PC-NOW, IPPS/SPDP98, Orlando, USA, 1998.

[14] Al Geist, Adam Beguelin, Jack Dongarra, Weicheng Jiang, Robert Manchek, Vaidy Sunderam *PVM: Parallel Virtual Machine A Users' Guide and Tutorial for Networked Parallel Computing* 1994. Published by MIT Press, Boston. http://www.netlib.org/pvm3/book/pvm-book.html

[15] http://www.experts-exchange.com

[16] A. Geist et al. *Harness, the next generation beyond PVM.* http://www.epm.ornl.gov/harness

[17] http://www.netlib.org/pvm3/index.html

DISTRIBUTED PROCESSING OF REMOTELY SENSED LANDSAT-TM IMAGERY USING MPI

J. A. GALLUD , J. GARCÍA-CONSUEGRA , AND A. MARTÍNEZ *

Abstract. One of the constraints in remotely-sensed images processing is the computational resources required. Distributed processing is applied in remote sensing in order to reduce spatial or temporal cost using the message passing paradigm. In this paper, we present a workbench developed to provide a framework to perform the distributed processing of Landsat images using a cluster of NT workstations. A set of functions and a message structure, called DIPORSI, have been designed to distribute the main algorithms employed in remote sensing. Thus, the large amount of time required by the sequential process drops when the distributed algorithm is used. Our application is based on the NT implementation (WinMPICH) of the MPI standard.

Key words. HPC on clusters, remote sensing, MPI, Windows NT

AMS subject classifications. 15A15, 15A09, 15A23, 68M14, 68N19, 68M20

1. Introduction. Remote sensing involves the manipulation and interpretation of digital images which have been captured from remote sensors on board of satellite or aircraft systems. Such images collect information about the Earth's surface, which allow scientists to perform many environmental studies.

Remotely sensed image processing is an interesting application area for distributed computing techniques, which has become more and more attractive both for the spatial resolution increase of the new sensor generation, and for the emerging use of Geographic Information Systems (GIS) in environment studies [1]. The large data volumes involved and the consequent processing bottleneck may indeed reduce their effective use in many real situations, and hence the need for exploring the possibility of splitting both the data and processing over several storing and computing units.

Remote sensed imagery processing involves several steps that begin when a image is acquired by the satellite, and continue with the image analysis and processing to obtain, finally, a variety of results. All the procedures involved in the digital image manipulation of such images may be categorized into one or more of the following four broad types of computer assisted operations: image rectification and restoration, image enhancement, image classification and data merging [5].

In this paper, we describe a distributed workbench designed to perform a considerable number of the former tasks by using a cluster of workstations composed by NT platforms which are connected by means of an ethernet network using the Message-Passing Interface standard (MPI). MPI provides an interface to design distributed applications that run on a parallel system [6, 7].

Thus, this paper shows how the long computation time required by remote

*Departamento de Informática, Universidad de Castilla-La Mancha, Campus Universitario, 02071 Albacete, Spain (`jgallud@info-ab.uclm.es`).

sensing procedures can be reduced without using high-cost parallel machines. All the distributed applications are implemented by splitting the original images into several small ones, which are processed in each node parallelly.

The following section explains the structure of our distributed workbench. In section 3 an example based on the georeferring process of Landsat-TM images is shown. Finally, in section 5 the conclusions and future work are presented.

2. Distributed Processing of Remotely Sensed Imagery. The basic idea behind remotely sensed image processing is simple. The digital image is fed into a computer one pixel at a time, usually together with its neighbours. The computer is programmed to insert these data into an equation, or series of equations, and then store the results of the computation for each pixel. These results make up a new digital image that may be displayed or recorded in a raster format or may itself be further manipulated by additional programs [2, 4].

Many remote sensing algorithms work in a parametric way, that is, the application performance is related to the initial parameters. The latest algorithms usually are classifiers and their behaviour are governed by a set of initial parameters. To get a classified image, the algorithm begins its computations with such inital values as yield the resultant image. This resultant image depends on both the initial parameters as well as the original multidimensional image. In many cases, the process must be repeated with other parameter values because the results are unacceptable. Thus, it is easy to understand the need to reduce both spatial and temporal costs when a test-and-error process is employed.

Our aim was to implement an environment to perform remotely sensed image processing distributely where both the process and data can be distributed. So, we designed DIPORSI workbench, which stands for *DIstributed Processing Of Remotely Sensed Imagery.* In figure 2.1, the functional diagram of DIPORSI can be seen where only one process is executed in each processor.

DIPORSI appears as a layer between MPI functions and the code of each process. DIPORSI offers a set of functions and a message structure to the user for performing easily and distributively whatever remote sensing algorithm it chooses. As explained in section one, DIPORSI runs in a batch way, thus all the user has to do is to generate a parametric file with the following information:

- The algorithm, or the sequence of algorithms, to compute: i.e. the georeferring algorithm using the bilinear interpolation method.
- The workload allocation: how many nodes and how much information in each node must be defined.
- The number and the location of the data images

What kind of functions does DIPORSI offer to the user? A set of functions have been defined to generate special messages to interpretate them, a number of functions for managing files of different kinds such as text files, data files, raster images, etc.

Our workbench allows us to work by distributing both spatially and temporally either of the remote sensing algorithms. That is, we can make all the nodes peform the same computations on different data and, if we want, we can

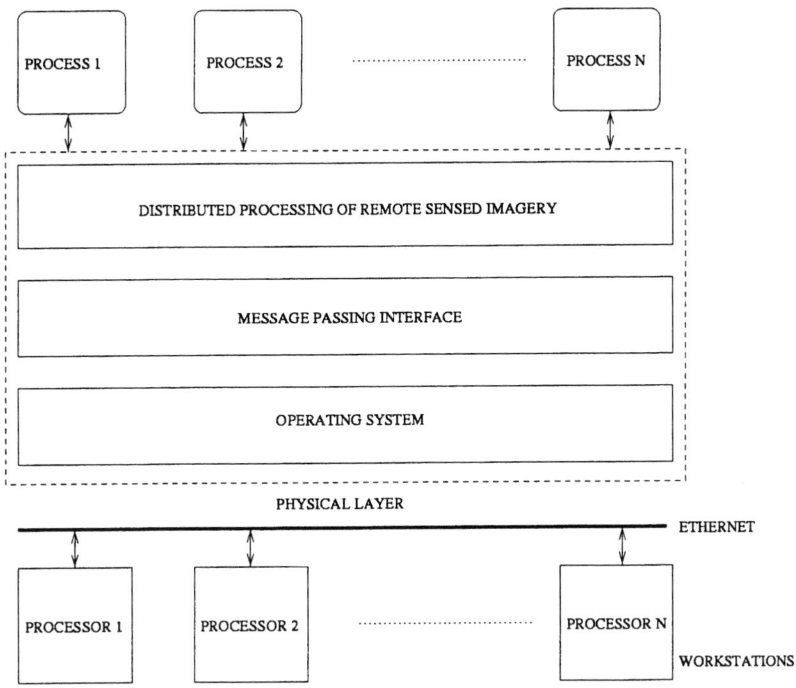

FIG. 2.1.

make each node do different computations on the same image. This process is showed in figure 2.2 where each process is executed on a different processor.

When a distributed approach of a particular algorithm is defined, its special features must be studied in order to improve the efficiency. DIPORSI follows a general schema which will be applied to all remote sensing algorithms. Such a schema is structured into three steps:

1. The images (in our example, the distorted images) are broadcasted into the nodes.
2. The computations are performed following the particular algorithm in each node.
3. The resultant image is restored, usually on the master computer by the nodes.

In order to confer a greater generality to our development, and with a view to further applications, two types of messages have been defined: control and data. The first one is used to specify the activity to be carried out and the parameters necessary for the algorithm, as well as for the control of the MPI. The second type of message is used for the passing of data or image files, as well as pixel streams.

MPI is a standard interface for message passing in distributed applications. There are different MPI implementations, most of them designed to run over

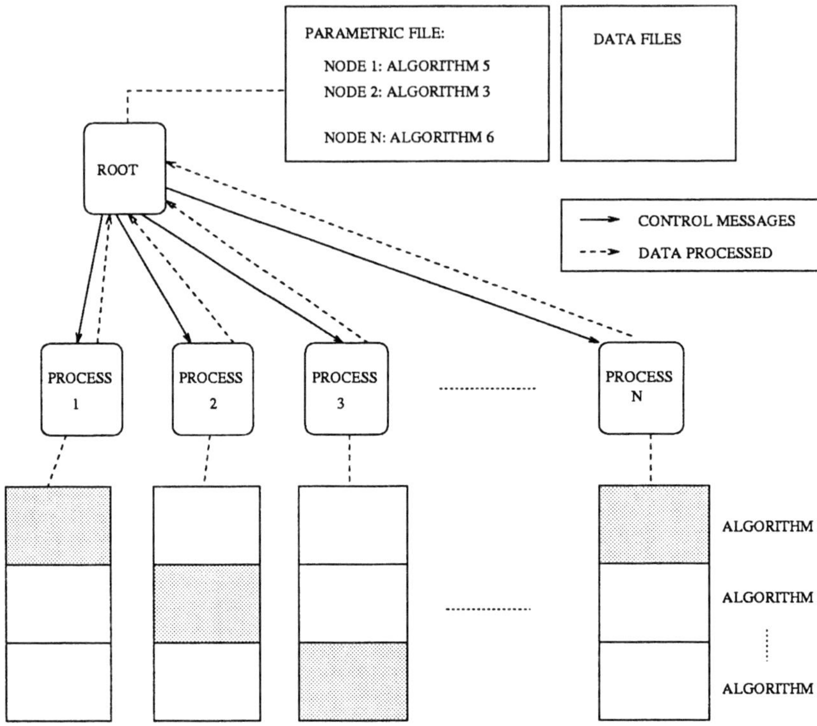

FIG. 2.2. *Workload distribution schema*

Unix or Linux workstations. We have used a MPI implementation on Windows NT named WinMPICH 0.9b version [7].

3. DIPORSI: the georeferring problem. In this section an example based on the georeferring problem is described. First the problem to be solved is presented with the sequential approach and then, the distributed approach using DIPORSI is shown.

When a image is remotely sensed, a number of different errors appear distorting it in such a way that they cannot be used as maps. The process of georeferring a satellite image consists in the application of a set of mathematical operations on the original image to obtain a geometrically corrected image. So, the purpose of geometric correction is to compensate for the distortions introduced by different factors (earth curvature, relief displacement, and so on) so that the corrected image will have the geometric integrity of a map [3].

This process is usually implemented using one of two possible procedures [2, 5]. In the first one, the procedure uses the orbital model reproducing the physical conditions of the image acquisition. The second procedure applies the traditional polynomial correction algorithm with or without using a digital model terrain. This paper is focused on the second step related to random distorsions. This kind of distorsion is corrected by analyzing well-distributed ground control points occurring in an image. The GCP (ground control points) are features of a known ground location that can be accurately located on the digital imagery. These values are then submitted to a least-squares regression analysis to determine coefficients for two coordinate transformation equations that can be used to interrelate the geometrically correct coordinates and the distorted image coordinates. Once the coefficients for these equations are determined, the distorted image coordinates for any map position can be precisely estimated by using this expression:

$$X = f1(x, y)$$
$$Y = f2(x, y)$$

Where (X,Y) are the distorted image coordinates, (x,y) are the correct coordinates (map) and f1 and f2 are the transformation functions. The process is actually made inversely. An undistorted output matrix of empty map cells is defined, and then each cell is filled in with the gray level of the corresponding pixel (digital number or DN), or pixels depending on the method employed, in the distorted image. That is to say, the process is performed using the following operations:

1. The coordinates of each element in the undistorted image are transformed to determine their corresponding location in the original distorted image.
2. The intensivity value or DN of the undistorted image is determined by using one of these usual methods: nearest neighbour, bilinear interpolation and cubic convolution.

Thus far, the sequential process has been defined. In what follows, the three steps schema explained in section 2 is going to be applied to the georeferring problem.

The first step is made by the master process, which opens a file that contains the information of the task to be solved. The root process is initiated with a parametric file, in which all the activities to be performed and their parameters are specified in a ordered way. The master process sends such information to all the nodes involved. Thus, each node knows what it must do (correction method) and how much information it must receive (number of bands -the resultant image to a given frequency-, resolution, the transformation functions, etc). At this point, the master process sends the Landsat image to all the nodes. The special features of the georeference algorithm force us to send all the data to all the nodes. As explained above, the resultant image is a combination of rotations and translations of the original distorted image.

On the other hand the MPI broadcast function allows us to distribute the image easily, but unfortunately at a high cost.

The second step is executed in each node, which acts on the region of the distorted image where the computations must do the corrections. As soon as a row of the resultant image is computed, it is sent to the master process, so computations and communications overlap. So, when a node is involved in a communication, the others can carry out correction computations.

The second and third step run at the same time. The master process receives partial data from nodes, together with the information to restore the resultant image. This is made by using a special message with information about the location (x and y coordinates and the number of the band) of the received data.

A Landsat image has 7 bands, 6 with 30x30mts and 1 with 120x120 mts of resolution respectively, with approximately 40Mb each band, which explains the high value of the response time (over two hours on a powerful workstation) when geometric correction is computed in a single machine. Our parallel algorithm works by splitting the original distorted image into number-of-rows/number-of-nodes blocks in accordance with an uniform workload allocation, then each node computes a small submatrix and the computation time can be reduced and the overall performance of the algorithm can be improved.

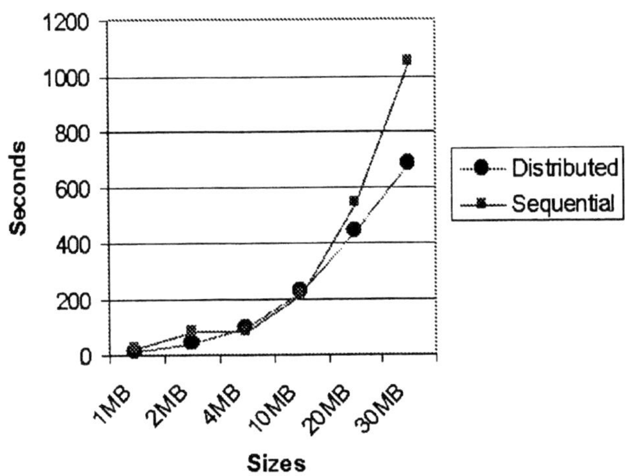

FIG. 3.1. *Distributed vs sequential georeferring*

In Figure 3.1 the results obtained with six nodes are shown. As can be observed the distributed georeferring is more efficient than the sequential as larger image sizes are used. It should be noted that the sequential algorithm is not the result of executing the parallel algorithm on a node. The single machine is a Pentium 166 MHz with 100 MB of RAM running on Windows NT Server 4.0.

Figure 3.2 shows the performance comparison between sequential and distributed algorithms working with 37 MB image sizes. If the algorithm works on smaller images, the speedup does not increase as should do it when the number of used nodes does. Figure 3.3 shows the workload distribution times when distributed systems of different sizes are used. In the example we have employed NT workstations connected by means of an ethernet. It must be taken into account that the underlying ethernet uses stream traffic, which is characterized by lengthy and fairly continuous transmissions. This reason explains that the

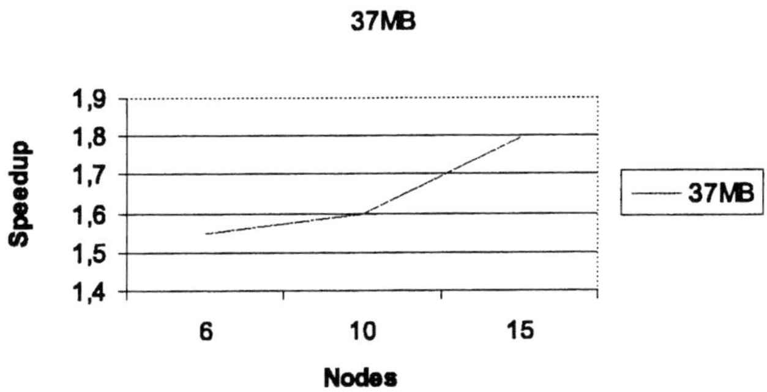

FIG. 3.2. *Speedup*

number of collisions influences in the time required to the data distribution when the number of nodes increases.

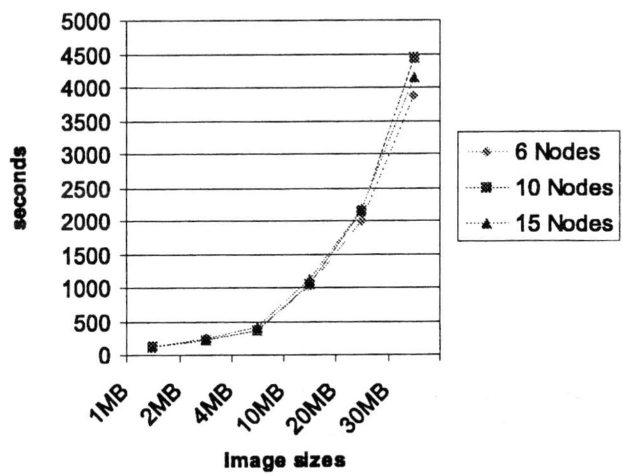

FIG. 3.3. *Workload distribution with different image sizes*

4. Conclusions and future work. This paper describes a distributed workbench to implement the main remote sensing algorithms, using a cluster of workstations, called DIPORSI. The implementation shows the timing results when different image sizes are used, as well as the time gained with the parallel algorithm for georeferring. MPI proved useful for implementing distributed applications on low-cost platforms, which can contribute to designing efficient solutions in remote sensing.

Future work admits of several possibilities: a comparative analysis when different sizes of streams are used, the implementation of other algorithms to solve geometric correction, the implementation of radiometric correction, automatic detection of the ground control points, the integration of Unix plattforms using the future release of WinMPICH, and other works intended to improve the communications between nodes.

REFERENCES

[1] McCormick, J.A., Alter-Gartenberg, R., Huck, F.O., *Image Gathering and restoration: information and visual quality*, Journal of Optical Society of America, Vol 6,No. 7, (1989), pp 987-1005.

[2] Lillesand, T.M., Kiefer, R.W., *Remote Sensing and Image Interpretation 2nd Edition*, J.Wiley & Sons.

[3] Markham, B.L., *The Landsat Sensors' Spatial Responses*, IEEE Transactions on Geoscience and Remote Sensing, Vol. GE-23,No. 6, (1986).

[4] Andersen, J.D., *Digital Image Processing: A 1996 Review*, Applied Parallel Computing - 3rd International Workshop Para 96. LNCS 1184, (1996).

[5] Mather, P.M. *Computer Processing of Remotely-Sensed Images*, John Wiley & Sons.

[6] MPI Forum, *MPI:A message-passing interface standard*, International Journal of Supercomputer Applications 8(3/4), (1994).

[7] Gropp, Lusk, Doss, Skjellum, *A High-Performance, Portable Implementation of the MPI Message Passing Interface Standard*, Parallel Computing, 1996.

THE DOGMA APPROACH TO PARALLEL AND DISTRIBUTED COMPUTING

QUINN SNELL, GLENN JUDD, MARK CLEMENT *

Abstract. Heterogeneous distributed computing has traditionally been a problematic undertaking which increases in complexity as heterogeneity increases. This paper presents results obtained using DOGMA–a Java based system which simplifies parallel computing on heterogeneous computers. The performance of Java just-in-time compilers currently approaches C++ for many applications, making Java a serious contender for parallel application development. DOGMA provides support for dedicated clusters as well as idle workstations through the use of a web based browse-in feature or the DOGMA screen saver. DOGMA supports parallel programming in both a traditional message passing form and a novel object-oriented approach. This research provides a unified environment for developing high performance parallel applications on heterogeneous systems.

Key words. Java, parallel programming, performance

1. Introduction. Researchers have long sought to utilize the computational power of heterogeneous clusters of computers in order to achieve fault tolerance, utilization of idle computers and resource sharing. Unfortunately, the complexity of heterogeneous computing has made these goals elusive. The Java programming language has eliminated some of the problems by making high performance applications portable across nearly all architectures. However, the Java environment does not directly support parallel computing. The Distributed Object Group Metacomputing Architecture (DOGMA) provides system management, data distribution and messaging facilities for Java based parallel applications.

Harnessing the computational power of clusters of heterogeneous computers requires both a hardware system capable of fast, reliable communication as well as a software system capable of allowing applications to make use of large numbers of computers. Recently the creation of distributed/parallel programs has been eased somewhat by developments such as MPI[33], PVM[20], and CORBA[23]. These standards have allowed parallel/distributed programs to be written that will function on several different platforms in both tightly and loosely coupled environments.

Despite the advances in source code level compatibility, traditional distributed programming environments require machine specific compilation and operating system customization. This makes the inclusion of a new architecture into an existing distributed computing platform non-trivial. With the advent of Java, code distribution is now relatively simple. Unfortunately, many have come to view Java as incapable of the performance required for scientific applications. However, while it is true that Java performance lags significantly behind C for some applications, there are many applications where Java just-in-time compiler

* Computer Science Department, Brigham Young University, Provo, Utah 84602-6576, ({snell, glenn, clement }@cs.byu.edu)

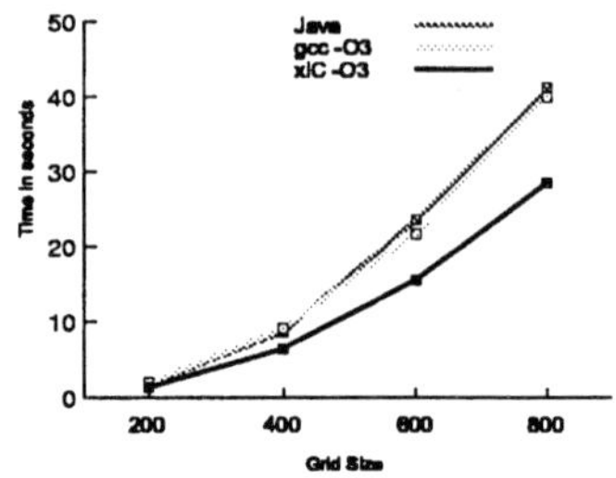

FIG. 1.1. *Java Performance Comparison*

performance is quite close to that of optimized C. Figure 1.1 shows the performance of a finite element algorithm on a single node of an SP2. The performance of the Java code is nearly indistinguishable from the fully optimized gnu gcc compiled executable. The custom IBM xlc compiler achieves higher performance, but scheduled improvements in JIT compiler technology promise to close this gap. The DOGMA system proposed in this research provides the portability of Java as well as high performance for heterogeneous parallel computing,

1.1. Related Work. Java's platform independent/internet-centric nature make it natural for use in distributed computing. This has lead several groups to begin research on distributed/parallel programming with Java. This section reviews these other avenues of research and differentiates DOGMA from these systems.

This comparison is made in the context of DOGMA's two main goals which are: to create a distributed computing platform which can harness the power of clusters of computers as well as anonymous idle computers in both Internet and intranet settings, and to provide mechanisms for easily writing programs capable of efficiently using the power of such a system.

System level comparison:. At the system level, DOGMA's architecture differs from most existing systems in that it provides a simple means to use both dedicated clusters of machines as well as anonymous volunteer machines. In addition, DOGMA includes a screen saver which provides an automatic means for volunteer computing. DOGMA provides a hierarchical management system that allows both volunteer machines and clusters to dynamically join a computation.

User API level comparison:. At the user API level, one significant difference between DOGMA and other efforts is that DOGMA architecture allows it to provide multiple APIs to users (three at present). DOGMA's most developed user API is MPIJ. We are working with the developers of mpiJava[41] and JavaMPI[42] on a proposal for Java MPI bindings. MPIJ differs from these efforts primarily in that it is written completely in Java. Currently, both mpiJava and JavaMPI rely on native MPI implementations.

Another key difference between MPIJ and other systems is communication performance. As will be demonstrated in experimental results, on Windows NT

MPIJ point-to-point communication performance is equivalent to the best MPI implementation currently available and far better than PVM 3.4 for Windows NT. No other Java based system has yet reported comparable communication performance.

Additional comparisons by system type.. Additionally, message passing systems such as IceT[7] JavaPVM[37] and JPVM[36] have not yet reached the same performance as MPIJ. Both Linda derivatives such as Jada[8], JavaSpaces[14], and Javalin[?] as well as shared memory systems such as JavaParty[13], Java/DSM[12], and Spar[34] simplify application development, but have not been able to reach the performance of MPIJ. Frameworks for controlling native code such as Lilith[16] and WWVM[31] are functionally orthogonal to DOGMA since DOGMA is not specifically designed to control native applications.

2. DOGMA.

The DOGMA architecture consists of two conceptual layers: the system layer and the user API layer.

System layer.. The system layer is responsible for linking multiple Java virtual machines into a single integrated system. This layer then provides simple services to the user API layer such as: job scheduling, primitive communication for job startup, etc.. The concrete implementation of the conceptual layer is known as the Distributed Java Machine.

Figure 2.1 illustrates how the Distributed Java Machine is constructed. The system is divided into units known as "configurations". Each configuration is controlled by a "configuration manager". Configuration managers are responsible for managing nodes within the configuration, and allowing those nodes to access nodes in other configurations. Each configuration manager generall manages under 50 nodes. To provide for greater numbers of nodes, configuration managers are linked in a hierarchical fashion as discussed in [40].

Within each configuration three types of nodes may join the system:

- Cluster based nodes - These are nodes which the user who started the configuration manager has login privilege. The configuration manager may bring these nodes into the system via a command such as rsh.
- Browser based nodes - These are nodes which have joined the system by browsing into the system homepage which is served by the configuration manager's http server.
- Screen saver based nodes - These are nodes which have the DOGMA screen saver installed and automatically join the system when the screen saver comes on.

User API layer.. The user API layer consists of multiple API's which allow users to write parallel applications which will run on the DOGMA system. The separation of user APIs from the system layer both eases the development of user APIs, and ensures that user API's can be ported to other parallel systems with much less difficulty. Currently, the user API layer consists of three API's: MPIJ, Dynamic Object Groups, and Distributed Object Groups.

2.1. MPIJ.

The Message Passing Interface Standard has proven to be a widely supported API for parallel programming. Unfortunately, no formal Java

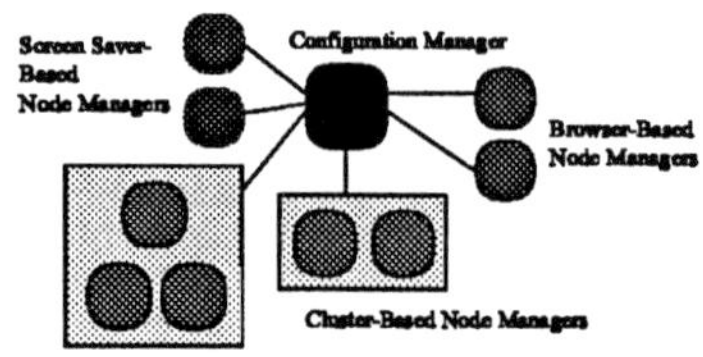

FIG. 2.1. *Sample System Configuration*

bindings for MPI exist. To overcome this, we have collaborated with researchers at the NPAC–Syracuse University, and the University of Westminster on a formal proposal for Java MPI bindings [43].

Based on these proposed bindings, we have implemented a pure Java version of MPI. Below is a short sample:

```
import mpij.*;
public class SampleMPIApplication {
        public void MPIMain(String[] args) {
        MPI.init(args);
        myNode = MPI.COMM_WORLD.rank();
        totalNodes = MPI.COMM_WORLD.size();
        ...
        }
}
```

This code sample is very similar to a C++ MPI implemented code, and it is fairly easy to port existing MPI code to this system. MPIJ programs communicate over Java sockets. One performance enhancement that has been incorporated into MPIJ is the use of native methods for argument marshalling. Tests have shown that this allows Java to remain very competitive with C sockets for sending arrays of primitive data. Porting of MPI programs from C to Java has proven to be very straightforward, and the performance obtained is promising.

MPIJ currently supports most major MPI functionality including point-to-point communication (all four modes for both synchronous and asynchronous methods), intracommunicator operations, and user defined operations.

Three major areas which are currently included in the proposed Java MPI bindings are net yet implemented in MPIJ: intercommunicators, process topologies, and user defined datatypes. It is worth noting that user defined datatype functionality may not be included in the final Java MPI bindings since their functionality can be handled entirely through the use of Java objects.

In order to ensure the quality of our implementation, we have ported the IBM MPI Test Suite[38] to Java. All capabilities which have been implemented have passed the corresponding tests, and as the standard evolves, additional functionality will be added.

2.2. Distributed Object Groups. The DOGMA system also allows programs to be written using an experimental API known as Distributed Object Groups. Distributed Object Groups allow data parallel programs to work with large groups of objects easily and efficiently. A master instantiates a Distributed Object Group made up of a number of objects which is distributed across the DJM. A Distributed Object Group is organized according to a data configuration scheme. The scheme defines how data will be partitioned, group elements will communicate, and what type of coordinates are used to define group element position. Through asynchronous group method invocation, the master can invoke methods on the entire group, blocking only when a return value is requested and unavailable.

Since DOGMA was created for the purpose of heterogeneous clustered computing, automated variable load balancing is built into the system to address the problem of varying node performance. Distributed Object Groups free the programmer from the traditional tasks of computing partition sizes, partition overlaps, element position, etc., and add the power of dynamic partitioning according to system topology and load. Arguments to methods can be partitioned automatically by the system. The compute speed and load of nodes on which group elements reside are considered in determining the appropriate partition size for each node. DOGMA currently supports partitioning of object data along a single dimension. A distributed data structure can be automatically distributed among the processors in one of three modes: EVEN, CAPACITY, and DYNAMIC [2]. EVEN partitioning ignores compute speed and assigns an equal amount to each processor. The latter two partitioning modes are based on a processor's Net QUIPS as reported by the HINT benchmark [1]. CAPACITY load balancing is based solely on Net QUIPS, while DYNAMIC also takes into account the current load on the system. Data returned by a group method invocation can also be reassembled automatically by the system. Alternatively, an array of results can be returned.

Distributed Object Groups differ from exisiting systems such as The Parallel Java with Global Object Space[19] and Mentat[17] substantially in that they allow data to be partitioned at run-time according to node speed and load.

Writing Distributed Object Group programs is fairly simple. As in Java Remote Method Invocation (RMI), an interface file must be written defining which methods in a given object (or object group) may be invoked remotely. Upon group method invocation, arguments of type Partition or one of its subclasses are automatically partitioned by the system while other arguments are simply sent to every node in the group. For example:

```
interface SkelElement extends Element {
        public OneDArrayFloatPartition
        addFloatToArray(
        OneDArrayFloatPartition myPartition,
        float floatToAdd)
        throws RemoteException;
}
```

In this case, `addFloatToArray` is defined to accept a `Partition` data structure, `myPartition`, that will contain only the processor's required subset of the data. Group elements then extend the element base class for the data configuration scheme to create the corresponding implementation of the distributed object. A master (a class which has a distributed object group as a member) may then instantiate a distributed object group as follows:

```
skelGroup =
        new SkelElementGroup("my.pkg.SkelElementImpl",
        minNodes, preferredNodes, maxNodes,
        new OneDArrayController(),
        DistObjectGroup.CCFG_NONE);
```

This example uses the `OneDArrayController` to allocate a one-dimensional array and automatically perform the data distribution. Methods may then be invoked on the entire group with their arguments being partitioned if they are of type Partition or one of its subclasses. As the invocation is asynchronous, a handle to the invocation is returned:

```
handle = dog.addFloatToArray(data, 7.0f);
```

This call invokes the `addFloatToArray` method on all available processors, sending each processor a piece of the array. The programmer then uses the handle to request the results of the method. The programmer may request that the results be automatically reassembled, or that an array of results be returned. The statement

```
partition = (OneDArrayFloatPartition)handle.getAssembledReturn();
```

causes the results to automatically be reassembled into the array `partition`

Group element communication is similar to other parallel systems. Note that objects may be sent as easily as primitive data as in the following statement. The object `histogram` is broadcast to all participating objects.

```
sendToAll(histogram);
Object[] otherHistogram = receiveFromAll();
```

The Distributed Object Group paradigm presented here provides a high level abstraction for parallelism that also achieves high performance.

2.3. Dynamic Object Groups. An additional API which is currently under design is the Dynamic Object Group API. This API provides a very simple mechanism for writing hierarchical master/slave applications. Dynamic Object Groups allow applications to easily scale to thousands of nodes. In addition, as the name implies, they are capable of allowing nodes to join or leave the computation at runtime. This capability also provides a very natural fault tolerance.

Dynamic Object Groups consist of two types of nodes: master nodes, and slave nodes. Master nodes operate both as masters and slaves while slave nodes act purely as slaves.

Consider the Dynamic Object Group shown in part a of figure 2.2 running on a single cluster of nodes. As nodes within this cluster become available or unavailable they join or leave the group respectively. When they are part of

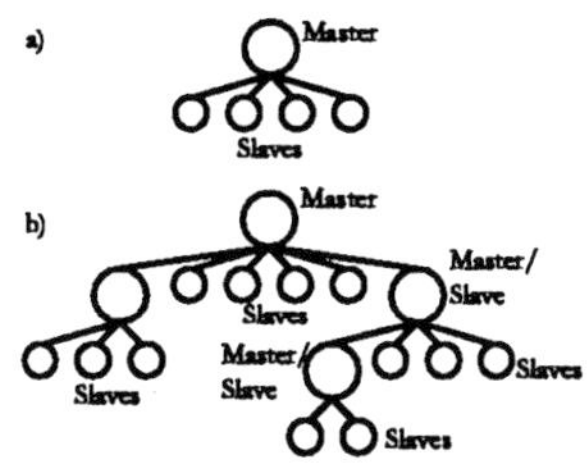

FIG. 2.2. *Dynamic Object Groups*

the group, they request tasks from the master node. As a new cluster becomes available, the first available node in that cluster is picked to act as the master for that cluster. This master node then requests large tasks from the original master. As far as the original master is concerned, the new cluster's master is simply a very fast slave.

As further clusters join the system, they are added below the closest master node which results in a configuration such as shown in part b of figure 2.2. Should an intermediate master node become unavailable, a new node within the same cluster will be promoted from slave to master. If an entire intermediate cluster becomes unavailable, master nodes below it are reallocated to the next closest master/slave node.

2.4. Fault Tolerance. Fault tolerance in DOGMA must be handled at both the system layer and the user API layer.

At the system layer fault tolerance is an active area of research. Currently, nodes which fail to contact their configuration manager are labeled as unavailable by the configuration manager. If the node has simply been disconnected temporarily from the configuration manager it will periodically try connecting again. When it reconnects the configuration manager then labels the node as available. Configuration managers follow a similar scheme when they are disconnected from each other.

At the user API layer, each user API is responsible for implementing its own fault tolerance scheme. Both MPIJ and Distributed Object Group applications are designed to be run on reliable machines and networks. Hence, they both implement only fault detection in the form of exceptions when a fault occurs. Dynamic Object Groups, on the other hand, are designed to scale to large numbers of machines where faults may be considered inevitable. The master/slave nature of these groups allows work not completed by a faulty node to be completed by other nodes.

2.5. Security. DOGMA security is also an area of active research. Current security policies are directed at protecting nodes which donate their resources to the system. These nodes are protected by the Java "sandbox" which will prevents applications from accessing system resources. In addition, Sun's JDK 1.2 allows the sandbox to be loosened to allow applications in the sandbox to

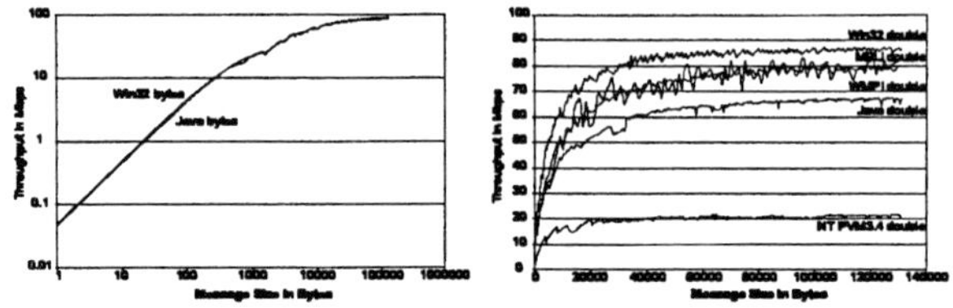

FIG. 3.1. *Native communication vs Java for bytes(left) and floating point data(right).*

make arbitrary network connections. This is a definite requirement for parallel processing.

3. Experimental Results. DOGMA has proven to be an effective, easy-to-use parallel programming environment. We have successfully run applications on large groups of heterogeneous nodes with no source code modification. The applications include: matrix multiplication, image FFT, image histogram equalization, finite differences, and ray tracing to name a few. The number of nodes included in the system has ranged from 1 to 180 with the nodes residing in 4 different domains. The system has also incorporated both browser-based nodes, which were able to execute applications and donate CPU power, as well as nodes running the DOGMA screen saver to donate idle CPU time to DOGMA. In addition, DOGMA is capable of seamlessly harnessing the power of multiprocessor machines by assigning multiple objects to the machine.

3.1. Communication Performance. High communication performance is essential in a parallel computing environment. In order to evaluate DOGMA's communication performance we tested DOGMA communication under Sun's JDK 1.1.5 on Windows NT nodes connected by 100 Mbps Ethernet. We chose this system becuase the maturity of the just-in-time compiler on Windows NT.

We then compared the performance measured with the following systems: Linux MPICH–this system was chosen because it is one of the most common environments in use in clustered computing. PVM 3.4 for Windows NT–this system was chosen because we desired to compare DOGMA on NT with a native parallel processing system on NT. At the time of testing, PVM 3.4 was one of the most mature parallel computing environments for Windows NT. WMPI–this system is a relatively new implementation of MPI under Windows NT, it was included because [39] showed that its communication performance was one of the best of available parallel computing systems for Windows NT.

We also included performance for Win32 sockets, Linux sockets, Java sockets (which are used by MPIJ), and Java RMI (which is used by Distributed Object Groups) to show the performance of our machines without the overhead of a parallel messaging protocol.

The left graph in Figure 3.1 compares native socket communication with Java socket communication for sending bytes. The graph clearly shows that the performance of Java communication using sockets is essentially equal to that of native sockets using the Windows NT Winsock interface when sending bytes.

This is reasonable because Java communication and native communication are calling the same system library to perform communication. So, the only real overhead associated with Java communication is a small increase in initial latency which becomes insignificant as message size increases.

However, the above results are only for byte communication. Most messages in a parallel program are not bytes, but are floating point data. Java communication is based on the InputStream and OutputStream classes; neither of which support communication with data types other than bytes. Therefore, in order to send an array of floating point data, the data must be converted into a byte array. Java is a strongly typed language and, as such, does not allow type casting of pointers. Unlike C programs which allow a floating point array to be directly treated as an array of characters, each Java data element must be type cast and copied into a byte array to be transmitted. This technique is termed data marshalling, and adds significant overhead.

The right graph in Figure 3.1 shows the results of double precision floating point communication tests. The overhead due to Java data marshalling is clear from the fact that while Java bytes are sent at the same rate as Win32 double–88 Mbps maximum, Java doubles are sent at a maximum of 68Mbps.

However, the graph also demonstrates that significant performance increases are possible in Java by performing the data marshalling in native code. This technique allows MPIJ to achieve 80Mbps which is equivalent to the performance of WMPI. While native marshalling of arguments is not currently a standard feature in Java, it could very easily be added for very large performance benefits.

The graph also shows the comparison of message passing performance between two DOGMA nodes versus communication between two PVM nodes. Both tests were run on the same two workstations. PVM uses native sockets as a communication medium, while DOGMA communication is based on Java sockets and the JNI marshalling methods. Surprisingly, DOGMA communication performance is better than PVM on Windows NT.

3.2. Aggregate Performance. The above results are meaningless unless they translate into aggregate cluster performance for parallel applications. In this section, we demonstrate MPIJ application performance in comparison with NT PVM and Linux MPI applications. The target applications were coded using the same algorithm in each environment. The applications of choice were: Gaussian elimination, and a finite differences code. These applications were chosen for their varying communication demands.

The application performance graphs in Figure 3.2 show the comparative performance results for the Gaussian elimination and finite element calculations. Each of the applications require successively less communication. As the communication demands decrease, the computational performance of the individual nodes is more important. In these cases, MPIJ application performance is better than NT PVM performance for larger numbers of nodes, but does not usually exceed Linux MPI application performance. It does, however, approach Linux MPI performance in all cases tested. In summary, these graphs show that

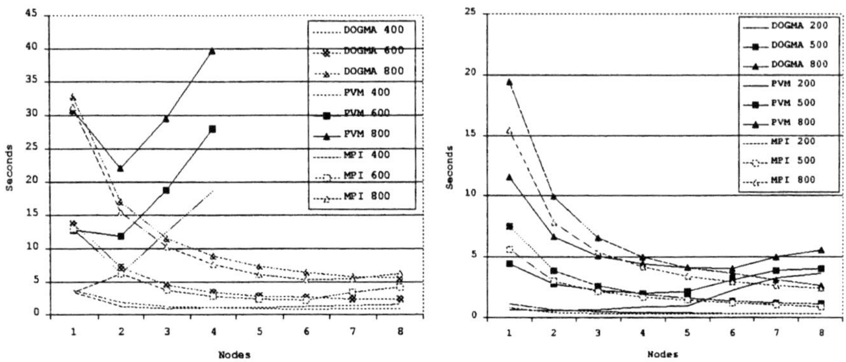

FIG. 3.2. *Comparison for Gauss Elim.(left) and Finite Element(right) Computations.*

MPIJ's aggregate performance is reasonably comparable to traditional native approaches.

4. Conclusions. Parallel computing is a field that demands high performance. Although performance results for interpreted Java is somewhat disheartening, current generation JIT compilers frequently provide the requisite computational performance while supporting a single executable format. The computation performance of Java Just In Time (JIT) compilers on sequential tasks can rival optimized C++ on some tasks. Java communication performance can be as good as or better than that obtained by parallel libraries like PVM and MPI on operating systems common in the clustered parallel computing environment. The aggregate performance of many parallel applications also rivals that of more traditional parallel language systems. In short, Java is ready for parallel computing and will usher in new opportunities for clusters.

The DOGMA system allows idle machines to be incorporated into parallel computing clusters irrespective of their CPU or operating system. Since use of these clusters is much less expensive than traditional parallel computing platforms, more researchers and average users can have access to high performance compute resources. Applications such as voice recognition, image processing and large database indexing (which often require much more compute power than is available on a single system) can be approached using DOGMA clusters.

Though there is much future research to be done, DOGMA has proven to be very capable of enabling clusters of computers and individual anonymous computers to act as a single powerful networked computing entity. DOGMA volunteer facilities also provide an excellent means to increase workstation utilization. Other issues such as security and fault tolerance enhancements are also being enhanced.

See the DOGMA homepage for more current information:
http://ccc.cs.byu.edu/DOGMA/

REFERENCES

[1] JOHN GUSTAFSON AND QUINN SNELL *HINT:A New Way to Measure Computer Performance* in The Fifth Annual Hawaii International Conference on System Sciences", January 1995.

[2] QUINN SNELL AND GLENN JUDD AND MARK CLEMENT *Load Balancing in a Heterogeneous Supercomputing Environment* in PDPTA, July 1998.

[3] C. CHAMBERS *The Design and Implementation of the Self Compiler, an Optimizing Compiler for Object-Oriented Programming Languages*, Stanford University, 1992.

[4] U. HOELZLE *Adaptive Optimization for Self: Reconciling High Performance with Exploratory Programming*, Stanford University, 1992.

[5] ARASH BARATLOO AND MEHMET KARAUL AND ZVI KEDEM AND PETER WYCKOFF *Charlotte: Metacomputing on the Web* in Proceedings of the ISCA International Conference on Parallel and Distributed Computing, 1996.

[6] SATOSHI HIRANO *The Magic Ccarpet for Network Computing*, http://ring.etl.go.jp/openlab/horb/, 1997.

[7] PAUL A. GRAY AND VAIDY S. SUNDERAM, *IceT: Distributed Computing and Java* in Proceedings of the ACM 1997 PPoPP Workshop on Java for Science and Engineering Computation, June 1997.

[8] DAVIDE ROSSI *Jada: Multiple Object Spaces for Java*, http://www.cs.unibo.it/~rossi/jada/, 1996.

[9] BRYAN CARPENTER AND YUH-JYE CHANG AND GEOFFREY FOX AND DONALD LESKIW AND XIAOMING LI *Experiments with "HPJava"* in Concurrency, Practice and Experience, June 1997, Vol. 9 No. 6, pp.579–619.

[10] JAMES GOSLING AND BILL JOY AND GUY STEELE *The Java Language Specification*, Addison-Wesley, 1996.

[11] BERND O. CHRISTIANSEN AND PETER CAPPELLO AND MIHAI F. IONESCU AND MICHAEL O. NEARY AND KLAUS E. SCHAUSER AND DANIEL WU *Javelin: Internet-Based Parallel Computing Using Java", in Proceedings of the ACM 1997 PPoPP Workshop on Java for Science and Engineering Computation, June 1997.*

[12] WEIMIN YU AND ALAN COX Java/DSM: A Platform for Heterogeneous Computing *in Proceedings of the ACM 1997 PPoPP Workshop on Java for Science and Engineering Computation, June 1997.*

[13] MICHAEL PHILIPPSEN AND MATTHIAS ZENGER JavaParty - Transparent Remote Objects in Java *in Proceedings of the ACM 1997 PPoPP Workshop on Java for Science and Engineering Computation, June 1997.*

[14] JAVASOFT JavaSpaces, *http://chatsubo.javasoft.com/javaspaces/, 1997.*

[15] HERNANI PEDROSO AND LUIS M. SILVA AND JOAO GABRIEL SILVA *Web-based Metacomputing with JET* in Proceedings of the ACM 1997 PPoPP Workshop on Java for Science and Engineering Computation, June 1997.

[16] D.A. EVENSKY AND A.C. GENTILE AND L.J. CAMP AND R.C. ARMSTRONG *Lilith: Scalable Execution of User Code for Distributed Computing* in Proceedings of the Sixth IEEE International Symposium on High Performance Distributed Computing, pp. 305–314 (1997).

[17] A. S. GRIMSHAW *An Introduction To Parallel Object-Oriented Programming with Mentat* University of Virginia, 1991, 91-07.

[18] TIM BRECHT, HARJINDER SANDHU, MEIJUAN SHAN, AND JIMMY TALBOT *ParaWeb: Towards World-Wide Supercomputing* in Proceedings of the Seventh ACM SIGOPS European Workshop, pp. 181–188, September 1996.

[19] L. V. KALE AND MILIND BHANDARKAR AND TERRY WILMARTH *Design and Implementation of Parallel Java with Global Object Space* in Proceedings of the International Conference on Parallel and Distributed Processing Techniques and Applications, pp. 235–244, (1997).

[20] A. GEIST AND A. BEGUELIN AND J. DONGARRA AND W. JIANG AND R. MANCHEK AND V. SUNDERAM *PVM 3 User's Guide and Reference Manual* Oak Ridge National Laboratory, September 1994, ORNL/TM-12187, User's guide for PVM version 3.3.

[21] JAVASOFT *Remote Method Invocation*, http://java.sun.com/products/jdk/1.1/docs /guide/rmi/index.html, 1997.

[22] SUN *Sun Announces Java Platform Roadmap*, http://java.sun.com/pr/ 1997/april/pr970402-04.html, 1997.

[23] OMG *The Common Object Request Broker: Architecture and Specification*, 2.0 ed., July 1997.

[24] KEES VAN REEUWIJK AND ARJAN J.C. VAN GEMUND AND HENK J. SIPS *Spar: A Programming Language for Semi-Automatic Compilation of Parallel Programs* in Proceedings of the ACM 1997 PPoPP Workshop on Java for Science and Engineering Computation, June 1997.

[25] SUSAN FLYNN HUMMEL AND TON NGO AND HARINI SRINIVASAN *SPMD Programming in Java* in Concurrency, Practice and Experience, June 1997, Vol. 9 No. 6, pp. 621–631.

[26] ALBERT D. ALEXANDROV AND MAXIMILIAN IBEL AND KLAUS E. SCHAUSER AND CHRIS J. SCHEIMAN *SuperWeb: Towards a Global-Based Parallel Computing Infrastructure* in Proceedings

of the 11th International Parallel Processing Symposium, April 1997.

[27] Lukasz Beca and Gang Cheng and Geoffrey C. Fox and Tomasz Jurga and Konrad Olszewski and Marek Podgorny and Piotr Sokolowski and Tomasz Stachowiak and Krzysztof Walczak *Tango - a Collaborative Environment for the World-Wide Web*, http://trurl.npac.syr.edu/tango/papers/tangowp.html, 1997.

[28] Objectspace *Voyager*, http://www.objectspace.com/voyager/, 1997.

[29] Zhikai Chen and Kurt Maly and Piyush Mehrotra and Praveen K. Vangala and Mohammad Zubair *Web Based Framework for Distributed Computing*, in Proceedings of the ACM 1997 PPoPP Workshop on Java for Science and Engineering Computation, June 1997.

[30] Wojtek Furmanski and Geoffrey Fox *WebFlow - A Visual programming Paradigm for Web/Java Based Coarse Grain Distributed Computing*, From handout material at Supercomputing '96, 1996.

[31] Kivanc Dincer and Geoffrey C. Fox *Building a World-Wide Virtual Machine Based on Web and HPCC Technologies* in Proceedings Supercomputing '96, November 1996.

[32] Bernd O. Christiansen and Peter Cappello and Mihai F. Ionescu and Michael O. Neary and Klaus E. Schauser and Daniel Wu *Javelin: Internet-Based Parallel Computing Using Java* in ACM 1997 PPoPP Workshop on Java for Science and Engineering Computation, June 1997.

[33] MPI Forum *MPI: A Message-Passing Interface Standard*, University of Tennessee, June 1995.

[34] Kees van Reeuwijk, Arjan J.C. van Gemund, Henk J. Sips *Spar: A Programming Language for Semi-Automatic Compilation of Parallel Programs* in ACM 1997 PPoPP Workshop on Java for Science and Engineering Computation, June 1997.

[35] Javasoft *Remote Method Invocation*, http://java.sun.com/ products/jdk/1.1/docs/guide/rmi/index.html/, 1997.

[36] A. Ferrari *JPVM*, http://www.cs.virginia.edu/~ajf2j/jpvm.html, 1997.

[37] D. Thurman *JavaPVM*, http://homer.isye.gatech.edu/chmsr/JavaPVM.html/, 1997.

[38] Richard Treumann *IBM MPI Test Suite*", ftp://info.mcs.anl.gov/pub/mpi/mpi-test/ibmtsuite.tar, 1995.

[39] Mark Baker and Geoffrey Fox *MPI on NT: A Preliminary Evaluation of the Available Environments*, 12th IPPS and 9th SPDP, Lecture Notes in Computer Science Jose Rolim (Ed.), Parallel and Distributed Computing, Springer Verlag, Heidelberg, Germany, April 1998, Vol. 9 No. 6, pp. 549–563.

[40] Mark Clement and Glenn Judd and Quinn Snell *High Performance Computing for the Masses* in International Workshop on Java for Parallel and Distributed Computing, April 1999.

[41] Bryan Carpenter and Geoffrey Fox and Guansong Zhang and Xinying Li *A draft Java binding for MPI*, http://www.npac.syr.edu/projects/pcrc/HPJava/mpiJava.html, November 1997.

[42] Sava Mintchev and Vladimir Getov M. Bubak and J. Dongarra and J. Waśniewski editors, *Towards portable message passing in Java: Binding MPI* in Recent Advances in PVM and MPI., volume 1332 of *Lecture Notes in Computer Science*, 1997, pp. 135–142, Springer Verlag.

[43] Bryan Carpenter and Vladimir Getov and Glenn Judd and Tony Skjellum and Geoffrey Fox *MPI for Java: Position Document and Draft Specification, Report JGF-TR-03*, Java Grande Forum http://www.javagrande.org/reports.htm, November 1998.

OVERLAP OF COMPUTATION AND COMMUNICATION ON SHARED-MEMORY NETWORKS-OF-WORKSTATIONS

TAREK S. ABDELRAHMAN* AND GARY LIU†

Abstract. This paper describes and evaluates a compiler transformation that improves the performance of parallel programs on Network-of-Workstation (NOW) shared-memory multiprocessors. The transformation overlaps the communication time resulting form non-local memory accesses with the computation time in parallel loops to effectively hide the latency of the remote accesses. The transformation peels from a parallel loop iterations that access remote data and re-schedules them after the execution of iterations that access only local data (local-only iterations). Asynchronous prefetching of remote data is used to overlap non-local access latency with the execution of local-only iterations. Experimental evaluation of the transformation on a NOW multiprocessor indicates that it is generally effective in improving parallel execution time (up to 1.9 times). The extent of the benefit is determined by three factors: the size of local-only computations, the significance of remote memory access latency, and the position of the iterations that access remote data in a parallel loop.

Key words. networks-of-workstations, distributed-shared memory, compiler optimizations, locality enhancement, latency hiding, loop transformations.

AMS subject classifications. 68N20, 65Y05, 68Q22

1. Introduction. Shared-memory multiprocessors built from Networks of Workstations (NOWs) are becoming increasingly popular as platforms for high-performance computing. In these systems, general-purpose workstations are connected together using a fast communication network, such as ATM or Fast Ethernet. Shared memory is supported using a Distributed Shared Memory (DSM) software, which makes the memory address space of each workstation part of a larger global address space. Hence, a process on one workstation can access data residing in this global address space, irrespective of the local address space in which the data actually resides. Examples of such systems include the Stanford Distributed FLASH [11], the SUN s3.mp architecture [12] and the POW system at the University of Toronto [13].

Although NOW multiprocessors support shared memory, data transfers and synchronization are realized using underlying message passing mechanisms. This results in high memory access latencies when data being accessed is not resident in the local memory of a workstation. Indeed, the latency of a non-local memory access can be orders of magnitude higher than the latency of a local memory access. Programs that makes a large number of non-local memory accesses are likely to exhibit poor performance. Consequently, it is imperative that the latency of non-local memory accesses be reduced.

In this paper, we describe and experimentally evaluate a compiler transformation for parallel loops in scientific programs on NOW shared-memory multiprocessors. The transformation utilizes data distribution directives provided by programmers, or determined by the compiler, to identify the iterations of a parallel loop that require non-local memory accesses. These iterations are peeled from

*Department of Electrical and Computer Engineering, The University of Toronto, Toronto, Ontario, Canada M5S 3G4 (tsa@eecg.toronto.edu).

†IBM Canada, Ltd, Toronto, Ontario, Canada M3C 1V7. (gary@ca.ibm.com).

the parallel loop, leaving iterations that only access local data (called *local-only iterations*). The peeled iterations are scheduled for execution after the local-only iterations, and asynchronous reads (in the form of prefetches) are inserted before the local-only iterations. This effectively overlaps the latency of the remote accesses with the computation time of local-only iterations, reducing the impact of the latency on performance. We refer to this transformation as Computation-Communication Overlap, or CCO.

Experimental evaluation of the CCO transformation using representative applications on a shared-memory NOW multiprocessor indicates that the transformation is generally effective in hiding the latency of remote accesses, and in improving parallel execution time. The performance of target parallel loops improves by a factor of up to 2.9; overall performance improves by a factor of up to 1.9. The extent of the benefit of the transformation is determined by three factors: (1) the size of the computation of the local-only iterations; (2) the significance of non-local memory access latency; and (3) the location in a parallel loop of the iterations that access remote data.

The remainder of this paper is organized as follows. Section 2 gives some background material on dependence and data distribution. Section 3 describes the computation-communication overlap transformation in details. Section 4 presents and discusses the results of our experiments. Section 5 reviews related work. Finally, Section 6 gives concluding remarks.

2. Background. The presentation of the CCO transformation requires familiarity with data dependence [17] and data distribution [8]. These topics are briefly described in this section.

2.1. Data Dependence. In a loop nest L, two statements S_1 and S_2 that reference a common array a are said to have a data dependence $S_1(\vec{i})\delta S_2(\vec{i'})$ if S_1 references the same array element in some iteration $\vec{i}$ as S_2 in some iteration $\vec{i'}$, where iteration $\vec{i}$ is executed before $\vec{i'}$. The dependence is called a *flow* dependence when S_1 writes a and S_2 reads a; an *anti*dependence when S_1 reads and S_2 writes; or an *output* dependence when both S_1 and S_2 write. S_1 is called the *source* of the dependence and S_2 is called the *sink* of the dependence. For each dependence $S_1(\vec{i})\delta S_2(\vec{i'})$, the dependence distance vector is defined as $\vec{d} = \vec{i'} - \vec{i}$. A dependence is said to be *loop independent* if its source and sink statements are in the same iteration, i.e., if $\vec{d} = 0$, otherwise it is *carried* by a loop. A loop is said to be *parallel* if it carries no dependence; otherwise the loop is said to be *sequential* or *serial.*

2.2. Data Distribution. Data distribution is an approach used by compilers for distributed memory multiprocessors, such as High-Performance Fortran (HPF) [10], to map array data onto separate address spaces. Although such partitioning of an array is not necessary in the presence of shared-memory, it can be used to enhance memory locality—the compiler can place an array partition in the physical memory of the processor that uses it the most [2]. Data distribution can be specified by the programmer using compiler directives, as in Fortran D [8] and HPF [10], or automatically derived by the compiler [15]. In either case, we assume that directives in the input program specify data distribution.

An array is distributed by specifying a partitioning scheme for the array and by specifying a processor geometry to which the array partitions map.

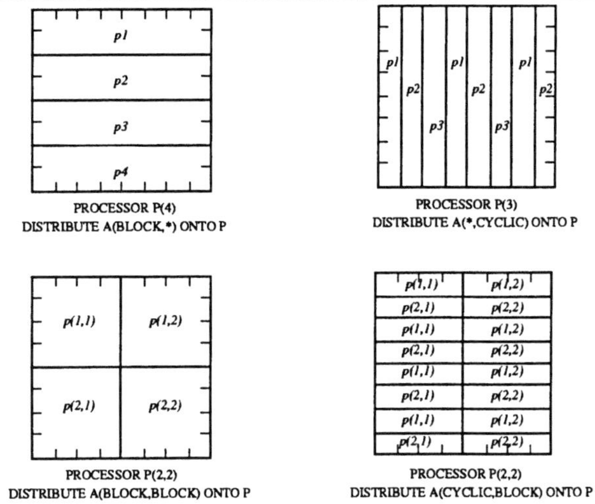

FIG. 2.1. *Data distribution examples.*

This is done using the `DISTRIBUTE` and `PROCESSOR` directives respectively. The `PROCESSOR` directive declares an n-dimensional Cartesian grid of virtual processors $\mathbf{V}(V_0, V_1, \cdots, V_{n-1})$, where V_i is the number of processors in the ith dimension of the grid, and $V_1 \times V_1 \times \cdots \times V_{n-1} = P$, the total number of processors. For example, `PROCESSOR P1(32)` declares a linear array `P1` of 32 virtual processors. Similarly, `PROCESSOR P2(4,6)` declares a 2-dimensional virtual processor grid `P2`, with 4 rows and 6 columns.

The `DISTRIBUTE` directive partitions an array by assigning a *partitioning attributes* to each dimension of the array. The `DISTRIBUTE` directive also maps the resulting array partitions onto a processor geometry declared using the `PROCESSOR` directive. The `BLOCK` attribute divides the corresponding dimension of the array in approximately equal size blocks such that a processor owns a contiguous range of that dimension of the array. The `CYCLIC` attribute divides the corresponding array dimension by distributing the array elements in this dimension to processors in a round-robin fashion. The `BLOCK_CYCLIC` attribute first groups array elements in the corresponding dimension in contiguous blocks of a given size, and then assigns the blocks to processors in a round-robin fashion. The block size is called the *block-cyclic factor*. Finally, the `*` attribute is used to indicate that the corresponding dimension of the array is not distributed.

The use of the partitioning attributes in the dimensions of a multi-dimensional array results in useful data distribution schemes, which is illustrated in Figure 2.1 using a 2-dimensional array `A`. The processor geometry on which the array is mapped determines the number of processors assigned to each distributed dimension of the array.

3. The CCO Transformation.

3.1. Overview. The goal of the CCO transformation is to overlap the latency caused by accesses to remote data in a parallel loop with the computations of the loop, effectively hiding remote access latency. This is accomplished by

```
PROCESSOR P(4)
DIMENSION A(100,100)
DIMENSION B(100,100)
DISTRIBUTE A(*,BLOCK) ONTO P
DISTRIBUTE B(*,BLOCK) ONTO P
        :
        :
DOALL j=2,99,1
  DO i=2,99,1
    A(i,j)=B(i,j-1)+B(i,j+1)
```

(a) Program segment

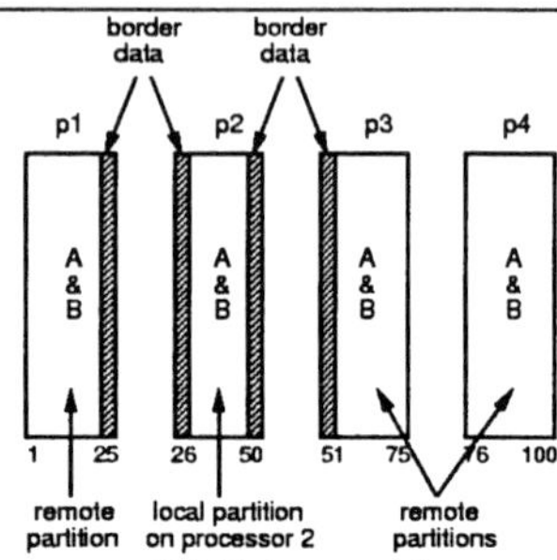

(b) Data partitions

```
DO j=26,50,1
  DO i=2,99,1
    A(i,j)=B(i,j-1)+B(i,j+1)
```

(c) Code on processor 2

```
prefetch B(2:99,25)
prefetch B(2:99,51)

DO j=27,49,1
  DO i=2,99,1
    A(i,j)=B(i,j-1)+B(i,j+1)

DO i=2,99,1
  A(i,26)=B(i,25)+B(i,26)
  A(i,50)=B(i,49)+B(i,51)
```

(d) Peeling and inserting prefetchs

FIG. 3.1. *Overview of the CCO transformation.*

peeling iterations that read[1] remote data in the parallel loop, and re-scheduling these iterations for execution after the iterations that read only local data (referred to as the *local-only iterations*). Asynchronous reads in the form of prefetch instructions are initiated before the local-only iterations to overlap the latency of these remote reads with local computations, effectively hiding the latency.

The transformation is illustrated using the short program segment shown in Figure 3.1(a). The outer loop with the index `j` is parallel. The arrays `A` and `B` are partitioned using `(*,BLOCK)`, i.e., in column blocks as shown in Figure 3.1(b). The code generated by the compiler for execution on processor 2 is shown in Figure 3.1(c). Iterations `26` and `50` of loop `j` in this code compute elements on the boundaries of the local data partition of array `A` residing in processor 2. These two iterations cause reads to elements of array `B` that are both local as well as remote. In contrast, iterations `27` to `49` read only local elements, and hence constitute the local-only iterations. Consequently, iterations `26` and `50` are peeled of the loop and rescheduled for execution after local-only iterations, as shown in Figure 3.1(d). The prefetch instructions are used to initiate remote memory reads to make needed elements of `B` residing in the memory modules of processors `1` and `3` into the local memory of processor 2.

There are 2 types of analyses that are used by the CCO transformation: (1) data distribution analysis, which is used to determine for a given processor which array elements are local and which elements are remote; and (2) communication analysis, which is used to determine which iterations of a parallel loop read only

[1] The use of data distributions and the owner-computes rule (described in the next section) dictates that all writes to array elements be local. Hence, the only source of remote accesses are reads.

local array elements and which iterations read remote data. The transformation is then implemented using loop peeling and by inserting appropriate calls to prefetch instructions.

3.2. Data Distribution Analysis. This analysis uses the array distribution directives in the input program to map array partitions to processors and to partition parallel loops, i.e., determine the subset of loop iterations that will be executed by each processor. This analysis is largely based on that of Fortran D [8], and hence, will only be overviewed.

The mapping of data partitions to processors is performed in two steps. In the first step, the array partitions are assigned to the virtual processors of the n-dimensional grid to which they are distributed. This is done using the `DISTRIBUTE` and `PROCESSOR` directives in the input program. In the second step, the virtual processors are assigned to the physical processors. The physical processors are viewed as a linear array, and are numbered $0, 1, \cdots, P-1$. Virtual processor $(v_0, v_1, \cdots, v_{n-1})$ is assigned to the physical processor numbered $\sum_{i=0}^{n-1} v_i \prod_{j=i+1}^{n-1} V_j$. Thus, for a 2-dimensional grid of virtual processors, this mapping scheme implies a column-major order assignment of virtual processors to physical processors.

The owner-compute rule [8] is used to partition parallel loops. This rule specifies that a processor executes a statement that *computes* an array element (i.e., writes to it) if and only if it *owns* the array element, i.e., has the element in its local memory. Consequently, the subset of loop iterations a processor executes is the subset of loop iterations that write local array elements. The partitioning of a parallel loop is performed by computing the *Local Index Set* for each distributed array on each processor. This is the set of indices of array elements that reside in the local memory of a processor. It is calculated using the array distribution directives provided by the programmer. The *Global Iteration Set* is computed for each array reference in the left hand side (`lhs`) of an assignment statement in the parallel loop. This set describes the iteration space spanned by the reference in the parallel loop, and is calculated using the inverse array subscript expressions appearing in the array reference. Finally, the *Local Iteration Set* is computed for the parallel loop on each processor. This set is the subset of loop iterations which are executed by each processor, and is computed by intersecting the Global Iteration Set with the set that describes the loop iteration space. The data distribution analysis is illustrated in Figure 3.2, which shows a simple example and the various index sets generated on a processor. The index sets are expressed using regular section descriptors, or RSDs [4]. An RSD is denoted by $[l_1 : u_1 : s_1][l_2 : u_2 : s_2] \cdots [l_n : u_n : s_n]$, where l_i, u_i and s_i are respectively the lower bound, upper bound and stride of the ith dimension of the RSD.

3.3. Communication Analysis. This analysis also uses the owner-compute rule to determine which array references are non-local to each processor. Such references must be on the right hand side (`rhs`) of the statements of the body of the loop since the owner-compute rule makes all references on the `lhs` local. The *Local Access Set* for each `rhs` array reference in a loop statement is calculated by determining array indices spanned by the loop's Local Iteration Set. The *Remote Index Set* for each array reference is then computed as the set difference of the Local Access Set for the array and the Local Index Set for the

```
PROCESSOR P(4,4);
DISTRIBUTE a (BLOCK,BLOCK) ONTO P;
DISTRIBUTE b (BLOCK,BLOCK) ONTO P;
    :
    :
DOALL i = 0, 63, 1       /* L1 */
   DOALL j = 1, 62, 1    /* L2 */
      a[i][j] = ( b[i][j-1] + b[i][j+1] ) / 2
```

(a) A parallel loop code segment.

Local Index sets of a and b	=	$[32:47:1][16:31:1]$
Global Iteration Set of a	=	$[0:63:1][1:62:1]$
Local Iteration Set of $L1$	=	$[32:47:1]$
Local Iteration Set of $L2$	=	$[16:31:1]$
Local Access Set of b	=	$[32:47:1][15:30:1] + [32:47:1][17:32:1]$
Remote Access Set of b	=	$[32:47:1][15:15:1] + [32:47:1][32:32:1]$ $+ [32:47:1][15:32:17]$
Remote ownership of b	=	{ $P(2,0)$: $[32:47:1][15:15:1]$, $P(2,2)$: $[32:47:1][32:32:1]$, others: none }

(b) Index sets for processor P(2,1).

FIG. 3.2. *Analysis for a simple loop nest.*

reference. Finally, the ownership of the array elements in the Remote Index Set is determined by intersecting the Remote Index Set with the Local Index Set for the array on each processor. The index sets generated by communication analysis in the above example are also illustrated in Figure 3.2.

3.4. Prefetch Insertion. The compiler inserts a call to a prefetch routine to initiate asynchronous transfer of data from remote to local memory. This is done whenever the Remote Index Set for an array reference in a parallel loop nest is non-empty. The call to the prefetch routine are inserted immediately preceding the outmost parallel loop in the nest. The RSD representation of the Remote Index Set of each array is passed as a parameter to the prefetch routine. The routine uses the RSDs and a table containing the starting address of each array (initialized at run-time) to generate the addresses of the pages that must be prefetched to transfer remote data.[2]

3.5. Loop Peeling. The peeling transformation itself is always legal since only parallel loops are considered. A parallel loop has no loop carried dependences and hence its iterations can be executed in any order. The iterations that access remote data are removed from the loop and re-scheduled after the iterations that access only local data.

However, in some loop nests, the index of a serial loop is used to access an array dimension that is distributed. The dependences that are carried by the serial loop become *cross-processor* and force the serial loop to be executed in a pipelined "wave-front" fashion [8]. In this case, reordering the iterations of the loop is not legal because of the dependences. Consequently, loop peeling is not applied in the presence of cross-processor dependences.

It is important to note that it is possible to only insert the prefetch instruction to read remote data without peeling and re-scheduling loop iterations that access non-local data. In this case, the benefit of the CCO transformation depends on the location of the iterations that access non-local data in the parallel loop. If such iterations are towards the end of a parallel loop, the computations

[2]The prefetch supported by our DSM software is page-based; see [6] for details.

(a) Parallel Loop (b) Application

FIG. 4.1. *Speedup of 256 × 256* `Jacobi` *with 640 iterations.*

of the parallel loop provide the necessary overalp. However, if the iterations are towards the beginning of the parallel loop, peeling is necessary to re-schedule the execution of the iterations after local-only computation and realize an overlap.

4. Experimental Evaluation.

4.1. Overview. The CCO transformation was implemented in a prototype compiler called *Jasmine*, which is being developed at the University of Toronto. The compiler has four major phases: parallelism detection, cache locality enhancement, memory locality enhancement and code generation [1]. The Polaris compiler [5] from the University of Illinois is used for parallelism detection. The Jasmine Compiler accepts data distribution directives and implements the CCO transformation as part of the memory locality enhancement phase.

The Jasmine complier was used to automatically apply the transformation to 3 representative applications: the well known `Jacobi` kernel, red-black SOR (`rbsor`) and the `swim` benchmark from `spec95`. The performance of the applications with and without the transformation was experimentally evaluated on the POW network-of-workstations multiprocessor [13], also developed at the University of Toronto. The POW multiprocessor consists of IBM RS/6000 workstations connected by Fast Ethernet. The experiments were conducted using 8 workstations. A version of TreadMarks [3] modified to support page-level prefetching [6] was used to provide cache-coherent shared-memory.

4.2. Results. The speedup (the ratio of execution time of the sequential program to execution time of the parallel program) of `Jacobi` is shown in Figures 4.1–4.3. A `(*,BLOCK)` data distribution is used for all arrays. In each figure, the speedup of only the target parallel loop targeted by the transformation as well as the speedup for the complete application are shown. In each case, 3 sets of results are presented. The first gives the speedup without any optimizations, and it is used for reference. The second set gives the speedup with only prefetches inserted, but without loop peeling. The final set gives the speedup after prefetches are inserted and loop peeling is applied.

The speedup curves reflect that the performance of both the target parallel loop in `Jacobi` and of the overall `Jacobi` do benefit from the CCO transformation. The ratio of the parallel execution time at 8 processors with both prefetching and peeling applied to the parallel execution time (at 8 processors) with no optimization is shown in Table 4.1. The table indicates that the performance of the parallel loop improves by up to 2.9 times. The performance of the overall kernel improves by up to 1.9 times. However, the speedup of `Jacobi`

(a) Parallel Loop (b) Application

FIG. 4.2. *Speedup of 512 × 512* `Jacobi` *with 640 iterations.*

(a) Parallel Loop (b) Application

FIG. 4.3. *Speedup of 1024 × 1024* `Jacobi` *with 640 iterations.*

at 1 processor is only 0.50, because of the overhead that is introduced by parallelization and loop peeling in the parallel program. When the parallel program on 1 processor is slower than the sequential program. Furthermore, the speedup of the program is not scaling because of the high communication overhead that remains even after peeling and overlap.

The speedup curves also indicate the need for the peeling component of the transformation. Although there is benefit from just using prefetching, there is added benefit from combining peeling with prefetching. As discussed in Section 3.5, the prefetch instructions alone benefit performance when the iterations that access remote data are towards the end of the parallel loop. The loop computations provide sufficient overlap and there is little or no need to use the peeling component of the transformation to provide further overlap. However, when the iterations that access remote data are at the beginning of the parallel loop, there is no sufficient computation to overlap with the prefetches, and processors idle waiting for remote data. In this case, peeling is necessary to delay the execution of these iterations. In the case of `Jacobi`, there are accesses to remote data both at the beginning and at the end of the parallel loop. Consequently, there is benefit to performance by using the prefetches alone and added benefit from peeling.

The speedup curves and Table 4.1 also indicate that the extent of the benefit of the transformation depends on the size of the data array and on the number of processors. The improvement in performance is higher when the input size is smaller. The transformed parallel program with both prefetching and peeling is 1.9 times faster than the original parallel program without optimization at 8 processors when a data size of 256 × 256. However, the transformed parallel program is only 1.3 times faster when the data size is 512 × 512, and only 1.1

TABLE 4.1
Ratio of parallel execution times at 8 processor with and without transformation (640 iterations).

Problem Size	Loop Only	Overall Application
256 × 256	2.9	1.9
512 × 512	1.3	1.3
1024 × 1024	1.1	1.1

TABLE 4.2
Average ratio of un-successful prefetches at 8 processors (640 iterations).

Data Size	Average Ratio
128 × 128	6.03E-3
256 × 256	1.11E-3
512 × 512	0
1024 × 1024	0

times faster when the data size is 1024 × 1024. This is because the size of the data determines the amount of local computation performed by each processor in the parallel loop. When the size of the data is relatively small (256 × 256), the amount of local computation in the parallel loop is small, and the impact of the remote memory accesses is more pronounced. Hiding the latency of remote accesses has a significant impact on performance. In contrast, when the size of the data is relatively large (1024 × 1024), the impact of remote memory accesses on performance is relatively small; the amount of local computation grows by $O(n^2)$ while the amount of non-local memory accesses grow by $O(n)$, where $n \times n$ is the problem size. Consequently, for larger data sizes there is less benefit to overall performance.

The computation time of the local-only iterations also determines the effectiveness of the CCO transformation in hiding the latency of remote accesses. Table 4.2 shows the average ratio of un-successful prefetches (i.e., prefetches that are issued by a processor, but are not complete by the time data is needed by the processor) to total prefetches for various data size of the `Jacobi`. When the size of the data is small, the amount of local-only computation is small and a fraction of prefetches are unsuccessful. However, when the size of the data is large, there is enough local-only computation to overlap with remote accesses and all of the prefetches that are issued succeed.

The speedup of `rbsor` and of `swim` is shown in Figures 4.4 and 4.5, respectively. The magnitude of the performance improvement in each case that is less than that in the case of `Jacobi`. The is because of the large amount of local-only computation time compared to the time of non-local memory accesses. Furthermore, in the case of `swim`, the location of the iterations that access remote data is towards the end of the parallel loops, resulting in minimal benefit from peeling.

5. Related Work. There is a large body of work on the use of hardware and software prefetching to improve the performance of programs, on both single- and multi-processor systems (see [7]). These techniques differ from this work in two main aspects. First, the above techniques prefetch data into the *cache* of a processor. In contrast, the prefetch mechanism we use (developed by Chan [6]) brings data into the local memory of a processor, making the benefit of prefetching smaller. However, it avoids potential cache pollution problems. Second, the above techniques generally prefetch a single cache line. In contrast,

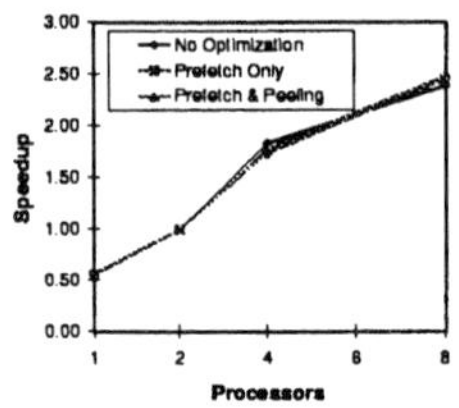

FIG. 4.4. *Speedup of* `rbsor`.

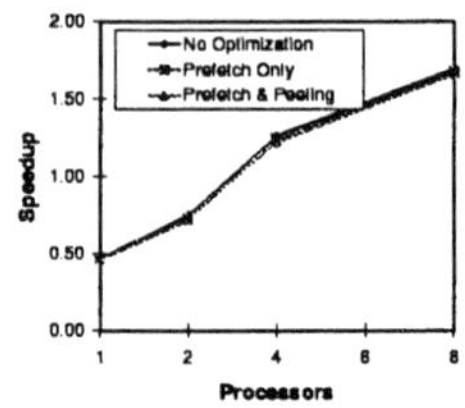

FIG. 4.5. *Speedup of* `swim`.

the prefetch mechanism we use brings a whole page into memory, which makes it possible to implement prefetching with no hardware support [6].

There is also a large body of work on communication optimization in message passage programs that are compiler-generated using Fortran D or High-Performance Fortran [8, 9, 14]. Pugh and Rosser [14] describe *iteration slicing* which can be used to separate iterations that need non-local data from those that do not and use it for communication optimization. The CCO transformation is similar to *iteration reordering* described by Hiranandani, Kennedy and Tseng [9]. The CCO transformation can be considered as extending the applicability of iteration re-ordering to shared memory multiprocessors. However, there are some important differences. The use of prefetch instructions in a shared address space relieves the compiler from calculating "owners" of remote data and from using explicit send/receive instructions. On the other hand, while iteration reordering uses message passing to move exactly the needed data from remote to local memory, the prefetches move data in units of pages, which may contain un-needed data, and results in more overhead. In addition, the prefetches are non-binding and cannot be used for synchronization in a manner similar to message receives. Hence, if no sufficient local-only computation time exist, the full latency of remote accesses is incurred in addition to the overhead of prefetching.

6. Conclusions. This paper described and evaluated a transformation called CCO for hiding the latency of non-local memory access in parallel loops on shared-memory NOW multiprocessors. Experimental evaluation of the transformation indicates that it is effective in improving parallel performance. The benefit is highest when the impact of non-local memory accesses is high, and there is sufficient local computation to hide non-local memory accesses. The extent of the benefit also depends on the location in a parallel loop of the iterations that access remote data; the benefit is higher when such iterations are towards the beginning of the parallel loop.

Acknowledgements. This work has been supported by research grants from the Natural Sciences and Engineering Research Council of Canada (NSERC) and the Information Technology Research Centre of Ontario (ITRC).

REFERENCES

[1] T. ABDELRAHMAN, N. MANJIKIAN, G. LIU AND S. TANDRI, *Locality enhancement for large-scale shared-memory multiprocessors*, in Proc. of the 4th Workshop on Languages, Compilers and Run-Time Systems for Scalable Computers, 1998, pp. 335–342.

[2] T. ABDELRAHMAN AND T. WONG, *Compiler support for array distribution on NUMA multiprocessors*, The Journal of Supercomputing, 4, (1998), pp. 349–371.

[3] C. AMZA, ET AL., *TreadMarks: shared memory computing on networks of workstations*, IEEE Computer, 2, (1996), pp. 18–28.

[4] V. BALASUNDARAM, *A mechanism for keeping useful internal information in parallel programming tools: the data access descriptor*, Journal of Parallel and Distributed Computing, 6, (1990), pp. 154–170.

[5] W. BLUME, ET AL, *Parallel programming with Polaris*, IEEE Computer, 12, (1996), pp. 78–82.

[6] C. CHAN, *Tolerating latency in software distributed memory systems through non-binding prefetching*, M.Sc. Thesis, Department of Computer Science, University of Toronto, 1997.

[7] T. CHEN AND J. BAER, *A performance study of software and hardware data prefetching schemes*, in Proc. of the Int'l Symposium on Computer Architecture, 1994, pp. 223–232.

[8] S. HIRANANDANI, K. KENNEDY AND C. TSENG, *Compiling Fortran D*, Communications of the ACM, 8, (1992), pp. 66–80.

[9] S. HIRANANDANI, K. KENNEDY AND C. TSENG, *Evaluation of compiler optimizations for Fortran D on MIMD distributed-memory machines*, in Proc. of the Int'l Conference on Supercomputing, 1992, pp. 1–14.

[10] C. KOELBEL, D. LOVEMAN, R. SCHREIBER, G. STEELE, JR. AND M. ZOSEL, *The High Performance Fortran Handbook*, The MIT Press, Cambridge, MA, 1994.

[11] J. KUSKIN, ET AL, *The Stanford Dash multiprocessor*, in Proc. of the Int'l Symposium on Computer Architecture, 1994, pp. 302–313.

[12] A. NOWATZYK ET AL, *The s3.mp scalable memory multiprocessor*, in Proc. of the Int'l Conference on Parallel Processing, 1995, pp. 1–8.

[13] *The POW multiprocessor project*, The University of Toronto. A WWW document available at `http://www.eecg.toronto.edu/parallel/sigpow`, 1997.

[14] W. PUGH AND E. ROSSER, *Iteration space slicing and its application to communication optimization*, in Proc. of the International Conference on Supercomputing, 1997, pp. 221–228.

[15] S. TANDRI AND T. ABDELRAHMAN, *Automatic partitioning of data and computation on scalable shared memory multiprocessors*, in Proc. of the Int'l Conference on Parallel Processing, 1997, pp. 64–73.

[16] B. VERGHESE, S. DEVINE, A. GUPTA AND M. ROSENBLUM, *OS support for improving data locality on CC-NUMA compute servers*, in Proc. of the 7th Int'l Conference on Architectural Support for Programming Languages and Operating Systems, 1996, pp. 279-289.

[17] M. WOLFE, *High performance compilers for parallel computing*, Addison-Wesley Publishing Company, Redwood City, CA, 1996.

AGGRESSIVE COMMUNICATION OPTIMIZATIONS FOR CLUSTERS OF WORKSTATIONS*

GAGAN AGRAWAL †

Abstract. Because of the increasing computational power of workstations and the PCs, the peak processing power of clusters of workstations has been increasing at a rapid pace. However, the sustained performance on a variety of applications lags far behind, because these systems offer lower communication performance. In this paper, we focus on improving the communication performance of the applications run on the clusters through aggressive compiler optimizations. We present a general interprocedural technique for performing communication optimizations across procedure boundaries. Our technique uses the result of local analysis to model the communication as a communication loop, and then performs flow-sensitive interprocedural data-flow analysis to avoid redundant communication, and to perform communication aggregation. Our experimental results and the projected analysis on the clusters shows that aggressive communication optimizations from compilers are very important for system with low communication performance and high computational power.

1. Introduction. Technological advances in recent years have made clusters and network of workstations very attractive alternatives to the dedicated parallel machines. Because of the increasing computational power of the individual nodes of the clusters, the peak processing power of these systems is increasing at a rapid pace. Several clusters of workstations or PCs are now listed in the top 500 supercomputers in the world.

Though the peak computational power of clusters has increased rapidly, the sustained performance on a large variety of applications lags far behind. This is primarily because the clusters or the networks offer lower communication to computation performance, as compared to the dedicated parallel machines. Improving communication performance of a variety of applications is the key to long-term success of clusters of workstations.

The performance of individual applications can be improved through aggressive tuning of MPI code; however, we believe that optimizing compilers for message passing architectures can play an important role in improving performance of these systems. Compiling for message passing architectures has been an area of increasing significance over the last few years. Design of initial academic systems like Vienna Fortran Compiler [14] and Fortran D system [10], lead to the definition of High Performance Fortran (HPF) language. HPF compilers are available from several vendors today. Because of the portability of MPI, these compilers can be easily targeted for generating code for clusters or network of workstations.

Improving communication performance in the presence of limited bandwidth and high communication latency has been one of the important goals of the compilers of these machines. All message passing compilers perform some commu-

*THIS RESEARCH WAS SUPPORTED BY NSF CAREER AWARD ACI-9733520 AND NSF GRANT CCR-9808522

† Department of Computer and Information Sciences, University of Delaware, Newark DE 19716, (302)-831-2783, Email: agrawal@cis.udel.edu

nication analysis and communication optimizations to both reduce the volume of communication (by avoiding redundant communication) and the frequency of communication (by aggregating messages). The existing research in the area of communication analysis and communication optimization can be classified into three levels:

Single Loop Nest Level:. The earliest compilers performed analysis within a single parallel loop, or even a single Fortran 90 array statement [5]. Such communication analysis aggregated the off-processor elements required in the different iterations of the same loop, but did not aggregate messages or avoid redundant communication across loops.

Single Procedure Analysis:. Several researchers improved upon the single loop level analysis by performing data flow analysis within a single procedure. The Rice Fortran D compiler performed a number of communication optimizations between loops which were related through simple flow of control [10], like message vectorization and message aggregation. Gupta *et al.* used partial redundancy elimination [7] and greedy analysis on the SSA form [6] to improve the performance of regular applications. Hanxleden proposed a data flow framework called *Give-N-Take* for performing communication placement within a single procedure [9].

Interprocedural Analysis:. The only work in the area of flow-sensitive interprocedural analysis for communication has been restricted to performing placement of collective communication calls and communication preprocessing calls, after communication aggregation has been done within single procedures [2, 1]. These techniques consider the communication calls as a pure function, and use the mod-ref information on the parameters of the pure function for performing the placement. One particular limitation of this work has been to consider each array as a single entity, and modification or reference to any element of the array as a modification to the entire array. As part of the Fortran D system in Rice university, flow-insensitive analysis has been implemented for communication optimizations [8]. This work only applies to programs for which the call graph is a directed acyclic graph (i.e. non-recursive programs).

Because of the lower communication performance (as compared to the computational power) of the cluster of workstations, aggressive communication optimizations become increasingly important for these systems. In this paper, we present a new technique for aggregating communication across procedure boundaries.

Our technique initially summarizes the result of local analysis for communication in terms of a novel abstraction, called a *communication loop*. We use a full program representation called *FPR* [2, 1] to propagate information about communication through flow-sensitive interprocedural analysis, allowing redundant communication elimination and communication aggregation. Next, we use some heuristics to avoid unnecessarily early placement of communication.

The rest of the paper is organized as follows. We introduce the problem in Section 2. Local communication analysis is presented in Section 3. Program representation used for interprocedural analysis is presented in Section 4 and the

```
Program Foo                          Procedure P(X,Y,Z)
  Template T                           forall(i=2:N:2)
  Align A, B, C, D with T              X(i) = ..Y(i+1) + Z(i+1)
                                     End
  Call P(A,B,D)
  if foo                             Procedure Q(X,Y)
    Call Q(A,D)                        forall(i=1:N:1)
  else                                 X(i) = Y(i+1)
    Call Q(A,D)                      End
  endif                              Procedure R(X,Y)
  Call R(C,B)                          forall(i=1:N-1:2)
End                                    X(i) = Y(i+1)
                                     End
```

FIG. 2.1. *An Example Program*

actual analysis is presented in Section 5. Experimental evaluation is presented in Section 6 and conclusions are presented in Section 7.

2. Problem Definition. We initially list the goals of our analysis. Obviously, we require that the communication placement done as a result of the analysis must not change the semantics of the program, i.e. all required off-processor elements must be available whenever required for correct execution of the program.

Our analysis aims to achieve the following:

- Decrease the overall communication bandwidth required by avoiding redundant communication
- Decrease the effect of latency on the overall performance by aggregating messages, i.e. decreasing the frequency of communication

Consider the example program presented in Figure 2.1. In both the procedures P and R, off-processor elements of the global array B are required (array B is renamed as Y in both these procedures). The code inside procedure P requires even numbered indices whereas the code inside the procedure R requires odd numbered indices. However, the request for these elements can be coalesced into one message, which will reduce the number of messages required. Also, the code inside the procedure P and both the invocations of the procedure Q requires off-processor elements of the global array D (renamed as Z inside the procedure P and as Y inside the procedure Q). If the message for Q is moved earlier in the code, no further communication will be required for the access of array D in the procedure P.

Our analysis framework has two main phases, a local analysis phase where the communication requirements of individual loop nests are summarized, and an interprocedural propagation phase.

Local Communication Analysis. All compilers for message passing machines perform analysis on single loop nests or a single basic blocks to identify off-processor elements required [5, 10]. More recently, even the distributed shared memory compilers perform such analysis for reducing the synchronization overheads [12]. In our framework, the result of this step is to summarize the off-processor references in the form of an abstraction called a *communication loop*, which is described in more details later in this paper.

Interprocedural Propagation. The main phase of the analysis uses interprocedural data flow to perform communication aggregation, redundant communication elimination and communication placement. We use our novel program representation, called *FPR* [2, 1]. We use the set of *communication loops* as the lattice for data flow analysis.

Before interprocedural analysis can be done, we need to summarize the local communication requirements. We present the abstraction used for summarizing the local communication requirements in the next section.

3. Local Communication Analysis. All the current compilers for distributed memory machines perform analysis within a single parallel loop for determining the communication requirements [5, 10]. We do not propose any specific technique for performing such local analysis, but we are interested in summarizing the result of this analysis using a novel representation called *communication loop.*

Previous global and interprocedural frameworks have chosen a range of different abstractions for summarizing local communication requirements. In contrast to the previous approaches [7, 9], we believe that communication analysis should be done before knowing the number of processors on which the code is to be executed. There are two main reasons for this:

- There is an increasing trend to use a network of non-dedicated workstations for executing parallel code. For such a configuration, the compiler needs to generate code which is independent of the number of processors. We are interested in developing a uniform analysis framework which can optimize communication even for such systems.
- We believe that to the extent possible, phases of data parallel compiler should be independent of the number of processors, to allow easy recompilation to a different number of processors.

With the above considerations, we have defined a new abstraction for communication requirements, which we call a *communication loop.* To motivate this abstraction, consider the following parallel loop, which we denote by `L1`.

```
L1:  forall( i = 1:N-2:1)
     A(i)  =  B(i) + C(i) + D(i+2)
```

If the arrays A, B and C are identically distributed and if owners compute rule is used for loop partitioning, the local communication analysis can determine that the above loop will not involve any off-processor references to the elements of the arrays B and C. However, off-processor references will be required to the elements of array D. The precise set of off-processor references depends upon the number of processors on which this code is to be executed. We can represent the communication requirement of this loop as follows:

```
communicate( i = 1:N-2:1)
A(i)  =   D(i+2)
```

The above abstraction will allow us to eliminate communication of the elements of array D, if they are being assigned to the elements of array A in another loop. However, if the identical elements of the array D are being assigned to a different array in another loop, the above abstraction not be adequate for removing such redundancy. Consider, for example, the following loop (denote by L2):

```
L2:  forall( i = 1:N-2:1)
     B(i) = C(i) + D(i+2)
```

If the distribution of the arrays A and B are identical, the communication requirements of the two forall loops will be identical. If there is no modification to the array D in any control flow path from the first loop to the second loop, the required off-processor elements of D can be communicated and stored in a buffer location and used for both the loops. This will reduce the communication volume by a factor of two and improve the overall speedup.

To allow better reuse of the off-processor data, we improve our abstraction by using the notion of *templates* from languages like HPF and Fortran-D [10]. Typically, arrays with identical distributions are aligned with the same template. For example,

```
Template T(N)
Distribute T(block)
Align  A, B, C, D with T
forall(i = 1:N-2:1)
A(i)  =  B(i) + C(i) + D(i+2)
```

We represent the communication associated with this forall loop by the following communication loop:

```
communicate( i = 1:N-2:1)
T(i)  =   D(i+2)
```

The communication requirements of the loop involving assignment to B will also be represented using an identical communication loop which will make identifying the redundancies easier.

4. Full Program Representation. One key aspect of interprocedural analysis is the choice of program representation. Therefore, before presenting the details of the analysis, we describe the full program representation we use. We have developed a new full program representation which preserves information about the call sites but is more concise than a Supergraph.

A procedure can be partitioned into a set of basic blocks, a set of call statements and a set of exit statements, An exit statement ends the closure of the current procedure. Each call statement is a *call site* of the procedure invoked there.

Full Program Representation: (*FPR*) is a directed multigraph $G = (V, E)$, where the set of nodes V consists of nodes of four types:

- Procedure entry nodes; for a procedure i, the entry node is denoted by

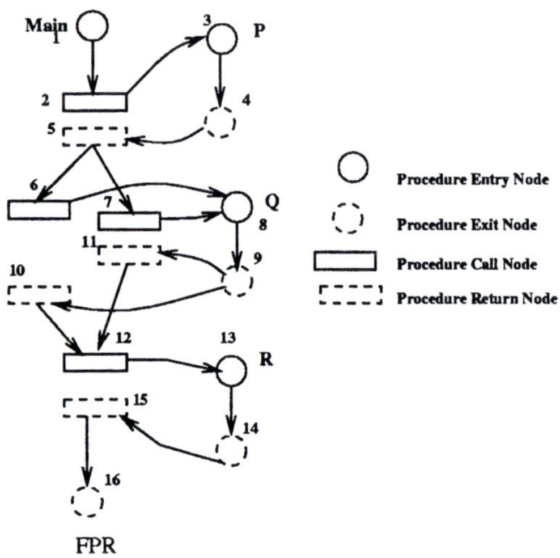

FIG. 4.1. *FPR for the code in Figure 2.1*

pn_i.

- Procedure exit nodes; for a procedure i, the return node is denoted by px_i.
- Call Site node; for a procedure call site j, the procedure call node is denoted by cs_j.
- Call return node; for a procedure call site site j, the procedure return node is denoted by cr_j.

Edges are inserted to show the flow of control (both intraprocedurally and interprocedurally between these nodes). An example of FPR is shown in Figure 4.1. For presenting our scheme, we introduce the notion of *procedure closure.*

Procedure Closure.. Closure of a procedure p is a the smallest set of procedures $\mathcal{S}$ such that

(a) The procedure p is in the set $\mathcal{S}$.

(b) Any procedure which is called by a procedure in the set $\mathcal{S}$ is in $\mathcal{S}$.

When we refer to a procedure closure p, we mean the set of procedures in the set S as defined above.

The following information is pre-computed and assumed to be available during our analysis phase. For each block of code in *FPR*, we compute the array sections that are modified. This information can be computed by intraprocedural analysis. For simplicity, we restrict ourselves to computing rectilinear sections, which can be represented by a forall loop. We perform flow-insensitive analysis for calculating the array sections modified by each procedure closure.

5. Interprocedural Communication Analysis. The goal of the interprocedural analysis is to avoid redundant communication and aggregate communication wherever possible. For achieving these two goals, our analysis uses the notion of *anticipability* from the classical data flow analysis literature. Anticipability has been used as part of more general frameworks like partial redundancy elimination for code placement. Suppose we are considering placement of an expression. This expression is anticipable at a point p in the program if there is an occurrence of this expression on all paths leading from p and none of the variable in the expression are modified between p and the point of occurrence.

By placing the communication at the earliest point where it is anticipable, we can avoid redundant communication and try to aggregate communication. However, this will often lead to unnecessarily early placement of communication, which can increase the buffer requirements. Later in this section, we describe a set of heuristics that can be used for avoiding redundant motion in most of the cases.

Collective communication in distributed memory programs can be broadly classified to be of two kinds: *gathers* or *pre-comp* communication and *scatters* or *post-comp* communication. By gather, we mean a routine which, before entering a data parallel loop, collects the off-processor elements referred to in the loop. By scatter, we mean a routine which, after a data parallel loop, updates the off-processor elements modified by the loop. The details of analysis presented here are for optimization of gather communication only. The analysis presented here can be applied in the opposite direction on the graph for optimizing scatter communication.

We introduce the following definitions for presenting our analysis.

COMM(n)	:	Communication anticipable at a node n in the graph
GEN(n)	:	Communication generated at a node n in graph
PLACE(n, m)	:	Communication placed at a node n in the graph
MOD(n, m)	:	Array sections modified along the edge (n, m)
PMOD(p)	:	Array sections modified by the procedure closure p

The significance of the above terms is as follows. The term GEN(n) is computed using local analysis and is used to initialize the value of COMM(n). The term COMM(n) represents the communication which is to be placed at the points preceding to the current one and is propagated using interprocedural analysis. PLACE(n) is the communication which is placed at a node n in the graph. PLACE(n, m) is the communication to be placed along an edge (n, m). Precise placement of such communication requires further intraprocedural analysis. All these values are stored as a set of communication loops, an abstraction for communication we defined earlier.

The functions MOD(n, m) and PMOD(p) are used to propagate communication terms. Consider a set of communication loops, $S = < l_1, \ldots, l_i >$. MOD(n, m)[S] or PMOD(p)[S] will include l_1 only if:

- None of the array elements on the right hand side has been modified by the block of code or the procedure closure.
- The template on the left hand side of the communication loop has not been redistributed.

We first describe how the term GEN(n) is initialized following the local communication analysis. For procedure exit nodes and procedure call nodes, the set GEN(n) is set to be null. Consider a node n which is a procedure entry node, i.e. let $n = pn_i$. If a certain communication loop occurs on all the paths from the start of the procedure i, and these paths do not involve any procedure calls, and the right hand side array elements in the communication loop are not modified, then GEN(n) includes this communication loop. Alternatively, consider any node n which is a call return node, i.e. $n = cr_j$. If a certain communication loop occurs on all the paths from the call site j, and these paths do not involve any procedure calls, and the right hand side array elements in the communication loop are not modified, then GEN(n) includes this communication loop.

Next, we describe how the term COMM(n) is propagated using backward interprocedural data flow analysis. Consider a node n, which is either a procedure entry node or a call return node.

$$\text{COMM}(n) = \text{GEN}(n) \bigcup (\bigcap_{(n,m)\in E} \text{MOD}(n,m)[\text{COMM}(m)])$$

The above equation ensures that the communication loops placed in the COMM(n) sets are anticipable at the node n.

Along each such edge (n, m), the communication to be placed is given as

$$\text{PLACE}(n,m) = \text{COMM}(m) - \text{COMM}(n)$$

The final placement of this communication is done by further analysis on the block of code (n, m).

Next, consider a node n which is a procedure exit node.

$$\text{COMM}(n) = \bigcap_{(n,m)\in E} \text{COMM}(m)$$

Note that for a procedure exit node, we may also need to rename the variable names across procedure boundaries. We have ignored this detail here, as it can be trivially handled in implementation.

Finally, we consider a node n which is a call site node. In propagating the value of COMM(n) at a procedure call node, we need to address the problem of *unrealizable* or *invalid* paths in our program representation. This problem arises in any flow-sensitive interprocedural analysis, irrespective of the program representation used. An unrealizable or invalid path in the graph is a path which does not correspond to any actual execution of the program. The reason such paths can arise in the program representation is as follows: Consider any procedure p which is invoked at two call sites $cs1$ and $cs2$. The program representation will show a path from the call site node at $cs1$, to procedure entry for p, to procedure exit for p to call return node at $cs2$. Such a path can never be taken during any actual execution of the program and is referred to as an *unrealizable* or *invalid* path.

Such paths can bring significant inaccuracy in our analysis. Suppose a communication loop is anticipable at the call return node at $cs1$ but not at call return node for $cs2$. In this case, this communication will not be anticipable inside procedure p. Propagating backwards using just the predecessor relationship, we will determine that this communication loop is not anticipable at the call site node for $cs1$. However, this will not be accurate if the array on the right hand side of this communication loop is not modified in the procedure closure of p.

To accommodate this fact, we make the following modification in the way we propagate the anticipability of a communication loop. Given a call site node n, let n' be corresponding call return node and let p be the procedure invoked at this call site.

$$\text{COMM}(n) = \text{PMOD}(p)[\text{COMM}(n')] \bigcup \bigcap_{(n,m)\in E} \text{COMM}(m)$$

Consider any communication which was placed at the call return node n'. This communication needs to be placed here if it cannot be moved up the procedure exit node (that is the predecessor of the node n') or the corresponding call site node n. Let us denote the (unique) predecessor node of n' by m'. The communication to be placed at the node n' will be

$$\text{PLACE}(n') = \text{COMM}(n') - \text{COMM}(m') - \text{COMM}(n)$$

We finally briefly describe some heuristics for avoiding unnecessarily early code motion. Consider a node or an edge in the graph along which a communication loop is determined to be placed by the analysis performed so far. The analysis performed so far has determined this placement because this is the earliest place where the operation is still anticipable. However, in several cases, there is no further aggregation or redundancy elimination achieved by moving the operation this early. Unnecessarily early placement results in unnecessary high buffer requirements. To avoid such an early placement, we propose the following heuristic.

Starting from the node or an edge where PLACE includes a communication loop l_i, we traverse the FPR in the forward direction (i.e. the opposite of the direction in which communication was initially propagated). For each node n encountered, we check if COMM(n) includes l_i, and if GEN(n) includes l_i. Communication can be placed at any node where COMM(n) includes l_i and where GEN(n) does not include l_i.

6. Experimental Results. To demonstrate the efficacy of our technique, we have experimented with two real applications. All our experiments were performed on a 16 processor IBM SP-2, which is a cluster of workstations.

6.1. Direct Simulation Monte Carlo. Direction Simulation Monte Carlo is a well known technique for studying the interaction of particles in cells [4]. The program we used in our experiments, `dsmc-3d` was originally developed

No. of	w/o opt.			with opt.		
Proc.	Comp.	Comm.	Total	Comp.	Comm.	Total
1	37.1	0	37.1	37.1	0	37.1
2	18.5	1.8	20.3	18.5	0.8	19.3
4	9.3	1.8	11.1	9.3	0.8	10.1
8	4.7	2.6	7.3	4.7	1.1	5.8
16	2.3	2.0	4.3	2.3	0.8	3.1

FIG. 6.1. *Performance improvements through interprocedural communication optimizations (*DSMC*)*

by Richard Wilmoth at NASA Langley [11]. The version of the code we used comprised of 10 procedures and nearly 3000 lines of code. Communication is required in 4 different procedures in each time-step. We experimented with 388K particles. By applying our analysis by hand over the communication in the existing version, we were able to combine communication and also delete redundant communication. The executions times, with and without the optimizations, are shown for 1, 2, 4, 8 and 16 processors in Figure 6.1. Communication was already optimized through analysis within a procedure in our unoptimized versions. Thus, the performance gains shown in our optimized versions are the additional gains possible through flow-sensitive interprocedural analysis. Execution times are reported for 20 iterations. For both the optimized and unoptimized versions, we have shown the computation time, communication time and the total wall-clock time. The computation time decreases by a linear factor as the number of processors is increased. This is because all portions of the code are parallelized and there is no replicated code as the program is executed in parallel.

The overall communication time decreased by nearly 60% in execution over 2, 4, 8 or 16 processors. As the number of processors is increased, the communication time becomes an increasing fraction of the total execution time. As the result, the overall improvement in performance ranges from only 5% for 2 processors, when the communications costs are low, to nearly 27% on 16 processors, when the communication costs become very high.

6.2. Multi-block CFD solver. We also experimented with a version of a multi-block computation fluid dynamics application that solves the thin-layer Navier-Stokes equations over a 3D surface (multi-block `TLNS3D`). The original sequential version of this code was developed by Vatsa *et al.* [13] at NASA Langley Research Center. In previous work by the author and his colleagues a template was extracted to include portions of the entire code that are representative of the major computation and communication patterns of the original code [3]. This template comprised of nearly 2,000 lines of code and 8 procedures. This code was parallelized by a prototype Fortran 90D (a version of HPF) compiler originally developed at Syracuse university [5] and extended to handle multi-block applications at Maryland [3]. We applied the analysis proposed here by hand over the compiler generated code and removed redundant communication.

No. of Proc.	w/o opt.			with opt.		
	Comp.	Comm.	Total	Comp.	Comm.	Total
1	12.31	0	12.31	12.31	0	12.31
2	6.16	0.67	6.83	6.16	0.46	6.62
4	3.07	0.73	3.80	3.07	0.48	3.55
8	1.54	0.60	2.14	1.54	0.35	1.89
16	0.76	0.55	1.31	0.76	0.32	1.08

FIG. 6.2. *Performance improvements through communication optimizations (*TLNS3D*)*

The execution times, with and without the proposed optimizations, are shown in Figure 6.2. Experiments were performed on 100 iterations over a $49 \times 9 \times 9$ mesh. The decrease in communication time is nearly 30% over execution on 2, 4, 8 or 16 processors. This results in an overall reduction in execution time of 3% on 2 processors to 18% on 16 processors.

7. Conclusions. In this paper, we have addressed the problem of performing communication optimizations across procedure boundaries. We have developed a novel abstraction for summarizing local communication requirements and using it as the basis for data flow analysis. We have presented a general flow-sensitive framework for communication analysis across procedure boundaries and redundant communication elimination and communication aggregation. We have presented experimental results to demonstrate the performance gains from interprocedural communication optimizations. Our experimental results and the projected analysis on the clusters shows that aggressive communication optimizations from compilers are very important for system with low communication performance and high computational power.

REFERENCES

[1] G. Agrawal and J. Saltz, *Interprocedural compilation of irregular applications for distributed memory machines*, in Proceedings Supercomputing '95, IEEE Computer Society Press, Dec. 1995.

[2] G. Agrawal, J. Saltz, and R. Das, *Interprocedural partial redundancy elimination and its application to distributed memory compilation*, in Proceedings of the SIGPLAN '95 Conference on Programming Language Design and Implementation, ACM Press, June 1995, pp. 258–269.
ACM SIGPLAN Notices, Vol. 30, No. 6.

[3] G. Agrawal, A. Sussman, and J. Saltz, *An integrated runtime and compile-time approach for parallelizing structured and block structured applications*, IEEE Transactions on Parallel and Distributed Systems, 6 (1995), pp. 747–754.

[4] G. A. Bird, *Molecular Gas Dynamics and the Direct Simulation of Gas Flows*, Clarendon Press, Oxford, 1994.

[5] Z. Bozkus, A. Choudhary, G. Fox, T. Haupt, S. Ranka, and M.-Y. Wu, *Compiling Fortran 90D/HPF for distributed memory MIMD computers*, Journal of Parallel and Distributed Computing, 21 (1994), pp. 15–26.

[6] S. Chakrabarti, M. Gupta, and J.-D. Choi, *Global communication analysis and optimization*, in Proceedings of the SIGPLAN '96 Conference on Programming Language

Design and Implementation, ACM Press, May 1996, pp. 68–78. ACM SIGPLAN Notices, Vol. 31, No. 5.

[7] M. GUPTA, E. SCHONBERG, AND H. SRINIVASAN, *A unified data flow framework for optimizing communication*, in Proceedings of Languages and Compilers for Parallel Computing, Aug. 1994.

[8] M. HALL, S. HIRANANDANI, K. KENNEDY, AND C.-W. TSENG, *Interprocedural compilation of Fortran D for MIMD distributed-memory machines*, in Proceedings Supercomputing '92, IEEE Computer Society Press, Nov. 1992, pp. 522–534.

[9] R. v. HANXLEDEN AND K. KENNEDY, *Give-n-take – a balanced code placement framework*, in Proceedings of the SIGPLAN '94 Conference on Programming Language Design and Implementation, ACM Press, June 1994, pp. 107–120. ACM SIGPLAN Notices, Vol. 29, No. 6.

[10] S. HIRANANDANI, K. KENNEDY, AND C.-W. TSENG, *Compiling Fortran D for MIMD distributed-memory machines*, Communications of the ACM, 35 (1992), pp. 66–80.

[11] B. MOON AND J. SALTZ, *Adaptive runtime support for direct simulation Monte Carlo methods on distributed memory architectures*, in Proceedings of the Scalable High Performance Computing Conference (SHPCC-94), IEEE Computer Society Press, May 1994, pp. 176–183.

[12] C.-W. TSENG, *Compiler optimizations for eliminating barrier synchronization*, in Proceedings of the Fifth Conference on Principles and Practices of Parallel Programming, 1995, July 1995.

[13] V. VATSA, M. SANETRIK, AND E. PARLETTE, *Development of a flexible and efficient multigrid-based multiblock flow solver; AIAA-93-0677*, in Proceedings of the 31st Aerospace Sciences Meeting and Exhibit, Jan. 1993.

[14] H. P. ZIMA AND B. M. CHAPMAN, *Compiling for distributed-memory systems*, Proceedings of the IEEE, 81 (1993), pp. 264–287. In Special Section on Languages and Compilers for Parallel Machines.

EXPERIENCES WITH THE SEMPA RESOURCE MANAGER FOR REAL WORLD SCIENTIFIC COMPUTING IN NETWORKS OF WORKSTATIONS*

URSULA MAIER[†], PETER LUKSCH[†], AND ARNDT BODE[†]

Abstract. The Sempa Resource Manager is a resource management system for parallel applications in a network of workstations that enables the utilization of idle resources for parallel computing and shortens the execution time of parallel applications by dynamic load balancing at runtime. The network of workstations runs in a non-dedicated mode, where the Sempa Resource Manager assigns hosts that are not required by interactive users to its batch jobs. The flexible structure of the Sempa Resource Manager guarantees scalability and results in functions for transparent process migration and dynamic reconfiguration of the parallel execution environment. We present performance measurements with an industrial computational fluid dynamics program proving the efficiency of the Sempa Resource Manager.

Key words. resource management, load balancing, networks of workstations, parallel applications, PVM, scientific computing

1. Introduction. Parallelization of scientific computing applications is widely propagated to compute larger problems and to reduce the runtime of applications. In recent years, networks of workstations have gained acceptance as easily accessible and cost-effective hardware platforms for the computation of parallel applications in contrast to dedicated massively parallel systems.

Although the number of parallel applications is increasing, the usability of many parallel codes is restricted because of either low performance or missing runtime support, primarily resource management, for parallel applications in networks of workstations. The reason for low performance of parallel applications often is a lack of experience with parallelization concepts and tools for code development and performance analysis. In the SEMPA project guidelines are proposed for a structured way of parallelizing scientific computing applications. These guidelines are not only focused to the parallelization of scientific computing applications but also give important hints for debugging and performance analysis of parallel applications.

However, SEMPA not only deals with the development of parallel applications but also provides a runtime system to support the computation of parallel applications in a real-world production environment. In this article, we present the Sempa Resource Manager that makes a network of workstations transparent to the user and provides for an efficient computation of parallel applications. Usually, a network of workstations is a non-dedicated system running in time

*This work has been funded by the German Federal Department of Education, Science, Research and Technology, **BMBF** (**B**undes**m**inisterium *für* **B**ildung, *Wissenschaft*, **F**orschung *und Technologie*) within the research project **SEMPA** (**S**oftware **E**ngineering **M**ethods for **P**arallel **A**pplications in Scientific Computing).

[†]Technische Universität München, Institut für Informatik, Lehrstuhl für Rechnertechnik und Rechnerorganisation (LRR-TUM), 80290 München, Germany, {maier, luksch, bode}@in.tum.de, http://wwwbode.in.tum.de

sharing mode and providing resources primarily for interactive users. However, for most of the time the resources in a network of workstations are not completely utilized by interactive users. A resource management system makes the idle hosts accessible for parallel computing and improves user-friendliness by introducing services like batch queuing, automatic selection of idle hosts and control of the application's execution. The Sempa Resource Manager starts parallel applications and balances the load in the network of workstations to satisfy both the users of parallel applications and the interactive users.

This article is structured as follows. Section 2 gives a short overview of the objectives of the SEMPA project. The aims and the concept of the Sempa Resource Manager are presented in §3 followed by details about structure and implementation of the Sempa Resource Manager in §4. Performance measurements with the Sempa Resource Manager and a real-world test case are shown in §5. The article finishes with some concluding remarks and an outlook on future work.

2. The SEMPA project. Today's grand challenge problems in high performance computing (and many other domains) can only be solved in joint interdisciplinary efforts of partners from industry and academia. The interdisciplinary research project SEMPA (***S**oftware **E**ngineering **M**ethods for **P**arallel **A**pplications in Scientific Computing*) has brought together mechanical engineers, numerical analysts and computer scientists [8]. The partners of the SEMPA project are:

(i) AEA Technology GmbH: develops and markets commercial computational fluid dynamics software packages, e.g. TfC.

(ii) Institute for Computer Applications III: contributes know–how on numerical algorithms for partial differential equations and parallel computing.

(iii) GENIAS Software GmbH: develops and markets software tools for high performance computing, client/server computing and for workstation clusters, e.g. the batch queuing and resource management system Codine.

In SEMPA, we focus on two major aspects of software engineering: we define guidelines for systematic software design based on well established technology making optimal use of available tools and we explore how to use new programming paradigms in a real-world context [15]. Our objective is to provide guidelines how to make optimal use of widely available technology for efficient parallelization. The term "efficient" in this context refers to programmer's productivity as well as efficiency of the resulting code with respect to runtime and resource requirements. These guidelines are derived from experience gained in parallelizing a large scale industrial software package. The project's major objectives have been to

(i) develop software engineering methods for parallelizing large-scale scientific software packages. Parallelization of the state-of-the-art computational fluid dynamics package TfC is the case study to derive and evaluate the proposed methods.

(ii) explore the potential of new programming paradigms such as data parallelism and object-orientation in the domain of scientific computing.

(iii) develop a resource management system that allows for production runs of parallel applications in batch mode on networks of workstations using idle resources and avoiding interference with interactive users.

3. Aims of the Sempa Resource Manager. The Sempa Resource Manager is intended to support the execution of parallel applications in a network of workstations by providing services for batch queuing, scheduling of batch jobs and load balancing [11]. Existing resource management systems, e.g. Codine [3], Condor [7], LSF [10], DQS [4] have been developed for sequential applications and lack of mechanisms to communicate with parallel programming environments. Therefore, full control of parallel applications is missing which leads to major drawbacks in the support of parallel applications, e.g. process migration and preemptive load balancing cannot be applied to parallel applications. To overcome these deficiencies, the Sempa Resource Manager defines an interface between a resource management system and a parallel programming environment that allows to exchange information about resources, processes and load information while a parallel application is running. Both resource management system and parallel programming environment benefit from the additional information from each other to extend their range of functionalities.

The Sempa Resource Manager is designed to receive information from the parallel programming environment each time a new parallel process is created. This information enables the Sempa Resource Manager to gain control of the process and thus perform various operations on the process, e.g. stop the process, migrate the process, collect accounting information about the process, limit the resource usage of the process, etc. Existing resource management systems only have control of the first process of a parallel application but not of further processes that are created by the parallel programming environment [6].

The two common message-passing environments, PVM [2] and MPI [1], have no access to load information about the hosts which forces them to use a round-robin scheduling for process mapping within the virtual machine. In the Sempa Resource Manager load information measured by the resource management system is made available to the parallel programming environment to be used for scheduling or load balancing within the virtual machine [12].

Automatic reconfiguration of the virtual machine is offered by the Sempa Resource Manager to support load balancing and avoid intervention of the user as it is required for dynamic reconfiguration of the virtual machine in PVM. A parallel programming environment working together with the Sempa Resource Manager extends a virtual machine by requesting an idle host from the resource management system, e.g. to migrate a process to that idle host.

4. Architectural design and implementation of the Sempa Resource Manager. The main design issue of the Sempa Resource Manager was to benefit from batch queuing services and initial placement mechanisms for parallel applications of an existing resource management system. Thus, the batch queuing and resource management system Codine of the SEMPA project partner GENIAS builds the foundation of the Sempa Resource Manager. Advanced control structures, interfaces and scheduling algorithms have been integrated in Codine to form the first part of the Sempa Resource Manager. Its second part is composed by the interface to the parallel programming environment. The first generation of the Sempa Resource Manager is bound to PVM because PVM comprehends dynamic host and process management and offers a resource management interface. MPI-1 misses these functionalities und is therefore unable to integrate and benefit from the concepts of the Sempa Resource Manager. Transparent process migration in the Sempa Resource Manager is available through the checkpointing mechanism CoCheck.

The major issues concerning the implementation of the Sempa Resource Manager are presented below.

4.1. Interface between Codine and PVM. As described in the previous section, the interface between Codine and PVM is of major interest to exchange information about resources and processes. The implementation of the interface in the Sempa Resource Manager is based on the PVM resource manager concept that allows to define an interface between a resource management system and PVM [2]. A major advantage of the PVM resource manager interface is that it does not necessitate any changes in the PVM library or in the PVM applications.

A PVM resource manager is a PVM process written by the user that consists of a communication interface to receive requests and multiple handler functions to attend the requests. Usually, PVM calls are handled by the PVM daemons. If there is a PVM resource manager running in the virtual machine, the PVM calls concerning processes and hosts, e.g. `pvm_spawn` or `pvm_addhosts`, are redirected to the PVM resource manager and performed by the handler functions. The handler functions are not part of PVM but have to be implemented by the user to replace the default PVM strategies for scheduling and resource management. In the Sempa Resource Manager the handler function for `pvm_spawn` allows to use load values for the scheduling of processes within the virtual machine. The handler function for `pvm_addhosts` initiates a request to Codine to return an idle host.

The PVM resource manager takes a central position within the Sempa Resource Manager's concept because it incorporates the multiple components and functions of Codine, PVM and CoCheck. Concept and use of the PVM resource manager in the Sempa Resource Manager are explained in [9].

4.2. Control of the processes. The concept of the Sempa Resource Manager implies that processes created by PVM must be put under the control of Codine to use the full range of Codine's functionalities.

For each job the Codine execution daemon cod_execd starts a subordinate shepherd process that builds up the execution environment for a job. The shepherd starts the job by forking a process and thus is parent of the started job with the capability to control the job. In the current version of Codine there is only a single shepherd existing for each parallel job, i.e. Codine only has control of the process forked by the shepherd but not of processes that are spawned by PVM. Thus, operations such as resource limitation and the collection of accounting information can only be performed for the master process forked by the shepherd but not for the spawned slave processes.

A pvm_spawn call in the Sempa Resource Manager is redirected to the PVM resource manager that selects a host executing the process and notifies the PVM tasker on the selected host. The PVM tasker is a further concept of PVM to change the default way of forking a new process and enable the user to implement an own process creation routine. In the Sempa Resource Manager the PVM tasker initiates the cod_execd to start the process corresponding to the Codine control structure. The consequence is that for each PVM process a shepherd exists that controls the process.

Fig. 4.1 depicts the structure of the Sempa Resource Manager with the various Codine and PVM components joined together by the PVM resource manager. The process control structure in Codine with cod_execd and shepherd is clearly recognizable.

4.3. Load balancing. There are two ways to integrate a load balancing algorithm into the Sempa Resource Manager. One way would be to add some functions to Codine utilizing all the information about hosts and applications that is available in Codine. However, we decided against this central approach and preferred a distributed solution affiliating the load balancing algorithm to the PVM resource manager because a distributed approach is more scalable and avoids the bottleneck caused by a central component in larger computational environments. The load balancing algorithm of the Sempa Resource Manager is responsible for the mapping of newly created PVM processes with respect to the load situation within the virtual machine and the computational power of the hosts. Besides that, it decides about process migration if the load on a host exceeds a certain threshold or interactive users return to their machines.

CoCheck (**Co**nsistent **Check**points) is used for process migration to balance the load in the virtual machine or remove processes from a host where an interactive user has returned. CoCheck is an extension to message-passing libraries that allows the creation of checkpoints of parallel applications and the migration of processes. A checkpoint is written using the Condor single process checkpointing library [7]. There are implementations of CoCheck for PVM [14] and MPI [13]. The CoCheck functions for PVM are implemented as handler functions in the PVM resource manager.

5. Performance measurements. The Sempa Resource Manager has been designed and implemented to support the execution of parallel applications in a real-world production environment. The aims of the Sempa Resource Manager are to improve user-friendliness of the computational environment and provide efficient execution of the user's parallel batch jobs avoiding interference with interactive users. As user-friendliness of a system is hard to quantify we will turn towards the performance measurements with the Sempa Resource Manager

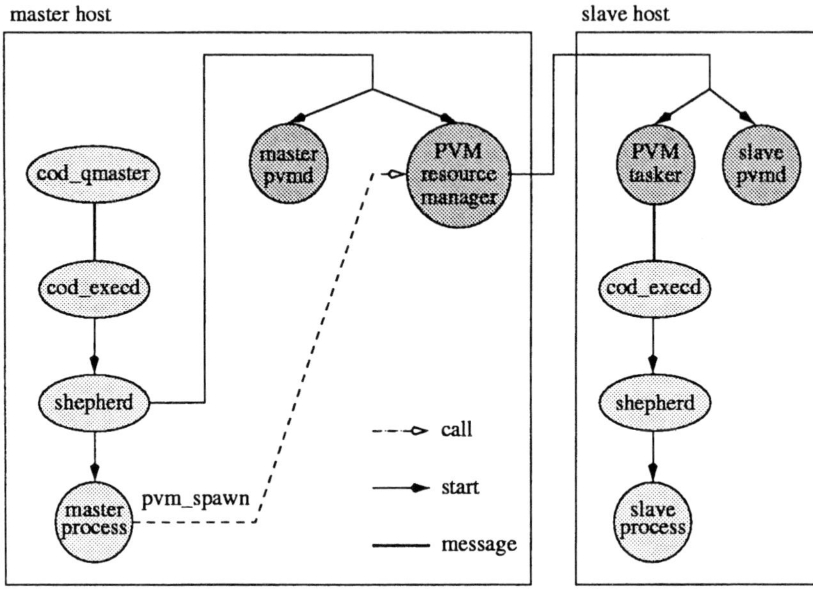

FIG. 4.1. *Process control structure in the Sempa Resource Manager*

demonstrating its efficiency and the benefits of process migration to equalize imbalanced load in a network of workstations.

We used the computational fluid dynamics package ParTfC as a real-world application for the performance measurements and measured CPU and wallclock time for master and slave processes of ParTfC using three test cases with varying numbers of grid nodes as depicted in Table 5.1. Each grid was divided into four partitions and each partition has been computed on an own host. All the measurements were performed on a network of SGI workstations.

TABLE 5.1
Test cases for ParTfC

test case	grid nodes
Grid1	3150
Grid2	22100
Grid3	71250

5.1. Efficiency of the Sempa Resource Manager. Three different experiments have been made to prove that advanced control structures and interfaces in the Sempa Resource Manager hardly cause overhead:

NO_RM :

PVM and ParTfC are started by the user. Neither Codine nor a PVM resource manager are running.

CODINE :

ParTfC is submitted as PVM batch job to Codine. Codine starts PVM and ParTfC, a PVM resource manager is not running.

SRM :

ParTfC is submitted as PVM batch job to Codine. Codine starts PVM, the PVM resource manager and ParTfC.

Tables 5.2, 5.3 and 5.4 show the CPU and wallclock time of ParTfC master and slave processes for the three test cases Grid1, Grid2 and Grid3. CPU time of the master process is higher than for slave processes because the master process has additional work with reading input data and writing output data. CPU time of ParTfC in NO_RM, CODINE and SRM hardly differs because the CPU time represents the real computation time of ParTfC that is not affected by resource management functions. The wallclock time for master and slave processes of ParTfC differs slightly because of the synchronization between master and slave processes.

TABLE 5.2
CPU and wallclock times for Grid1

	CPU		wallclock	
	master	slave	master	slave
NO_RM	84.002 s	64.760 s	221.300 s	220.367 s
CODINE	83.984 s	64.219 s	228.740 s	227.640 s
SRM	83.260 s	63.873 s	233.800 s	230.000 s

TABLE 5.3
CPU and wallclock times for Grid2

	CPU		wallclock	
	master	slave	master	slave
NO_RM	270.767 s	252.256 s	490.567 s	490.022 s
CODINE	270.500 s	252.760 s	493.980 s	492.760 s
SRM	270.080 s	252.673 s	501.100 s	497.393 s

TABLE 5.4
CPU and wallclock times for Grid3

	CPU		wallclock	
	master	slave	master	slave
NO_RM	616.620 s	586.507 s	1044.600 s	1043.133 s
CODINE	609.300 s	583.467 s	1055.000 s	1053.500 s
SRM	611.733 s	583.233 s	1061.000 s	1056.111 s

The most interesting result provides the comparison of the master process wallclock time in NO_RM, CODINE and SRM as plotted in Fig. 5.1 because it represents the response time of the application to the user. The wallclock time is slightly increasing in the order of NO_RM, CODINE and SRM because additional daemons are running and control structures are build up. In the case of NO_RM only the PVM daemons are running and the PVM calls are executed by the PVM daemons. If ParTfC is started by Codine, the Codine daemons are running additionally but the difference between the experiments NO_RM and CODINE is less than 1 % for the larger test cases because the Codine daemons are sleeping for most of the time. With the Sempa Resource Manager PVM taskers are started and the PVM processes are controlled by Codine, therefore, the wallclock time in the experiment SRM increases about 2 % compared to NO_RM.

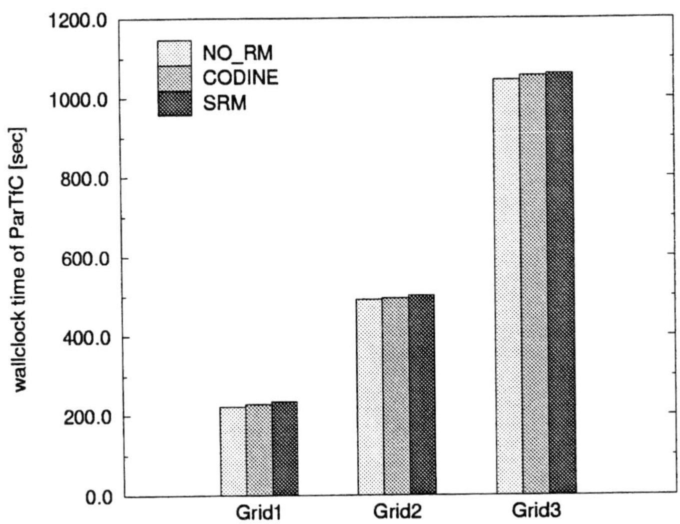

FIG. 5.1. *Runtime of ParTfC in different resource management environments*

5.2. Process migration. Process migration is a fundamental prerequisite for preemptive load balancing to transfer a running process from an overloaded host to an idle host [5]. Although process migration is quite costly, it is able to shorten application runtimes in an execution environment with unbalanced load. The following measurement results demonstrate the effects of process migration to the runtime of ParTfC. Two different kinds of process migration were compared: The first one is transparent process migration with CoCheck as described in §4. A second possibility of process migration is based on the existing checkpointing mechanism in ParTfC that is available for reasons of fault tolerance, i.e. to save results of the computation at runtime. In contrast to CoCheck ParTfC is not able to write the checkpoint of a single process, only the whole application can be checkpointed.

Process migration is initiated by overloading a host running a ParTfC process with a computational intensive program. Four experiments have been made to compare the two migration mechanisms:

NO_LOAD :
ParTfC is running in an unloaded computational environment.

NO_MIGRATE :
One host running a ParTfC process is overloaded but the ParTfC process running on that host is not migrated to an idle host.

COCHECK :
One host running a ParTfC process is overloaded and the ParTfC process on that host is migrated to a an idle host using the CoCheck process migration mechanism.

PARTFC_CKPT :
One host running a ParTfC process is overloaded and ParTfC writes a checkpoint of the whole application. The application is restarted avoiding the overloaded host.

Fig. 5.2 plots the wallclock time of ParTfC in the different experiments for Grid1, Grid2 and Grid3. Both types of process migration provide lower wallclock times than NO_MIGRATE for Grid1 and Grid2. ParTfC checkpointing becomes inefficient for larger grids which can be seen for Grid3 because the size of input and checkpointing files increases and the overhead for reading and writing these files outweighs the benefits of migrating a process to a lower loaded host. However, the performance of CoCheck also decreases for larger grids because the checkpoint grows due to the larger data space of the application but it still outperforms NO_MIGRATE for Grid3. In a real-world production environment grids and runtimes are larger than in Grid3 but process migration usually will take place less frequently so that the parallel application will still benefit from load balancing in a network of workstations.

COCHECK outperforms PARTFC_CKPT for about 10 % because CoCheck is designed for migration whereas the overall intention of ParTfC checkpointing is to save results during the computation and restart the application after a system failure. A more efficient implementation of the restart mechanism in ParTfC would certainly improve the results of the experiment PARTFC_CKPT.

Tables 5.5, 5.6 and 5.7 show CPU and wallclock time for master and slave processes of ParTfC in the different migration experiments for Grid1, Grid2 and Grid3. CPU time in COCHECK and PARTFC_CKPT is higher compared to the CPU times in the non-migration experiments which reflects the overhead required for the migration.

TABLE 5.5
Runtime of ParTfC in the migration experiments for Grid1

	CPU		wallclock	
	master	slave	master	slave
NO_LOAD	83.260 s	63.873 s	233.800 s	230.000 s
COCHECK	93.305 s	64.970 s	271.950 s	270.167 s
PARTFC_CKPT	98.030 s	65.100 s	302.330 s	300.010 s
NO_MIGRATE	84.117 s	64.817 s	416.567 s	414.233 s

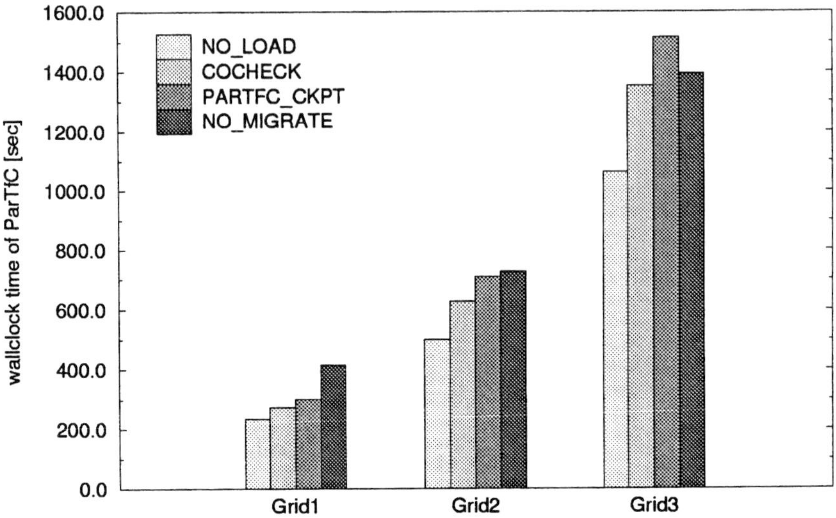

FIG. 5.2. *Process migration with CoCheck and ParTfC checkpointing*

TABLE 5.6
Runtime of ParTfC in the migration experiments for Grid2

	CPU		wallclock	
	master	slave	master	slave
NO_LOAD	270.080 s	252.673 s	501.100 s	497.393 s
COCHECK	298.367 s	278.367 s	627.700 s	625.733 s
PARTFC_CKPT	291.700 s	258.278 s	709.433 s	706.567 s
NO_MIGRATE	271.033 s	253.956 s	726.400 s	725.722 s

TABLE 5.7
Runtime of ParTfC in the migration experiments for Grid3

	CPU		wallclock	
	master	slave	master	slave
NO_LOAD	611.733 s	583.233 s	1061.000 s	1056.111 s
COCHECK	671.500 s	623.933 s	1353.000 s	1350.556 s
PARTFC_CKPT	675.800 s	600.967 s	1516.000 s	1512.100 s
NO_MIGRATE	611.150 s	583.317 s	1393.000 s	1391.500 s

6. Conclusion and future work. The SEMPA project provides guidelines for the parallelization of scientific computing applications, and the test phase and production run of parallel applications. In this article we have introduced the Sempa Resource Manager, a resource management system that supports the execution of parallel applications in a real-world production environment. It provides a simple but powerful interface to the user and hides the details of hardware and software configuration of a network of workstations. Resources and running parallel applications are monitored to detect load imbalance and migrate processes if required by the load situation.

Initial placement of parallel applications on idle hosts and dynamic load balancing provide for efficient resource utilization in the network of workstations and low response times of the parallel applications. Performance measurements with the real world scientific computing application ParTfC show that the advanced control structures of the Sempa Resource Manager do not influence the efficiency of the Sempa Resource Manager. Process migration has proved to be a powerful technique for load balancing whereas transparent process migration with CoCheck provides better results than the application oriented checkpointing mechanism that is available in ParTfC. Some investigations of checkpointing and restarting in ParTfC are necessary to optimize application oriented migration with ParTfC.

The restriction of the Sempa Resource Manager to PVM applications is inevitable because the MPI-1 standard misses some issues required for the Sempa Resource Manager's concept. In the meantime, the MPI-2 standard is available that allows dynamic process management and provides an external interface to connect components from outside [1] but dynamic configuration of the virtual machine is still missing in the MPI-2 standard. We are just working on an MPI interface to support MPI applications with the next generation of the Sempa Resource Manager.

The Sempa Resource Manager is focused to networks of workstations as a computational environment but we have already made some efforts towards metacomputing environments as alternative hardware platforms for parallel scientific computing. Problems in a metacomputing environment that connects thousands of hosts and local area networks are caused by its enormous size and its distributed nature which requires further efforts and new concepts in resource management. With the design of the Sempa Resource Manager we have already considered some of these aspects particularly flexibility and scalability. Currently we are working on an hierarchically organized resource management system based on cooperating Sempa Resource Managers with load balancing in a metacomputing environment.

REFERENCES

[1] M. P. I. Forum, *MPI-2: Extensions to the Message-Passing Interface*, Nov. 1996.

[2] A. Geist, A. Beguelin, J. Dongarra, W. Jiang, R. Manchek, and V. Sunderam, *PVM: Parallel Virtual Machine – A Users' Guide and Tutorial for Networked Parallel Computing*, Scientific and Engineering Computation, The MIT Press, Cambridge, MA, 1994.

[3] GENIAS Software GmbH, *CODINE Manual, Version 4.2*, 1998.

[4] T. P. Green and J. Snyder, *DQS, A Distributed Queuing System*, Technical Report FSU-SCRI-92-115, Supercomputer Computations Research Institute, Florida State University, Aug. 1992.

[5] M. Harchol-Balter and A. B. Downey, *Exploiting Process Lifetime Distributions for Dynamic Load Balancing*, in 1996 ACM SIGMETRICS Conference on Measurement

and Modeling of Computer Systems, Philadelphia, PA, USA, ACM Press, 1996, pp. 13–24.

[6] J. P. Jones and C. Brickell, *Second Evaluation of Job Queuing/Scheduling Software: Phase 1 Report*, NAS Technical Report NAS-97-013, NAS High Performance Processing Group, NASA Ames Research Center, Moffett Field, CA, June 1997.

[7] M. Litzkow, T. Tannenbaum, J. Basney, and M. Livny, *Checkpoint and Migration of UNIX Processes in the Condor Distributed Environment*, Technical Report 1346, University of Wisconsin-Madison, Computer Sciences Department, Apr. 1997.

[8] P. Luksch, U. Maier, S. Rathmayer, M. Weidmann, F. Unger, P. Bastian, V. Reichenberger, and A. Haas, *SEMPA: Software Engineering Methods for Parallel Applications in Scientific Computing, Project Report*, vol. 12 of Research Report Series LRR-TUM, Shaker Verlag, Sept. 1998.

[9] U. Maier, G. Stellner, and I. Zoraja, *Resource Allocation, Scheduling and Load Balancing based on the PVM Resource Manager*, in Parallel Computing: Fundamentals, Applications and New Directions, E. H. D'Hollander, G. R. Joubert, F. J. Peters, and U. Trottenberg, eds., vol. 12 of Advances in Parallel Computing, Elsevier Publishers, 1998, pp. 711–718.

[10] Platform Computing Corporation, *LSF Documentation*, North York, Ontario, Canada, Dec. 1996.

[11] W. Saphir, L. A. Tanner, and B. Traversat, *Job Management Requirements for NAS Parallel Systems and Clusters*, NAS Technical Report NAS-95-006, NAS Scientific Computing Branch, NASA Ames Research Center, Moffett Field, CA, Feb. 1995.

[12] B. A. Shirazi, A. R. Hurson, and K. M. Kavi, eds., *Scheduling and Load Balancing in Parallel and Distributed Systems*, IEEE Computer Society Press, 1995.

[13] G. Stellner, *CoCheck: Checkpointing and Process Migration for MPI*, in Proceedings of the International Parallel Processing Symposium, Honolulu, HI, Apr. 1996, IEEE Computer Society Press, pp. 526–531.

[14] G. Stellner and J. Pruyne, *Resource Management and Checkpointing for PVM*, in Proceedings of the Second European PVM User Group Meeting, Lyon, Sept. 1995, Editions Hermes, pp. 131–136.

[15] M. Weidmann, *Object-Oriented Redesign of a Real-World Fortran 77 Solver*, in Modern Software Tools for Scientific Computing, E. Arge, A. M. Bruaset, and H. P. Langtangen, eds., Birkhäuser, 1997, ch. 15, pp. 325–338.

TASK SCHEDULING ON BUS-BASED NETWORKS OF WORKSTATIONS*

WEI-MING LIN AND QIUYAN GU †

Abstract. In this paper, we propose a heuristic algorithm based on dynamic critical path (DCP) to solve the problem of task scheduling on networks of workstations (NOW). The algorithm takes into account both the characteristics of DCP and NOW by intelligently pre-allocating network communication resources so as to avoid potential communication conflict. It has a reasonable computational complexity of $O(v^2(1+p))$, where v is the number of nodes in the task graph and p is the number of processors in the NOW. It is suitable for regular as well as irregular task graphs. The algorithm when tested under various task graphs shows performance much superior to previously known techniques.

1. Introduction. In a parallel computing system, an application is divided into many modules (tasks) which are located on several processors and communicate with each other if necessary. Thus task scheduling is vital to the performance of such a system. Network of workstations (NOW) is regarded as a potential while very practical parallel computing environment for its low cost and flexibility. Although there have been various high-speed switches and communication protocols deigned to speed up communication in a NOW, a bus-based configuration still represents the most economic and widely available parallel computing platform.

Task scheduling has been regarded as one of the most challenging problems in the area of parallel and distributed computing for over a decade. It's known to be NP-complete in its general form and even in very simple special cases. There are only a few special cases known for which optimal polynomial time algorithms exist, for examples, scheduling tree-structured task graphs with identical computation costs on arbitrary number of processors, and scheduling arbitrary task graphs with identical computation costs on two processors [?]. Various heuristic algorithms have been proposed to solve different forms of task scheduling problems ([3],[6],[7],[11]). Most of the algorithms suit for fully-connected networks. In [6] a promising algorithm based on dynamic critical path which is suitable for fully-connected network is proposed, while in [5] a general task scheduling algorithm which can be used for any network topology is presented. Few of known research works [5] discuss task scheduling algorithm suitable for bus-based NOW. Task scheduling on bus-based NOW is different from that on a fully-connected network since two independent communication tasks cannot take place at the same time when a shared bus medium is used in a bus-based NOW. In this paper, we propose a heuristic algorithm based on dynamic critical

*THIS RESEARCH WAS SUPPORTED IN PART BY THE OFFICE OF NAVAL RESEARCH UNDER GRANTS N00014-95-1-0514 AND N00014-96-1-0897, AND IN PART BY THE DEPARTMENT OF DEFENSE/AIR FORCE OFFICE OF SCIENTIFIC RESEARCH UNDER GRANT F49620-96-1-0472.

† Division of Engineering, The University of Texas at San Antonio, San Antonio, TX 78249, Email: wlin@voyager1.utsa.edu

path (DCP) to solve the problem of task scheduling on networks of workstations. The algorithm takes into account both the characteristics of DCP and NOW by intelligently pre-allocating network communication resources so as to avoid potential communication conflict. It has a reasonable computational complexity of $O(v^2(1+p))$, where v is the number of nodes in task graph and p is the number of processors. It is suitable for regular as well as irregular task graphs. The algorithm is tested under various task graphs randomly generated showing performance much superior to previously known techniques.

The rest of this paper is organized as follows. Problem model and basic definition of terminologies are described in the next section. In section 3, several well-known scheduling techniques are described for comparison. It is then followed by the presentation of our proposed algorithm in section 4. Experimental results are then presented in section 5, with concluding remarks made in the last section.

2. Problem Model. In general, a task is defined as an indivisible module of an application. The purpose of task scheduling is to minimize execution time of the application by distributing tasks to different processors in a multiprocessor environment. Such an application is usually expressed by a directed acyclic graph (DAG) $G = (V, E)$, where V is the set of all nodes and E is the set of all edges in the graph. A node in a DAG represents a task and a directed edge originating from one node to another indicates that data dependency exists between the two tasks and communication is needed to satisfy such dependency from the former to the latter if the two tasks are assigned to different processors. The number of nodes in the graph is denoted as $|V| = v$ and the number of edges in the graph is $|E| = e$. Computation cost of a task is represented by a weight associated with the corresponding node, with $w(n_i)$ denoting the weight of node n_i where $n_i \in V$. Cost of a data dependency, i.e. communication cost if needed, is also represented by a weight associated with the corresponding edge, with c_{ij} denoting the weight of edge e_{ij}, where $e_{ij} \in E$ originates from node n_i and ends at node n_j. Thus an edge in DAG represents precedent relation between two nodes in the DAG. A task can begin to execute only after all its precedent relations are satisfied, i.e. after all the data it requires are provided by its direct parent(s) in the graph.

In most scheduling processes, one node is chosen from the task graph to be scheduled each time. Consequently, how to identify a meritorious scheduling sequence of the nodes is important to the efficiency of the final scheduling result. Such a sequence can be static which is predetermined before scheduling and remains unaltered throughout the scheduling. On the other hand, a sequence can be dynamic in which order of unscheduled nodes can be rearranged according to current partial scheduling outcome. Critical path (CP) [6] of a task graph gives critical information on how a graph can be efficiently sequenced. In the following, several relevant important notations which will be used throughout this paper are given. Some of them have been well-known and are given here for the sake of completeness, while some others are redefined to reflect the new meaning in scheduling for a NOW environment.

- CP: **Critical Path**. The CP of a task graph is the longest path from an entry node to an exit node, of which the sum of computation (node) costs and potential communication (edge) costs is the maximum. For example, the CP of the task graph shown in Figure 1 is the path through n_1, n_4, n_5 and n_7.

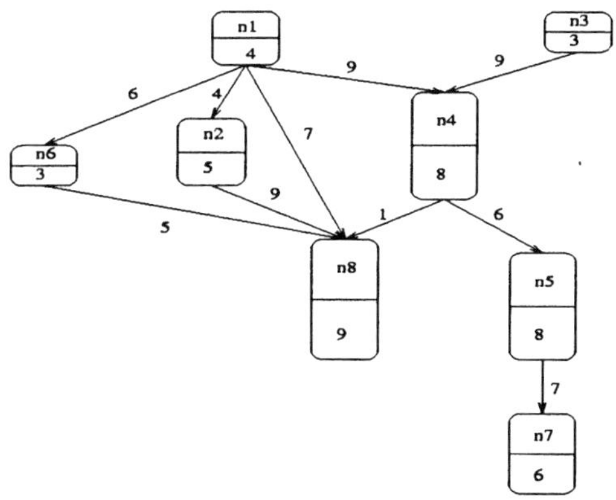

FIG. 1. *A Task Graph*

- CPL: **Critical Path Length**. The CPL of a task graph is the sum of all costs along the CP. Note that the task graph in Figure 1 has a CPL of 48.
- DCP: **Dynamic Critical Path**. The DCP of a task graph is the CP of it when partially scheduled. CP of a task graph may change due to the fact that some dependency costs (communication) never materialize when tasks involved in such dependency are scheduled onto the same processor. Note that the DCP at the end of scheduling represents the final schedule length if the target network is fully connected.
- DCPL: **Dynamic Critical Path Length (DCPL)**. The DCPL of a task graph is the sum of all costs along the DCP during the scheduling.
- REST: **Relative Earliest Start Time**. REST(n_i) is used to represent the relative earliest start time of a yet-to-schedule node n_i in a task graph, as opposed to the AEST (Absolute Earlist Start Time) in [6] for scheduling on a fully connected network. If n_i is an entry node, REST(n_i) is zero; otherwise, REST(n_i) $= \max_{1 \le k \le p}\{\text{REST}(n_{i_k}) + w(n_{i_k}) + c_{i_k i}\}$ if n_i has p parents with n_{i_k} being its k-th parent. REST of all nodes in Figure 1 are listed in Figure 2.
- RLST: **Relative Latest Start Time**. RLST(n_i) is used to represent the relative latest start time of a yet-to-schedule node n_i in a task graph, as opposed to the ALST (Absolute Latest Start Time) in [6] for scheduling on a fully connected network. If n_i is an exit node, RLST(n_i) is DCPL $-W(n_i)$; otherwise, RLST(n_i) $= \min_{1 \le k \le p}\{\text{RLST}(n_{i_k}) -$

node	REST	RLST
n1	0	0
n2	8	25
n3	0	1
n4	13	13
n5	27	27
n6	10	31
n7	42	42
n8	22	39

FIG. 2. *REST and RLST of Nodes in Figure 1*

$w(n_{i_k}) - c_{ii_k}\}$ if n_i has p children with n_{i_k} being its k-th child. RLST of all nodes in Figure 1 are also listed in Figure 2.

- CC: **Critical Child**. Among all the children of a node, CC is the one that has the smallest difference of its RLST and REST.
- EEST: **Exact Earliest Start Time**. EEST(n_i, p_j) is defined as the exact earliest start time of n_i when it is scheduled onto processor p_j.
- CCR: **Communication-to-Computation Ratio**. CCR of a task graph is its total potential communication costs divided by its total computation costs. CCR of a graph indicates the relative demand of data communication compared to amount of computation, and has been widely used to classify application programs for the purpose of performance comparison among scheduling algorithms. With this definition, the CCR of the task graph in Figure 1 is 1.4 (63/46).

REST and RLST are useful in providing critical information on how urgent a node yet to be scheduled needs to be scheduled. That is, they are used to determine the next candidate node to schedule. The REST of a node that has been scheduled will be replaced with its corresponding EEST value for updating information on others.

3. Related Work. In this section, two well-known scheduling algorithms, one static and one dynamic, which are related to our work are briefly described.

3.1. Bubble Scheduling and Allocation (BSA) Algorithm. BSA [5] is designed for general network topologies. The algorithm first serializes all nodes into a sequence which is then injected into a single processor (so-called pivot PE), chosen according to the network's topological character. Then some of the nodes are migrated to other processors in order to improve schedule length. **BSA** divides all nodes in a task graph into three classes: CPN, a node on critical path; IBN, a node not a CPN, but from which there is a path reaching a critical path; and OBN, a node that is neither a CPN nor an IBN. Node sequencing is based on CPN-first order and the IBNs reaching a CPN are always placed in front of the corresponding CPN. IBN's are sequenced following a recursive condition that the yet-to-sequence parent node of a CPN (or an IBN already sequenced) that has the largest edge weight to the CPN (or the IBN) will be placed just ahead of the CPN (or the IBN). OBNs are then appended to the sequence in a topological order so that no precedence constraints are violated. **BSA** will migrate a node from the pivot PE to an adjacent processor if either assigning the node to the new processor leads to a shorter start time, or the parent node of this node with the latest message arrival time has been assigned to the new processor. This algorithm is inherently static, thus any changes to the critical path by scheduling a node are not reflected in the decision-making for subsequent scheduling steps. Also, the major deficiency lies in the fact that when a node is to be scheduled, only the node itself is considered. Completely ignoring impact from future scheduling situations may jeopardize the **BSA**'s chances in leading to a desirable schedule length.

When **BSA** is applied to the task graph in Figure 1, the static CPN-order list is n_1, n_3, n_4, n_5, n_7, n_2, n_6 and n_8 as shown in Figure 3. Scheduling results are shown in Figure 4, with the resulted earliest start time of each node listed in Figure 3.

step	node	channel needed	EEST	processor
1	n_1		0	p_0
2	n_3		0	p_1
3	n_4	3-12	12	p_0
4	n_5		20	p_0
5	n_7		28	p_0
6	n_2		4	p_0
7	n_6		9	p_0
8	n_8		34	p_0

FIG. 3. *Scheduling Sequence and EEST Results of Figure 1 by* **BSA**

3.2. Dynamic Critical Path (DCP) Algorithm. **DCP** [6] schedules task graph with arbitrary computation and communication costs to a multiprocessor system with unlimited number of fully-connected identical processors. **DCP** differs from **BSA** in its dynamically reassigning priorities to the nodes at each step based on the dynamic critical path as well as selecting a suitable processor for a node by looking ahead the potential start time of the node's critical child on that processor. Candidate node is dynamically selected and its critical child (CC) is also scheduled to have the earliest start time. When computing the EEST of the node on a processor, the **DCP** also considers the possibility in inserting this node to a slot which is not large enough by pushing node(s) already scheduled forward further in time. This may lead to a shorter schedule for some cases but with a considerable price to pay in scheduling time efficiency. Altogether, DCP then schedules the candidate node to the processor which leads to the smallest sum of the EEST of the node and that of its CC.

A problem can arise from the above scheduling procedure in **DCP** when computing the EEST of the candidate's CC. If not all the parents of the CC have been scheduled, the EEST of this CC on a processor can be useless and sometimes misleading. Furthermore, while the **DCP** algorithm avoids some disadvantagies of other CP algorithms, it is not suitable for a bus-based NOW

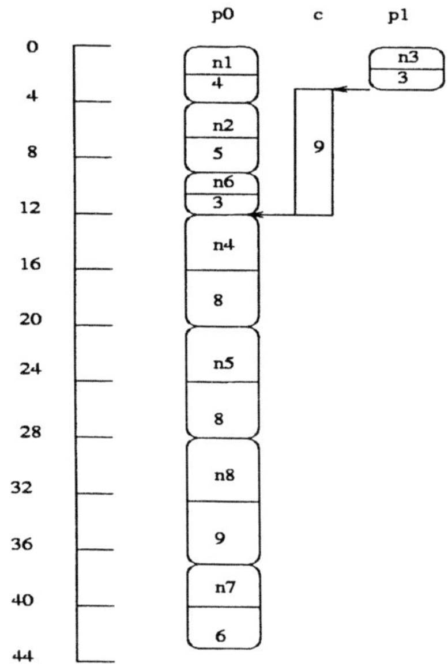

FIG. 4. *Schedule of the Task Graph in Figure 1 by* **BSA** *(Schedule Length = 43 Units)*

where network conflicts will affect execution time seriously. By applying the **DCP** algorithm to the task graph in Figure 1, a schedule length of 29 units as shown in Figure 5 on a fully connected network is obtained. Figure 6 displays

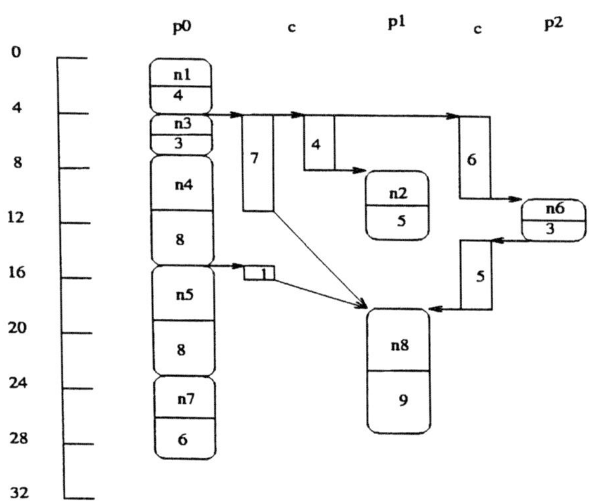

FIG. 5. *Schedule of the Task Graph in Figure 1 by* **DCP** *on a Fully Connected Network (Schedule Length = 29 Units)*

the sequence of scheduling as well as the final EEST results. When the schedule

step	node	channel needed	EEST	processor
1	n_1		0	p_0
2	n_3		4	p_0
3	n_4		7	p_0
4	n_5		15	p_0
5	n_7		23	p_0
6	n_2	4-8	8	p_1
7	n_6	4-10	10	p_2
8	n_8	4-11; 13-18; 15-16	18	p_1

FIG. 6. *Scheduling Sequence and EEST Results of Figure 1 by* **DCP**

is employed on a bus-based NOW, due to network conflicts, the actual schedule becomes the one with 36 units shown in Figure 7.

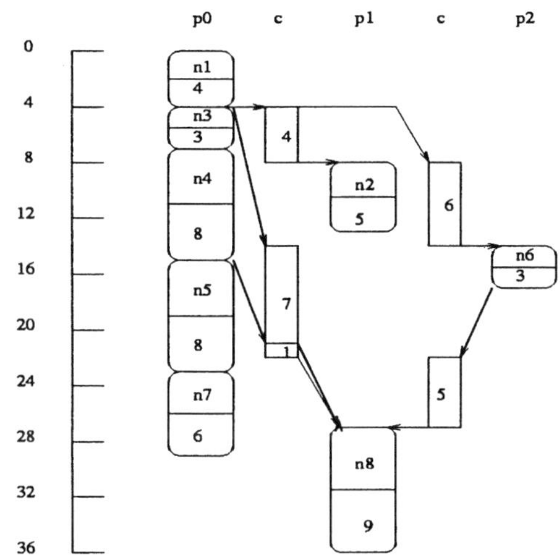

FIG. 7. *Schedule of the Task Graph in Figure 1 by* **DCP** *on a Bus-bsed NOW (Schedule Length = 36 Units)*

4. DCP-NOW Algorithm. The two major problems aforementioned in the **DCP** algorithm are taken into account in our proposed algorithm, the **DCP-NOW**. After a node in task graph is scheduled to a processor, REST of the nodes not yet scheduled may be affected, as well as the critical path. In our algorithm, the candidate node is selected based on dynamic critical path during each scheduling step. It also looks ahead for a node's critical child if all parents of the critical child have been scheduled; otherwise, only the node itself is considered. This avoids any potential misleading information induced by the **DCP** algorithm. If all the parents of the critical child have been scheduled, the candidate node will be scheduled to a processor which minimizes the sum of the node's EEST and its critical child's EEST.

The algorithm is presented in Figure 8 along with REST and RLST calculation algorithms. EEST calculation for each node is described in Figure 9. In **REST**(n_i) and **RLST**(n_i) algorithms, the REST and RLST calculation is

```
DCP-NOW( )
1. for each node n_i ∈ V
      REST(n_i); RLST(n_i);
2. while (not all nodes have been scheduled) do
3.    select the node to be scheduled:
        n_i = the highest node with the smallest difference between its RLST
          and REST;
        if there is a tie, select the one which has the smaller REST;
        if they have the same REST, randomly select one;
4.    select processor for n_i:
        let n_{i_m} be the CC of n_i;
        if (all n_{i_m}'s p parents have been scheduled except n_i and
              the k-th parent is assigned to p_k, 1 ≤ k ≤ p)
          assign n_i to p_j if p_j leads to the smallest EEST(n_i, p_j) + EEST(n_{i_m}, p_j);
        else assign n_i to p_j if p_j leads to the smallest EEST(n_i, p_j), 1 ≤ j ≤ p;
   update net slot list (nsl) accordingly (using the nsl' found in EEST(n_i,p_j));
5. Update REST and RLST for n_i and its descendants:
      REST(n_i) = EEST(n_i, p_j); RLST(n_i);
      for each n_j, a descendant of n_i
        REST(n_j); RLST(n_j);
6. End while

REST(n_i)
1. if (n_i is an entry node) REST(n_i) = 0;
   else {
         if n_i has p parents and n_{i_k} is the k-th parent of n_i;
           REST(n_i) = max_{i≤k≤p} { REST(n_{i_k})+w(n_{i_k}) + c_{i_k i} };
       }

RLST(n_i)
1. if (n_i is an exit node) RLST(n_i) =DCPL-w(n_i);
   else {
         if n_i has p children and n_{i_k} is the k-th child of n_i;
           RLST(n_i) = min_{i≤k≤p} { RLST(n_{i_k}) - w(n_{i_k}) - c_{i i_k} };
       }
```

FIG. 8. **DCP-NOW** *Algorithm*

performed according to the aforementioned definition for each of the two parameters. In Figure 9, the **EEST**(n_i,p_j) algorithm calculates the earliest start time of a node n_i if it is scheduled to p_j. It first finds in p_j's schedule all unscheduled slots each of which is large enough for $w(n_i)$. Note that as network conflicts must be considered when a node is to be scheduled, a 'net slot list' (nsl) with a format of $[s_1, e_1], [s_2, e_2], \dots [s_m, +\infty)$ to indicate at which time segment

```
EEST(n_i, p_j)
/* find the earliest start time of n_i if it is scheduled to p_j */
1. find slot on p_j:
     if p_j contains a sequence of scheduled nodes {n_j1, n_j2, ..., n_jm},
     find if there exits some "k" such that
        EEST(n_j(k+1), p_j)-EEST(n_jk, p_j) - w(n_jk) >= w(n_i);
     let ssl be the schedule list of all slots [begin, end], in a time-wise
        ascending order, satisfying the above condition, where
     begin = EEST(n_jk, p_j) + w(n_jk) and end = EEST(n_j(k+1), p_j);
2. find the earliest time that n_i gathers all data needed from its parents, that is,
   data arrival time (dat):
     sort all m parents of n_i according to their finish times in a
        nondescending order: n_i1, ..., n_im;
     for(k = 1; k <= m; k++)
       {
         if (n_ik was scheduled onto p_j) dat_on_p_j = finish time of n_ik on p_j;
         else
           {
             nsl' = nsl;
             let [s_i, e_i] be the first one in nsl' that satisfies
             finish time of n_ik >= s_i and finish time of (n_ik + c_iki) <= e_i;
             dat_not_on_p_j = max(s_i, finish time of n_ik + c_iki)
             update nsl': substitute [s_i, e_i] with [s_i, finish time of n_ik] and
               [finish time of (n_ik + c_iki), e_i];
           }
       }
     dat = max(dat_on_p_j, dat_not_on_p_j);
3. In ssl (determined in step 1) find a slot [begin, end] such that
     begin <= dat and dat + w(n_i) <= end,
   if found, return(dat);
   else return(max(finish time of n_jm, dat));
```

FIG. 9. **EEST** *Algorithm*

the network is still available. It has an initial value of of $[0, +\infty)$, and, for example, will change to $[0, a], [b, +\infty)$ if a communication happens in the slot $[a, b]$. For each of the direct parents of n_i that is not scheduled to p_j, a slot in nsl needs to be identified to support the needed communication. This leads to an earliest possible start time for n_i considering limitation from the communication channel. Among all the slots found in p_j's schedule, this algorithm then tries to find the earlist one that can accommodate this limitation from communication.

4.1. An Example for DCP-NOW Algorithm. In this section, the task graph in Figure 1 is used to illustrate the proposed **DCP-NOW** algorithm. Sequence of scheduling is shown in Figure 10. Each scheduling step is explained as in the following:

step 1: The highest CP node n_1 is scheduled to the first unused processor p_0.

step	node	channel needed	EEST	processor
1	n_1		0	p_0
2	n_3		4	p_0
3	n_4		7	p_0
4	n_5		15	p_0
5	n_7		23	p_0
6	n_2	4-8	8	p_1
7	n_6	8-14	14	p_1
8	n_8	14-21; 21-22	22	p_1

FIG. 10. *Scheduling Sequence and EEST Results of Figure 1 by* **DCP-NOW**

step 2: The next DCP node is n_4 which has an unscheduled parent n_3. To satisfy data precedence, n_3 must be scheduled before n_4. If n_3 is scheduled to p_0, it can start at time 4 and its critical child n_4 can start at 7. If n_3 is scheduled to a new processor p_1, it will start at time 0 while its critical child n_4 has to be scheduled to p_0 to get a better start time of 12. The sum of REST of n_3 and n_4 in the former case is 11 and that of the latter is 12. Thus, n_3 is scheduled onto p_0. The scheduling of n_3 will change REST and RLST values of its descendants.

step 3: After n_4 is scheduled to p_0, REST values of n_5, n_7, n_8 become 21, 22 and 36 respectively, and DCPL is 42.

step 4: n_5 is scheduled to p_0 since EEST(n_5, p_0) + EEST(n_7, p_0) = 15 + 23 = 38 and EEST(n_5, p_1) + EEST(n_7, p_1) = 21 + 29 = 50.

step 5: n_7 is scheduled to p_0 since EEST(n_7, p_0) = 23 and EEST(n_7, p_1) = 30.

step 6: n_2 becomes the candidate node and consumes channel from time 4 to time 8 when it is scheduled to p_1. EEST(n_2, p_0) = 29 and EEST(n_2, p_1) = 8. n_2 is scheduled to p_1.

step 7: n_6 is scheduled to p_1 to get the earliest start time of 14 because EEST(n_6, p_0) + EEST(n_8, p_0) = 29 + 32 and EEST(n_6, p_1) + EEST(n_8, p_1) = 14 + 22. Communication from n_1 to n_6 will start from time 8, the earliest time when channel is free.

step 8: n_8 is scheduled to p_1 to obtain the earliest start time of 22.

The schedule generated by **DCP-NOW** is shown in Figure 11 with a final schedule length of 31 units, better than the results from the aforementioned techniques.

5. Experimental Results. To compare performance of **DCP-NOW** with that of the **BSA** and **DCP** algorithms in a general case for a spectrum of various task graph characteristics, three categories of task graphs are used for our experiments. Mean value analysis (MVA) task graphs as shown in Figure 12(a) and fast Fourier Transform (FFT) task graphs as shown in Figure 12(b) are generated with various numbers of nodes (between 10 and 250) and CCR values (between 2 and 20). Comparisons are made in terms of schedule length improvement versus CCR values, with results shown in Figure 13 for MVA graphs and Figure 14 for FFT graphs. Each test point for MVA graphs corresponds to an

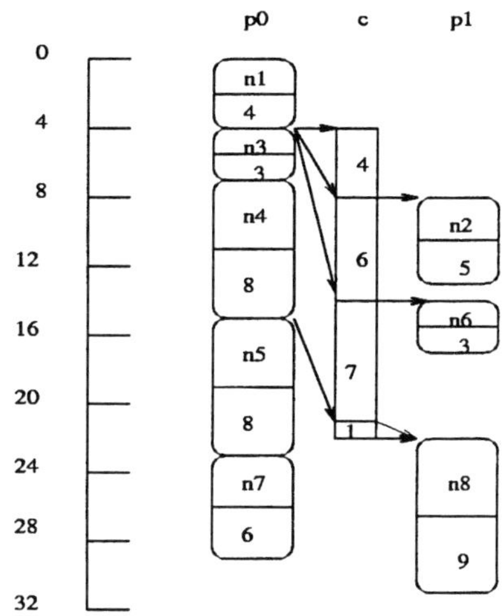

FIG. 11. *Schedule of the Task Graph in Figure 1 by* **DCP-NOW** *(Schedule Length = 31 Units)*

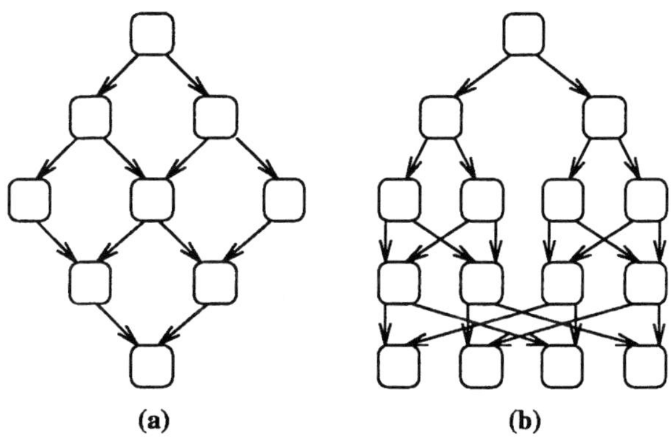

FIG. 12. *Task Graph Example for (a) a Mean Value Analysis and (b) an FFT*

average of 5 task graphs of different values of width. Each point for FFT graphs results from an average of 3 task graphs of various numbers of data points. Another set of randomly generated task graphs are also tested. Results are shown in Figure 15. Each point corresponds to an average of 40 randomly generated graphs with node number ranging from 20 to 50.

From the above comparison results, the DCP-NOW algorithm consistently outperforms the other two by a margin of 10% to 60% in the MVA and FFT graphs and significantly further in randomly generated graphs.

6. Conclusion. A very structured and simple task scheduling algorithm was proposed to handle scheduling on a bus-based NOW environment. We

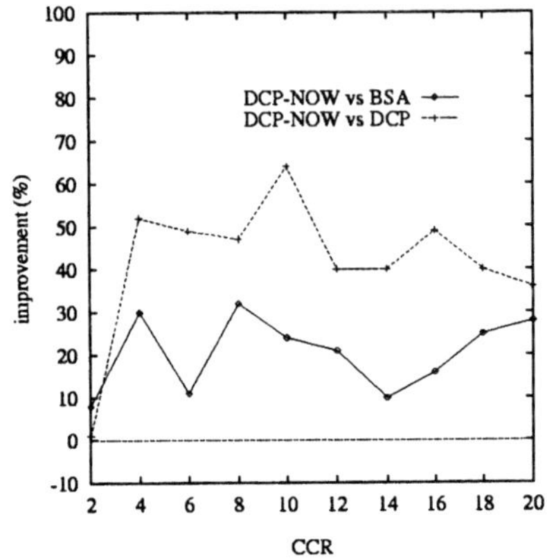

FIG. 13. *Performance Gain in Using* **DCP-NOW** *over* **BSA** *and* **DCP** *on MVA Task Graphs*

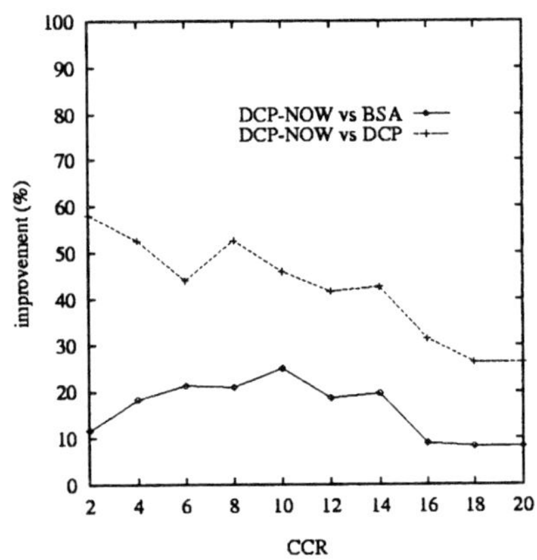

FIG. 14. *Performance Gain in Using* **DCP-NOW** *over* **BSA** *and* **DCP** *on FFT Task Graphs*

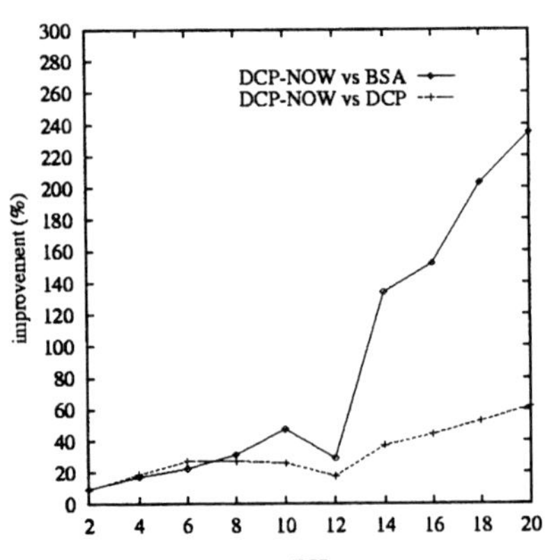

FIG. 15. *Performance Gain in Using* **DCP-NOW** *over* **BSA** *and* **DCP** *on Randomly Generated Task Graphs*

have shown that by looking ahead scheduling situations in a more reasonable manner and taking potential network conflicts into consideration the proposed algorithm easily outperform other known techniques. The proposed algorithm has managed to tackle the additional complexity from avoiding network conflicts with minimal added scheduling time requirement. It would be intersting to see the tradeoff between further improving scheduling performance and the resulted scheduling complexity.

REFERENCES

[1] S. Darbha and D. P. Agrawal, "A Fast and Scalable Scheduling Algorithm for Distributed Memory Systems," *Proceedings of Seventh IEEE Symposium on Parallel and Distributed Processing*, pp. 60-63, 1995.

[2] H. El-Rewini, H.H. Ali and T. Lewis, "Task Scheduling in Multiprocessing Systems," *Computer*, Vol. 28, No. 12, pp. 27-37, Dec. 1995.

[3] A. Gerasoulis and T. Yang, " A Comparison of Clustering Heuristics for Scheduling Directed Acyclic Graphs on Multiprocessors," *Journal of Parallel and Distributed Computing*, Vol. 16, pp. 276-291, 1992.

[4] K. Ghose and N. Mehdiratta, " A Universal Approach for Task Scheduling for Distributed Memory Multiprocessors," *Proceedings of IEEE Scalable High Performance Computing Conference*, pp. 577-584, 1994.

[5] Y-K. Kwok and I. Ahmad, "Bubble Scheduling: A Quasi Dynamic Algorithm for Static Allocation of Tasks to Parallel Architectures," *Proceedings of Seventh IEEE Symposium on Parallel and Distributed Processing*, pp. 36-43, 1995.

[6] Y-K. Kwok and I. Ahmad, "Dynamic Critical-Path Scheduling: An Effective Technique for Allocating Task Graphs to Multiprocessors," *IEEE Trans. on Parallel and Distributed Systems*, Vol. 7, No. 5, pp. 506-520, May 1996.

[7] C.L. McCreary, A.A. Khan, J.J. Thompson, and M.E. McArdle " A Comparison of Heuristics for Scheduling DAGS on Multiprocessors," *Proceedings of Eighth International Conference on Parallel Processing*, pp. 446-451, 1994.

[8] S. Pande, D. P. Agrawal, and J. Mauney, " A Scalable Scheme for Functional Parallelism on Distributed Memory Multiprocessor Systems," *IEEE Trans. on Parallel and Distributed Systems*, Vol. 6, No. 4, pp. 388-399, 1995.

[9] G.N.S. Prasanna and B.R. Musicus, "Generalized Multiprocessor Scheduling for Directed Acyclic Graphs," *Proceedings of Supercomputing '94*, pp. 237-246.

[10] R. Vemulapalli and H.H. Ali, "An Augmentation-Based Algorithm for Task Scheduling in Parallel Systems," *Proceedings of the 29th Annual Hawaii International Conference on System Sciences*, 1996.

[11] T. Yang and A. Gerasoulis, "DSC: Scheduling Parallel Tasks on an Unbounded Number of Processors," *IEEE Trans. on Parallel and Distributed Systems*, Vol. 5, No. 9, Sept. 1994.

HIGH-PERFORMANCE THREAD MIGRATION ON CLUSTERS OF SMPS

BORIS WEISSMAN AND BENEDICT GOMES*

Abstract. Thread migration is established as a mechanism for achieving dynamic load sharing and data locality. However, migration has not been used with fine-grained parallelism on workstation clusters due to the relatively high overheads associated with thread and messaging packages. This paper describes a portable, high performance thread migration system, implemented with user level threads and active messages. The thread system supports an extensible event mechanism which permits an efficient interface between the thread and active message system. Migration is supported by user level primitives; applications may implement different migration policies on top of the migration interface provided. The system runs on a cluster of SMPs and the performance obtained is orders of magnitude better than other reported measurements.

Key words. Thread Migration, SMP, Myrinet

1. Introduction. In recent years, the multi-threaded programming model has grown increasingly popular, propelled in part by the increasing availability of clusters of workstations and shared memory multi-processors (SMPs). Programming languages make use of the threaded model both for expressiveness (particularly in graphical user interfaces) and to exploit the parallelism available on an SMP. The convenience of the threaded model arises from the ease of sharing data between threads, and from the availability of automatic load balancing since threads, once blocked, may continue to execute on any available processor.

A major problem with using the threaded model for fine-grained concurrency is performance. While most modern thread packages are adequate for medium grained concurrency, the overhead costs are unacceptable for fine-grained parallelism. For instance, thread creation using Solaris threads on our SPARCstation 10 system takes 1 to 10 milliseconds; the median thread lifetimes for our application are of the same order. The performance of thread migration, which is necessary for load balance in the threaded model, is also affected by the thread system overheads.

There are several reasons for the poor performance of commercial thread packages. Kernel level threads, as found in NT [10] involve expensive kernel traps [2]. Even the user level thread packages available commercially have high thread creation costs; they appear to be targeted at medium grained parallelism, particularly in applications such as user interfaces where expressiveness rather than performance is the central issue. In addition to the problems of commercial thread packages, the performance of thread migration depends on the communication system. Many migration systems make use of kernel traps for either the thread system [10] or for the communication system [13] [15]. Performance also

*University of California at Berkeley and the International Computer Science Institute, 1947 Center Street, Suite 600, Berkeley CA. 94704, USA (510)642-4274x126, fax (510) 643-7684

depends on the degree of integration between the thread and communication systems. Nexus [7] presents an interface to a combined thread and communication systems; however, it makes use of off-the-shelf thread and communication components. A third potential reason for the poor performance of thread migration is the pointer fixing after migration that is performed by systems such as Ariadne [13] - see Section 3.1.

1.1. Improving Performance. We demonstrate a user level thread package, Active Threads, that achieves high performance with low overheads for thread creation and other thread operations. We also utilize user level messaging, with support for concurrent access to the network interface. A novel feature of the thread package is an extensible event mechanism that permits a close integration between the thread and message passing systems. The system provides primitives for thread migration, but does not dictate a particular thread migration policy. We demonstrate this flexibility by exploring the effect of different policies on several applications.

In summary, this paper makes the following contributions:

- A fine-grained, high-performance thread migration system with user level threads and messaging.
- An extensible thread event mechanism that permits the flexible and efficient integration of independent thread and communication systems.
- Detailed performance metrics for thread migration, and the ability to compare the effects of different migration policies on application performance.

An implementation of thread migration involves four basic components, each of which involves design decisions - the transfer of thread local data, the access of global data, the thread system and the messaging system. Our presentation will describe these four components, micro-benchmarks and then full program results.

2. Transferring State. In order to effectively move a thread to a different processor, it is necessary for the transferred thread to correctly access all related data and resources. All data that is local to the thread (the stack and any thread-local heap) may be copied to the destination processor. However, a problem may arise, since the addresses on the target processor may be different from the original addresses and internal pointers may no longer be valid. Furthermore, data that is not globally replicated or transferred along with the thread will not exist on the destination node.

2.1. Thread Local Data. Two approaches may be used to handle local pointers when threads are migrated. In the first approach, local pointer values may change after the thread has been migrated, and local pointers must be updated after migration [10], [12], [13]. This is both expensive and, if left to the user, error-prone.

The second approach is to partition the address space such that local pointers may maintain the same values after migration. Since we were interested in a portable, high performance system, we chose the alternate approach of storing the thread local data at the same location in the address space on the destination node, so that no local pointers need be updated. A pre-defined area of the virtual memory space is reserved for each thread stack on all nodes. This is essentially the same approach as used by Millipede [10], Amber [4] and UPVM [6].

2.2. Shared Data. In addition to thread local data i.e. the stack and the local heap, a thread may also access data that is shared between multiple threads. Examples of such shared data include resources located on a particular machine and global synchronization objects.

After a thread has migrated, if pointers to this shared state are to still be valid, it is necessary for the pointers to indicate the nodes on which the data resides. Our approach is to use global pointers, which create the illusion of a shared address space. Global pointers, which are commonly used in parallel languages, usually encode the node location in the unused bits of a standard pointer. Global pointers incur a certain overhead whenever they are dereferenced, even when the data is locally available since the location of the data must be ascertained before dereferencing. In the parallel language pSather (which uses Active Threads as a compilation target), the node location is encoded in the unused high bits of the address. In the C++ based library [9] we implemented a set of classes encapsulating global pointers using pointer overloading.

3. The Thread System. Active Threads is a general-purpose portable and extensible light-weight thread package for uni- and multiprocessors targeted at irregular applications. Active Threads is capable of handling millions of threads on a variety of hardware platforms. The details of the highly flexible Active Threads architecture, and API are given in [21]. The locality impact of thread scheduling on modern SMPs are considered in [22]. In this section, we concentrate on the aspects of the Active Threads organization that enable us to integrate threads with communications, efficiently implement thread migration primitives and to freely experiment with different migration policies.

3.1. Threads and bundles. Active Threads supports general-purpose blocking threads. Groups of logically related threads with common properties are organized into thread bundles, or simply bundles. All threads in a bundle share the same scheduling policy. Scheduling policies for different thread bundles can be completely independent from each other. A single application may create thread bundles with different scheduling policies such as FIFO, LIFO, priority, processor affinity scheduling, etc. Moreover, a scheduling policy for a bundle is not fixed and can change dynamically. While bundles were mainly designed to enable compositional development of parallel software and encapsulate scheduling policies together with other module resources, bundles and the associated scheduling event mechanism have proved to be an excellent abstraction to enable fine-grained thread mobility in distributed environments.

3.2. Scheduling Event Mechanism. Active Threads provides no hard-coded scheduling policy. Instead, it supports a general mechanism upon which different specialized scheduling policies can be built. All thread scheduling decisions are made by the bundle to which the thread belongs. The bundle is free to maintain any scheduling data structures that fit most closely the semantics of the thread group. Different susbsytems communicate with bundles by vectoring scheduling events. Bundles encapsulate all aspects of scheduling and must provide event handlers for all scheduling events. There are no restrictions on the implementation of such event handlers. All events are partitioned into two groups: internal Active Threads events and external (user-defined) events. Internal events deal with common thread operations: thread creation, termination, blocking, unblocking, dispatching by the processor, etc. A bundle encapsulates all scheduling decisions for a group of logically related threads. The system is extensible: new scheduling policies are implemented by extending the bundle library.

3.3. Scheduling Policies. An Active Threads bundle must implement event handlers for all eight internal events. No restrictions are placed on the bundle internals. The implementations are free to select the best data structures possible to implement the scheduler. For instance, if the number of threads is known statically (or even dynamically at bundle creation time), the scheduler may keep threads in an array to minimize rescheduling overhead.

4. Communications. Aside from context switching times, the other major overhead involved in thread migration arises from the system overhead of most messaging systems. Much of the overhead is caused by repeated copying of messages to and from buffers located in the OS kernel address space. The Active Message approach [19] eliminates much of the system overhead by handing control of the delivered message directly to a user-level message handler. Although the thread migration mechanism described in the following section does not rely exclusively on the communications style of Active Messages, user-level management of communications is indispensable for achieving low migration latencies and high throughputs. We have implemented a variant of the Berkeley Active Message communications system that supports the general Active Message communications style [19], but also extends the Active Message interface and functionality in several important ways.

The active message system, as originally conceived and available in the current Berkeley distribution, was not designed to run on multi-threaded SMPs. Multi-threading raises the possibility of contention for the network device; consequently, all accesses to the messaging system must be properly protected.

Some of the overhead involved in a message transfer (i.e. the message packaging) is actually incurred on the host processor. Therefore, on an SMP it is possible to increase the message throughput by pipelining message packaging and excuting some of the pipeline stages concurrently. We also extended the Active Message functionality to support remote thread creation, which is potentially a blocking operations

The performance of the message system is strongly affected by the processor performance. On our system, which consists of the network of 50 MHz Hyper-

SPARCs with 4 processors per node, a one way latency for a message with a payload of 5 words is around 17us. A bulk transfer of 1K takes 560us and is mostly constrained by the host processor and I/O bus speed rather than the network interface.

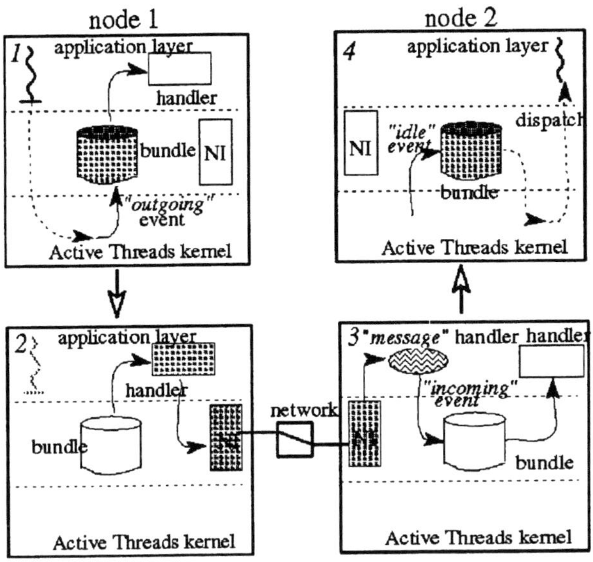

FIG. 4.1. *Events and thread migration.*

5. Thread Migration Mechanism. We view thread migration as a natural extension of thread scheduling for a single (possibly multiprocessing) node to a distributed environment. Migration is implemented by defining new bundles that are extended with special user-defined migration events. This enables seamless integration of migration with other thread subsystems. Migration happens transparently to other thread activities and bundles and threads that do not support migration need not be concerned with any new and unforeseen effects. Different migration policies are implemented by defining new bundles and can coexist in a single application. Though the mechanism is general, we show (Section 7) that we pay a very small price for this generality. In fact, thread migration in Active Threads outperforms other systems with hard-coded migration policies by orders of magnitude in some cases.

Figure 4.1 captures the essence of the underlying mechanism in the case of a thread relocating itself to a different node. In the first step, the user requests a migration, which generates a scheduling outgoing event. In the second step, the scheduler handles the event and transfers the thread state using the network interface. In the third step an incoming event is generated to restart the thread and, finally, the thread is run on node 2.

Operation	Ultra-1 167 MHz	Pentium Pro 200 MHz	Dec Alpha 250 MHz	HPPA 9000 99 MHz
thread create	1.3	1.4	1.0	2.0
null thread	5.6	4.4	2.9	7.2
context switch	1.7	1.5	1.1	3.0
uncontested mutex	0.4	0.5	0.3	1.0
uncontested sema.	0.4	0.5	0.3	1.0
mutex try	0.2	0.2	0.1	0.3
semaphore try	0.2	0.2	0.1	0.3
mutex ping-pong	6.0	3.4	2.9	7.9
sema. ping-pong	6.0	3.7	2.8	8.5

TABLE 6.1
Cost of thread and synchronization operations in Active Threads, microseconds.

6. Microbenchmarks. In the following section we present microbenchmarks that measure the performance of the thread migration system. We start by presenting the performance profile of the underlying thread system on a variety of modern platform. We then briefly discuss the organization of our NOW. We then present a detailed performance analysis of our thread migration system in terms or the following parameters:

- point-to-point latency
- initiating node overhead
- thread migration throughput

6.1. Threads and synchronization. We have measured the performance of Active Threads on a variety of hardware platforms: different models of SPARC symmetric multiprocessors, Intel Pentium Pro, DEC Alpha AXP, and HPPA 1.1. Performance measurements for Active Threads primitives on some of these platforms are shown in Table 6.1. For instance, on 167 Mhz Ultra-1, thread creation overhead is almost as expensive as null function call with window overflow and only about an order of magnitude more expensive than a null call that does not cause a window overflow.

A detailed comparison of the thread and synchronization performance of Active Threads and other modern research and commercial thread systems is given in [21].

7. Thread Migration. Our main platform is a cluster of SPARCstation-10 workstations connected together by Myrinet [1]. Each workstation has four 50 Mhz HyperSPARC processors. The Myrinet NI is an I/O card that plugs into the standard SBus. It contains a 32-bit RISC 'LANai' network processor, DMA engines, and local memory (SRAM). The NI's memory is mapped into the user process address space and can be accessed through load/stores to mapped main memory addresses. The Myrinet network consists of crossbar switches with eight bidirectional ports that can be linked into arbitrary topologies. The network is constructed of low-cost off-the-shelf commercial hardware that is readily available for a variety of architectures. The costs of different thread migration operations for this network configuration are presented in Figure 6.1. All graphs

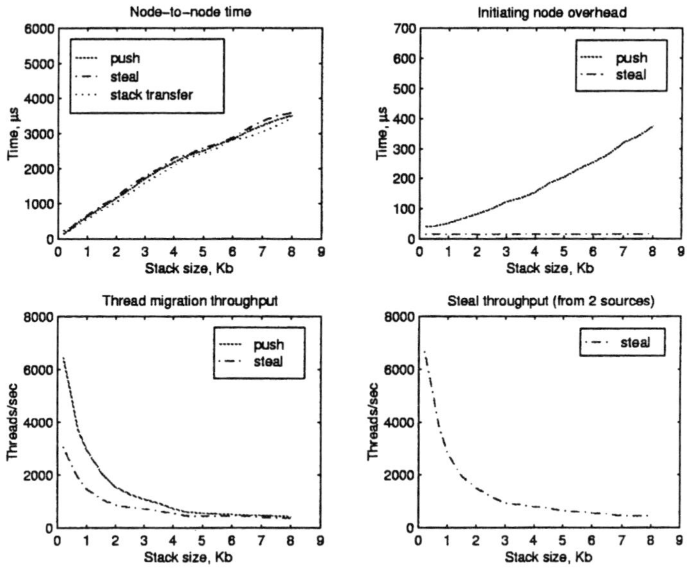

FIG. 6.1. *Migration latency and overhead in Active Threads.*

reflect an average over 1,000 migrations.

The overhead for a thread steal consists of two parts - the steal initiation on the requesting node and the service overhead on the remote node. The former is fixed and fairly small - only 8us on our system. The latter is exactly the thread push overhead. On our system, thread migration overheads are at least an order of magnitude lower than full point-to-point latencies for medium size stacks. For instance, the push overhead for a null thread is 40us and the overhead for a thread with an active stack size of 1Kb is only 52us.

For applications with small tasks, but highly dynamic and unpredictable loads, frequent thread migration may be necessary and throughput rather than latency can be the key factor. The migration throughput may also affect the programming style as well as application design. For instance, a single producer/multiple consumer pattern is well known for its simplicity and may be adequate to capture the semantics of many applications. However, designating a single node as a producer imposes a bandwidth constraint on the system in order to keep all the consumers busy.

From Figure 6.1, it is evident that Active Threads achieves a fairly high throughput, on the order of thousands of threads per second for small to medium thread stack sizes. Steal throughput is lower than push throughput, in particular for light-weight threads. This is due to the cost of the initiating message, the effect of which is amortized as the thread stack grows in size.

The last graph of Figure 6.1 demonstrates the scalability of our implementation. The throughput for small threads is essentially doubled when a node

TABLE 7.1
Migration time (in microseconds) on various systems as function of thread stack size.

1System	null	1K	2K
Ariadne (SS5, Ethernet)		1100	1400
Millipede (Pentium/fast Ethernet)	2000		?70000?
PM2 (ALPHA/1 processor)			2200
ActiveThreads Overhead (SPARC-10/Myrinet)	40	52	68
ActiveThreads Latency (SPARC-10/Myrinet)	150	630	1100

starts prefetching from two sources simultaneously.

7.1. Comparisons with other systems. It is hard to directly compare the performance of systems that support thread migration because of hardware differences such as processor and network speeds and the structure of memory hierarchy. Reported performance parameters also vary. Still, we find it instructive to list the performance characteristics of several recent thread migration systems, along with the hardware characteristics of each system.

In terms of pure processing power, Active Threads run on a very modest distributed platform - all the other systems employ hardware with the clock speed at least several times faster than our 50Mhz SPARCstation-10s. Our preliminary experiments on a Sun Enterprise 5000 demonstrate latencies reduced by a factor of 3.

Millipede [10] reports the 'average latency' of thread migration to be 70ms; however, the average thread stack size is not specified. In our own experiments, the average active stack size of a migrating thread was between 1K and 2K. The PM2 [15] latencies are for thread migration between processes on a single 1 processor DEC ALPHA workstation using PVM for interprocess communications.

In contrast to the other systems, Active Threads supports thread operations as well as communication at the user level. This allows us to keep operation overheads small, relative to the full operation latency. The overhead on other systems, although not reported, must account for most of the point-to-point latencies: Ariadne [13] traps to the OS kernel for TCP/IP communications; Millipede is based on kernel-level threads and must trap to the kernel for most thread operations; PM2 traps to the kernel for interprocess communication. As a result, Active Threads latencies are at least an order of magnitude lower than those of the other systems while the migration overhead can be several orders of magnitude lower.

8. Application Studies. We present the performance of the thread package on some parallel applications.

8.1. Quicksort. Our first distributed application is based on the threaded C++ implementation of quicksort. The structure of the application is rather simple: each recursive subdivision of the input results in new child threads; when the task size drops below a certain threshold, the algorithm switches to bubble sort.

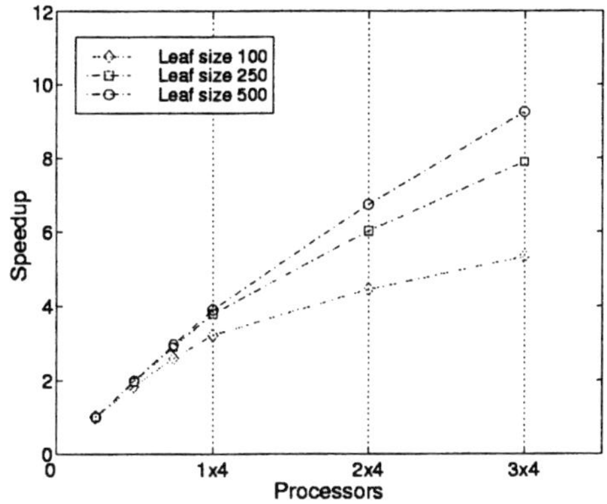

FIG. 8.1. *Quicksort scalability on a network of 4-way SS-10s connected by Myrinet.*

All input data is initially located on a single node. As processing starts, new threads are generated on that node. By default, Active Threads uses a simple thread stealing policy - whenever a processor on some node becomes idle and no local threads are available for execution, it tries to steal a thread from a randomly selected node. As the sort continues, generated threads are stolen from the nodes where they were created by idle processors of the other nodes. Dispatching stolen threads on processors that initiate migration results in the network transfer of the input arrays. On thread termination, a sorted subrange is transferred back to the originating node. Finally, a child thread informs a parent thread about its completion by signalling a (global) semaphore. Note that in this straight-forward implementation, records may be (and are) migrated several times between nodes before they actually end up in a correct place in the original array. Similarly, on their way back to the original node, records go through all intermediate hops. To preserve simplicity, we have intentionally avoided any optimizations of the original shared-memory code.

Figure 8.1 demonstrates scalability of this simple implementation for several different values of the threshold designating a switch to an elementary sorting algorithm.

9. Parallel grep. This application is a threaded version of 'grep', a standard Unix utility for regular expression-based search. It is based on a version of grep by Ron Winacott. at_grep supports the full functionality of 'grep'. It also supports several additional features such as the recursive traversal of directories. The application consists of search threads (which search through a single file) and cascade threads (which generate more search threads for all the files in a directory).

9.0.1. Steal-based migration policy. In the absence of any user migration specifications, Active Threads employ a simple thread stealing policy - whenever a processor is idle it tries to steal work from any remote node which has available work. The termination condition is detected when nodes have no

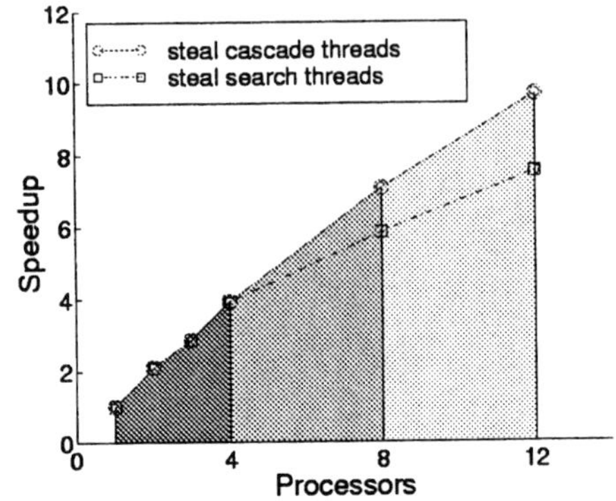

FIG. 9.1. *at_grep and thread steal*

threads and there are no pending network messages.

These minimal changes resulted in a fairly competitive distributed implementation of grep. Figure 9.1 and 9.2 present the speedup due to thread stealing for the command 'at_grep mutex' invoked on the Active Threads source tree. The effect of each additional multiprocessor on performance is indicated by shading the corresponding area under the speedup curve.

9.0.2. Push-based migration policy. To illustrate the flexibility of the Active Threads migration interface and to possibly achieve even greater performance, we next investigated taking direct control over thread migration from the runtime system by inserting explicit thread push calls.

Two heuristics were investigated. In naive round-robin a single node serves as a producer of work. Simple load-balancing augments the above scheme by having the producer send work to lightly loaded nodes. Figure 9.1 and 9.2 demonstrates the performance of at_grep under both push heuristics. While the load-balancing heuristic resulted in performance close to that of the best stealing heuristics, no further improvement was obtained. While simple, our load-balancing policy could be improved at the cost of introducing extra complexity.

10. Conclusions. We have demonstrated a thread migration system which achieves high performance by closely integrating user level threads with user level messaging. No compiler level support is necessary for pointer identification, resulting in a portable system that may be used for application programming or as a compilation target. The thread system defines an extensible event mechanism which permits a close integration between the thread and messaging systems, while maintaining the modularity of both components.

We have also defined a set of performance metrics, that make a clear distinction between the latency and the overhead of migration. Our micro-benchmarks indicate that the system is at least an order of magnitude better than existing systems. The performance could be further improved on more modern hardware

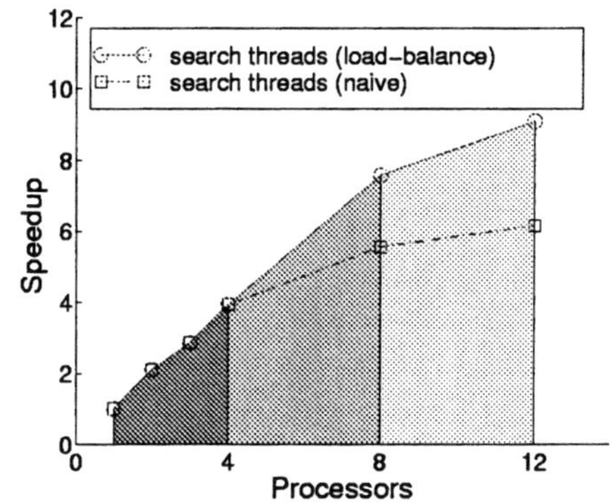

FIG. 9.2. *at_grep and thread push*

with the faster processors available today. Active Threads were used as a compilation target for Sather, an explicitly parallel object-oriented language, and for a distributed extension of C++.

REFERENCES

[1] NANETTE J. BODEN, DANNY COHEN, ROBERT E. FELDERMAN, AND ALAN E. KULAWIK, CHARLES L. SEITZ, JAKOV. N. SEIZOVIC, AND WEN-KING SU., *Myrinet: A Gigabit-per-second Local Area Network*, in IEEE Micro, 15(1), February 1995.

[2] BRIAN N. BERSHAD , *The Presto User Manual*, Oct 91. Available from: www.cs.washington.edu/research/compiler/papers.d/presto.html

[3] ROBERT D. BLUMOFE, CRISTOPHER F. JOERG, BRADLEY C. KUSZMAUL, CHARLES E. LEISERSON, KEITH H. RANDALL, AND JULI ZHOU , *Cilk: An Effcient Multithreaded Runtime System*, in Journal of Parallel and Distributed Computing, Vol. 37. No 1, August 1996. pp 55-69.

[4] JEFFREY S. CHASE, FRANZ G. AMADOR, EDWARD D. LAZOWSKA, HENRY M. LEVY, RICHARD J. LITTLEFIELD. , *The Amber System: Parallel Programming on a Network of Multiprocessors*, in ACM Symposium on Operating System Priciples, December 1989

[5] DAVID CRONK, MATTHEW HAINES, PIYUSH MEHROTRA , *Migration in the Presence of Pointers* , Proceedings of the Mini_track on Multithreaded Systems, 30th Hawaii International Conference on System Science, January 1997

[6] JEREMY CASA, RAVI KONURU, STEVE W. OTTO, ROBERT PROUTY, JONATHAN WALPOLE , *Adaptive Migration systems for PVM*,in Proceedings of Supercomputing '94, pp 390 - 399, Washington D.C., November 1994.

[7] IAN FOSTER, CARL KESSELMAN, STEVEN TUECKE , *The Nexus Approach to Integrating Multithreading and Communication* , in Journal of Parallel and Distributed Computing, Vol. 37. No 1, August 1996. pp 70-82.

[8] SETH COPEN GOLDSTEIN, KLAUS ERIK SCHAUSER, DAVID E. CULLER , *Lazy Threads: Implementing a Fast Parallel Call* , in Journal of Parallel and Distributed Computing, Vol. 37. No 1, August 1996. pp 5-20.

[9] MICHAEL HOLTKAMP , *Thread Migration with Active Threads*, International Computer Science Institute Technical Report TR-97-038.

[10] AYAL ITZKOVITZ, ASSAF SCHUSTER, LEA WOLFOVICH , *Thread Migration and its Applications in Distributed Shared Memory Systems* , in The Journal of Systems and

Software, 1997

[11] David K. Lowenthal, Vincent W. Freeh, Gregory R. Andrews, *Using Fine-Grain Threads and Run-Time Decision Making in Parallel Computing* , in Journal of Parallel and Distributed Computing, Vol. 37. No 1, August 1996. pp 41-54

[12] Eric Jul, Henry Levy, Norman Hutchinson, Andrew Black , *Fine-Grained Mobility in the Emerald System*, in: ACM Transactions on Computer Systems, Vol. 6, No. 1, pp 109 - 133, February 1988.

[13] Edward Mascarenhas, Vermon Rego , *Ariadne: Architecure of a Portable Threads System Supporting Thread Migration,*, in Software - Practice and Experience, Vol 26(3), pp 327 - 356, March 1996

[14] M.A. Malcolm, R.B. Simpson, *Local versus Global Strategies for Adaptive Quadrature*, ACM Trans. on Mathematical Software 1(2), pp. 129-146, 1975.

[15] R. Namyst and J. Mehaut, *PM2: Parallel Multithreaded Machine. A computing environment for distributed architectures*, www.fifl.fr/ñemyst/pm2.html

[16] M.L. Powell, S.R. Kleiman, S. Barton, D. Shah, D. Stein and M. Weeks , *Solaris SunOS5.0 Multithread Architecture*, White paper from Sun Microsystems, Mountain View, CA.

[17] Jurgen W. Quittek, Boris Weissman , *Efficient Extensible Synchronization in Sather*, in The 1997 International Scientific Computing in Object-Oriented Parallel Environments Conference (ISCOPE '97), Decmber 1997.

[18] D. Stoutamire and S. Omohundro , *The Sather 1.1 Specification*, International Computer Science Institute Technical Report TR-96-012.

[19] T. von Eichen, D. Culler, S. Golstein and E. Schauser , *Active Messages: a mechanism for integrated communication and computation* , in Proceedings of the 19th International Conference on Computer Architecture 1992

[20] Chih-Po Wen, Soumen Chakrabarti, Etienne Deprit, Arvind Krishnamurthy, Katherine Yelick, *Runtime Support for Portable Distributed Data Structure*, in Workshop on Languages, Compilers, and Runtime Systems for Scalable Computers, May 1995.

[21] Boris Weissman , *Active Threads: an Extensible and Portable Light-Weight Thread System*, International Computer Science Institute Technical Report TR-97-036

[22] Boris Weissman , *Performance Counters and State Sharing Annotations: a Unified Approach to Thread Locality*, Eighth International Conference on Architectural Support for Programming Languages and Operating Systems (ASPLOS-VIII), October 1998.

MULTIPLE-WRITER ENTRY CONSISTENCY *

HARJINDER SANDHU †, TIM BRECHT ‡, AND DIEGO MOSCOSO §

Abstract. In this paper, we present the design, implementation and evaluation of a new distributed shared memory (DSM) coherence model called multiple-writer entry consistency (MEC). MEC combines the efficient communication mechanisms of Lazy Release Consistency (LRC) with the flexible data management of the Shared Regions [17, 11] and Entry Consistency (EC) models [5]. This is achieved in MEC by decoupling synchronization from coherence (in contrast to the tight coupling of synchronization and coherence present in EC) while retaining the familiar synchronization structure found in Release Consistent (RC) programs. The advantage of MEC is that it allows region-based coherence protocols (those that manage data at the granularity of user-defined shared regions) to be used along side page-based protocols within an application and within the RC framework. Our experimental evaluation on an 8 processor system shows that using MEC reduces parallel execution times by margins ranging from 5% to 46% in five of the six applications that we study. However, the parallel execution time of the LRC version of the remaining application is lower than the MEC version by 48%. We conclude that offering both page-based and region-based models for coherence within the same system is not only practical but necessary.

Key words. parallel programming, network of workstations, distributed shared-memory, coherence models, memory consistency.

AMS subject classifications. 68-04, 68N99, 68M20.

1. Introduction.

Within the realm of Distributed Shared Memory (DSM) systems, several divergent streams of models have emerged. Among the most common are (1) those that rely on pages as the underlying abstraction for data management and use Release Consistency (RC) as the synchronization model presented to the user [7, 13], and (2) those that use user-defined *shared regions* as the underlying abstraction for data management coupled with a synchronization model called Entry Consistency (EC) that explicitly binds synchronization primitives with the data they protect [5, 11, 16]. Each of these models has their limitations. In RC-based systems, the reliance on pages as the unit of data management often causes these systems to transmit more data than necessary in order to maintain coherence due to the effects of false sharing, or to transmit data using more messages than necessary when shared data structures span multiple pages. Sophisticated coherence protocols such as *lazy release consistency* (LRC) reduce the impact of false sharing but cannot eliminate it entirely [13]. In EC-based systems, the problems that stem from the mismatch between the system's view of sharing and the granularity of sharing within the application

*This work was supported by the Natural Sciences and Engineering Research Council of Canada

† Department of Computer Science, York University, North York, Ontario, Canada M3J 1P3. email: hsandhu@cs.yorku.ca

‡ Department of Computer Science, University of Waterloo, Waterloo, Ontario Canada N2L 3G1. email: brecht@cs.uwaterloo.ca

§ Department of Computer Science, York University, North York, Ontario, Canada M3J 1P3. email: diego@cs.yorku.ca are avoided entirely by managing data at user-defined granularity. However, the EC synchronization model is more complex to program than RC and is often avoided as a result.

Ideally, a system should integrate both page-based and region-based protocols in a way that permits the programmer to begin with the simpler RC-based model, and then add EC annotations for just those data structures that are better suited to region-based rather than page-based data management. Unfortunately, RC and EC are difficult to integrate in this way due to the differences in their respective synchronization models. Adding EC annotations in an existing RC program requires modifying the program's synchronization structure and it may result in a program that contains too much synchronization. The study of LRC versus EC by Adve *et al.* [1], for instance, points out that their EC-based applications often suffered from this problem of over-synchronization.

In this paper, we present a new model called Multiple-Writer Entry Consistency (MEC). MEC manages data at a granularity defined by the user but, unlike EC, it decouples the primitives used for synchronization from those used for coherence. This decoupling of synchronization from coherence has two effects. The first is that it permits the efficient integration of both page-based and region-based protocols for coherence within the same RC framework. For synchronization, MEC retains the familiar *acquire* and *release* primitives of RC. Consequently, users can write programs for the simpler RC model, using an efficient page-based protocol such as LRC, and then, within the same synchronization framework, selectively add MEC annotations to those data structures that may benefit from region-based data management.

The second effect of decoupling synchronization and coherence in MEC is that user-defined shared regions can be concurrently modified by different processors. This presents greater flexibility than the single-writer multiple-reader behavior enforced by EC on regions defined by the user. Consider, for example, an application with interspersed fine-grained sharing among the elements of a large data structure. Under typical EC implementations, either each element would have to be bound to a separate synchronization object and guarded individually, or else the entire structure would have to be bound to a single synchronization object and guarded in a way that permits only one processor to modify it at a time. The former partitioning would be too fine-grained to be efficient in a DSM environment, while the latter solution would unnecessarily restrict concurrency.

We have implemented the MEC protocol within the Treadmarks distributed shared memory system (which itself implements page-based LRC) and conducted a detailed evaluation that compares the performance of LRC and MEC for six applications. The results of this investigation show that five of the six applications obtain better performance using MEC than LRC, with differences ranging from 5% to 46%. In the remaining application, however, there is a significant degradation (48%) using MEC. These results, which we consider to be among the key contributions of this paper, argue strongly in favor of using an integrated page-based and region-based solution as a platform for distributed shared memory.

An overview of this paper is as follows. Section 2 briefly describes the background to this work with a description of the RC, LRC, and EC models. Section 3 describes the MEC model and its implementation. Section 4 presents the results of a performance evaluation of LRC versus MEC, and is followed in Section 5 with a discussion of how these results relate to other work, including earlier work comparing LRC and EC. Section 6 presents the conclusions of this paper.

2. Background. Memory consistency models present a set of programming constraints to the user and guarantee correctness only for programs that obey those constraints. In the Release Consistency (RC) model [9] these constraints are (a) that only system recognized synchronization operations are used, (b) that all synchronization operations are labeled as *acquire* or *release* operations, and (c) that there are no data races in the program. Under RC, a processor may delay the propagation of coherence related information to other processors until it arrives at a *release* point in the program. A release point in the program indicates that the process is exiting a critical section, and that other processors must now be made aware of modifications to shared data within this critical section. A lazy implementation of release consistency (LRC) [13], however, takes advantage of the fact that a processor that wishes to use the data computed by another processor must first acquire a lock from the processor that has modified that data. Therefore, using LRC the propagation of coherence related information can be delayed until the acquire operation by another processor, rather than immediately upon a release operation.

DSM implementations using RC mitigate the impact of false sharing on pages both by delaying the propagation of coherence information and by permitting multiple processors to concurrently modify different portions of the same page. Munin, among the first DSM systems to use RC, introduced the notion of *twinning* and *diffing* to consolidate concurrent changes to a page from different processors [7]. Prior to modifying a page, a processor creates a twin (a local copy) of the page. Later, upon arrival at a release point, it compares the modified page to its unmodified twin and transmits to other processors only those portions of the page that have changed. Treadmarks' implementation of LRC delays the creation and transmission of *diff*s until modifications to the page are requested by another processor, thereby further reducing the number of messages required to maintain coherence.

Entry Consistency (EC) [5], and other models like it, such as the Shared Regions (SR) model [11, 17], avoid the problem of false sharing among virtual memory pages by managing data at a granularity defined by the user.[1] In SR, a *shared region* is a user-defined entity describing the granularity at which data is shared within the application. According to both EC and SR, each shared region is explicitly bound in the program to a token that is used for synchronization. In SR, the primitives *readaccess*, *writeaccess*, *readdone*, and

[1]For the purposes of discussion, we borrow terminology from both the EC and SR models; semantically, these models are equivalent.

writedone are used to guard access to a shared region. In addition to enforcing synchronization, the underlying system checks the state of the region when these primitives are invoked and, when necessary, initiates coherence actions to keep the region consistent. Each user-defined shared region follows a single-writer multiple-reader synchronization protocol. The EC or SR models have been used in a number of systems, including Midway [5], CRL [11], DiSom [16], ABC++ [4], Amber [8], and Hurricane [17].

3. Multiple-Writer Entry Consistency. The Multiple-Writer Entry Consistency (MEC) model described in this paper combines elements of both RC and EC in the interface that is presented to the user, and is akin to LRC in its implementation. This section describes the MEC model and its implementation.

3.1. Model. As in the Shared Regions (SR) model [17], we use the term *shared region* in MEC to denote a user-defined region of memory that is treated as a single unit for the purposes of coherence enforcement. Once a set of shared regions has been defined within the MEC framework, a set of operations, *readaccess* and *writeaccess*, are used in conjunction with a particular shared region to indicate when references to that shared region occur, and whether these references also modify that region. We refer to these operations generically as *access* operations.

From the programmers perspective, the main differences between MEC and the EC and SR models are twofold. First, the access operations in MEC enforce coherence but are non-synchronizing. For synchronization, MEC retains the familiar *acquire* and *release* operations of RC, and integrates the coherence enforced through the *access* operations with the synchronization performed by the *acquire/release* operations. The second difference between SR and MEC is that, in MEC, although the access operations are used prior to a series of references to a particular region, there is no need for corresponding operations to indicate the completion of this series of references to the region.

In MEC, regions defined by the user can be modified concurrently by different processors. Access operations are used to determine when to consolidate changes to a region. An *access* operation by processor P_i ensures that all modifications to region R *preceding* the *access* operation are seen by P_i. The use of the term *preceding* in MEC is equivalent to the *happened-before-1* relationship defined by Adve *et al.* [2]. That is, x can be said to *precede* y if: (a) x and y are on the same processor and x occurs before y in the order defined by the program, or (b) x is a release operation on one processor and y is an acquire operation on another processor, and y returns the value written by x. This relationship is transitive, so if x precedes y and y precedes z, then x precedes z in this partial order. Thus, modifications to R by processor P_i will be seen by processor P_j only when there is a transitive chain such that the modifications by P_i precede an *access* operation by P_j.

3.2. Implementation. Our implementation integrates MEC into the Treadmarks implementation of LRC [13]. In the standard Treadmarks implementation, a large shared data space is created in the initialization of the system, and all shared data is subsequently allocated within this space. A page table is used to keep track of the state of each page in this shared data area. The execution of each processor is divided into time intervals (where synchronization operations mark the beginning and end of an interval) and each processor maintains a list of the intervals it has seen from each of the other processors. On an acquire operation, a processor transmits its current interval time stamp and receives in return a list of intervals it has not seen and *write notices* containing the set of pages that were modified in that interval.

In our implementation of MEC, the shared data area is partitioned into two sections, a page-based area containing K virtual memory pages, and a shared region-based area containing the remaining space. The page table is converted into a page-region table, partitioned so that the first K entries keep track of pages in the page area, and the remaining entries keep track of user-defined regions in the shared region area. Shared data may be allocated in either area from within the program. Data allocated in the page-based area is managed using LRC in exactly the same way as in the unmodified Treadmarks system, using virtual memory protection to intercept faulting read/write references to pages and initiate coherence actions. For data in the shared regions area, page faults do not occur. Instead, *access* annotations in the program are used to determine when coherence actions are needed for a particular region.

In the integrated LRC/MEC implementation, both pages and shared regions are referred to by their index in the page-region table. On an acquire operation, a processor transmits its vector time stamp to the processor currently holding the lock, just as it does by default in LRC, but it receives in response *write notices* containing a list of both pages and regions that have been modified in intervals not seen by the acquiring processor. In MEC, a region is considered modified in interval q by P_i if P_i issued a *writeaccess* on that region in interval q.

The *diff* and *interval* management routines are identical for both page-based LRC and region-based MEC except for the granularity at which these actions are carried out. In our implementation, changes were made to the original Treadmarks *diff* management routines to support arbitrary regions of data, but the interval management routines were not modified from the originals. We also converted the Treadmarks communication layer from UDP to TCP to facilitate the transmission of large data regions in MEC. Comparisons between LRC in the original (unmodified) Treadmarks system and our modified version showed that neither of these changes had a significant impact on performance.

4. Performance Evaluation. In order to assess the performance of MEC as well as the value of integrating both MEC and LRC within the same system, we compared the performance of six application kernels executed first using LRC, and then with key shared data structures identified as shared regions in order to use MEC. These applications are: Blocked Matrix Multiplication (MM), Successive Over-Relaxation (SOR), Blocked-Contiguous LU-Decomposition (LU), Traveling Salesman Problem (TSP), Integer Sort (IS), and

Floyd-Warshall (FLOYD). TSP, SOR, and IS are from the suite of applications used in earlier TreadMarks studies [13, 14, 1], LU is from the Splash-2 benchmark suite [18], and MM and FLOYD were written locally.

All experiments were conducted on an 8 node cluster of workstations connected together by a Fore ATM switch. The workstations are IBM RISC System/6000s each with a 133 MHz PowerPC 604 processor, 16 KB L1 instruction cache, 16 KB L1 data cache, a 4-way associative 512 KB L2 cache, and 96 MB of memory. Virtual memory pages are 4 KB in size. Table 1 shows the problem sizes, execution times, and speedups of these applications running on this workstation cluster.

program	problem size	1 proc time	8 proc time		speedup	
			LRC	MEC	LRC	MEC
MM	1536x1536 (int) matrices , block size 32	257.7	58.1	50.1	4.4	5.1
SOR	2000x2000 (float) matrix, 100 iterations	108.5	34.9	18.8	3.1	5.8
LU	1536x1536 (double) matrix, block size 64	97.9	35.8	21.2	2.7	4.6
TSP	19 city tour	56.2	23.3	44.5	2.4	1.3
FLOYD	512 node graph	61.9	13.8	12.5	4.5	5.0
IS	2^{22} keys, bucket size 2^9, 10 iterations	24.9	4.0	3.9	6.2	6.3

TABLE 1
Problem sizes, execution times (in seconds), and speedups on 8 processors.

4.1. Summary of Results. Figure 1(a) shows the normalized parallel execution times of the applications used in this study. Execution times are divided into four components: (1) sync - synchronization time, (2) traps - time spent handling traps (protection traps to pages in LRC, *access* traps in MEC), which includes time spent fetching diffs and creating twins, (3) remote - time spent handling remote requests initiated from other processors, including time spent creating diffs on demand, (4) base - the time remaining, once sync, traps, and remote costs are accounted for. The base time is largely time spent performing computation in the application, although because trap and remote costs begin timing after asynchronously entering the signal handler, the base time will also include the cost of entering the signal handler. The accompanying graphs in Figure 1 show the number of messages communicated and the number of bytes transferred relative to one processor.

In the MEC version of our applications, shared data structures were partitioned into shared regions in what seemed to be the most obvious and natural fashion for each application. For the problem sizes used, MEC executions times are lower than LRC in MM, SOR, LU, FLOYD, and IS, by margins ranging from 5% in IS to 46% in SOR (Figure 1(a)). For MM, SOR, and LU, this difference is due largely to a reduction in the number of messages (Figure 1(c)), while in FLOYD, the difference is due to a reduction in the number of bytes (Figure 1(c)). In TSP, MEC execution time is significantly worse than LRC, by a margin of 48%, due to the overly simplistic way regions are used in the MEC version. Here, the number of messages is reduced using MEC by defining a shared region that spans many pages, but false sharing within this shared region leads to a significant increase in the number of bytes transmitted.

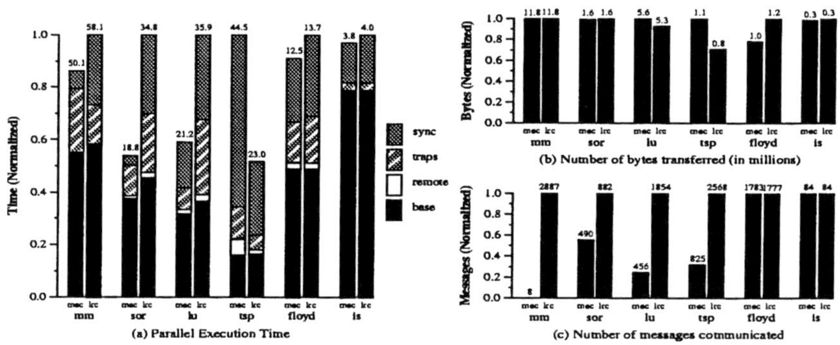

FIG. 1. *Eight processor performance of applications under LRC and MEC.*

The performance of MEC in these applications highlights the need for providing both page-based and region-based protocols within the same system. MEC requires more effort to program, and an improvement of 5% is not likely to justify this effort, whereas some of the larger improvements gained in other applications makes the corresponding effort appear justified. In order to provide insights into the underlying influences on the performance of MEC and LRC in these six applications, each of the applications is discussed in more detail below.

4.2. The Applications in Detail. MM implements a blocked matrix multiplication $C = A \times B$. The A and C matrices are partitioned into P contiguous sections among the P processors. In LRC the portions of A and C belonging to each processor, as well as all of B, are fetched one page at a time. B occupies 2304 pages, while the portions of A and C accessed by each processor occupy 288 pages each.[2] Fetching A, B, and C therefore requires on the order of 2800 messages in LRC. In MEC, on the other hand, each processor fetches exactly three regions, one containing matrix B, and two others containing the portions of A and C to be used by that processor, using a corresponding small number of messages. However, the advantage gained in MEC by reducing the number of messages is significantly hampered by increased contention that results from the size of the regions (9 MB for B and over 1 MB for each portion of A and C) and the fact that they are all accessed synchronously from one processor prior to beginning the computation. In the LRC version of MM, the interleaving of page requests with computation causes page requests to be distributed more randomly and therefore these requests experience less contention. Consequently, the dramatic reduction in the number of messages from several

[2]The number of pages occupied by B can be calculated as the size of the matrix ($1536 \times 1536 \times 4$) divided by the size of a page (4096 KB), and the number of pages occupied by the portions of A and C assigned to each processor are 1/8th of this each.

thousand to a handful in MEC results in a decrease in execution time of only 14%.

SOR uses a Red-Black Successive Over-Relaxation algorithm to solve partial differential equations. Sharing between processors occurs along the boundary rows of two $M \times N$ matrices. In the MEC version, a separate shared region is used for each row. For $N = 2000$, each row spans two pages. Rows of this size are page-aligned in LRC using the default Treadmarks memory allocation algorithm for page-based data, but unaligned in MEC using the memory allocation algorithm we implement for region-based data (where page alignment is unnecessary). The page-alignment in LRC means that false sharing plays no role in SOR's performance for this problem size. Most of the difference in execution time between MEC and LRC is due to the fact that each MEC region comprises two pages, so that the number of messages in MEC are half of those in LRC. Interestingly, using page-alignment in LRC degrades the cache performance of SOR, resulting in some loss in performance even before communication costs are accounted for. Not having page alignment in LRC, however, has more serious implications on performance (as discussed in Section 4.3).

LU decomposes a matrix into upper and lower triangular matrices. Sharing occurs along the blocks of an $N \times N$ matrix. As in the original SPLASH-2 version of this algorithm, data is allocated so that all of the blocks modified by a particular processor are allocated contiguously. Each 64 by 64 block, defined as a single region in the MEC version, occupies 32 KB, or 8 pages. Consequently, the LRC version uses 8 times as many messages to fetch a single block. False sharing exists within each block for both LRC and MEC but is limited by the page size in LRC. Thus, while MEC reduces the number of messages, it also transmits more bytes of data due to false sharing within blocks. In this case, however, the increase in the number of bytes due to false sharing in MEC, about 6%, is less significant than the decrease in the number of messages. As a result, the execution time using MEC in LU is 41% lower than when using LRC.

TSP solves the traveling salesman problem using a branch and bound algorithm. There are two data structures of interest in TSP, each of which is defined as a single shared region in the MEC version. The first (about 800 KB in size) is used to hold the partially evaluated tours, the priority queue consisting of pointers to tours in the pool, as well as associated data structures. The second (about 132 bytes in size) is used to keep track of the current shortest path. The size of the first region in MEC causes the number of messages to be reduced significantly compared to the LRC version. However, the number of bytes transmitted is about 40% higher in MEC because of the false sharing within regions. In TSP, this latter factor dominates, as execution time using LRC is 48% better than using MEC. Breaking up the larger data structure into smaller regions in the MEC version of TSP can avoid this performance degradation, but this requires more programming effort than the more obvious (albeit naive) way to use regions in this application.

FLOYD uses a dynamic-programming algorithm to solve the all-pairs shortest path problem on a directed graph. The distances and paths between each pair of nodes are computed and stored in separate two dimensional matrices. Each row of this matrix is defined as a region in MEC. Two regions, each equal to the size of one row, are also created and used to store a temporary copy of the current row of the distance and path matrix. The size of each row is less than one page. The number of messages is about the same for both MEC and LRC, though LRC suffers from some false sharing which causes it to transmit 27% more bytes than MEC. This results in a difference in execution times of about 9% in favor of the MEC version of FLOYD.

IS ranks an unsorted sequence of keys using bucket sort. In the MEC version only one region is created and is used for the shared array of buckets. We sort 2^{22} keys ranging from 0 to 2^9 for 10 iterations. With this problem size, a region occupies about half of a page, but this page contains no other data. As a result, the number of messages and bytes communicated is the same for both MEC and LRC (except for the first transfer of that data wherein LRC transfers the entire page unnecessarily), and execution times using either LRC or MEC are nearly identical.

4.3. Data Size and Alignment Sensitivity. Variations in problem size and data alignment have a significant impact on the relative behavior of LRC and MEC. We examined three of the applications (LU, SOR, and IS) in further detail by varying the problem sizes and thus changing the page alignments of the data structures in these applications (Figure 2). In each of the three applications examined, LRC and MEC execution times are nearly identical when data is page aligned and fits on one page, but small changes in the problem size cause data alignment to change in LRC and can result in significantly worse execution time for LRC. MEC behavior is insensitive to the alignment of data to pages. Consequently, in an integrated page-based and region-based system, the decision to use MEC in an application cannot be judged solely upon the performance of the application on a particular problem size. Rather, the performance of MEC versus LRC on a range of problem sizes must be taken into consideration, and the effort required to add MEC annotations for a particular data structure must be weighed against the effort required to avoid degradation in performance due to the misalignment of data and false sharing in LRC.

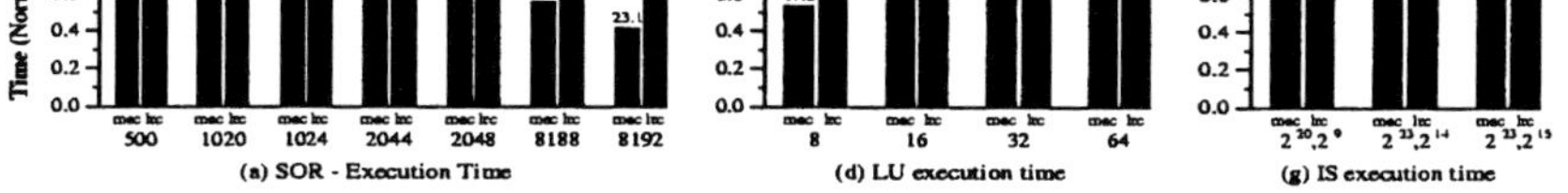

FIG. 2. *Varying input data characteristics in SOR, LU, and IS. In SOR, M* = 500 *and N is varied. In LU, the matrix size is fixed at 1024 and block size is varied. In IS, the number of keys and bucket sizes are both varied.*

5. Related Work. Adve *et al.* [1] conducted a performance comparison of lazy release consistency [9] and entry consistency [5] and conclude that there is no clear winner in terms of performance. They also point out that the performance of EC is hurt by extra synchronization and lock rebinding because all accesses to regions of shared memory may only occur after acquiring the corresponding lock. In contrast, the MEC model proposed in this paper uses no extra synchronization and requires no lock rebinding, yet retains the ability to manage data at region granularity. Further, in the three applications (SOR, TSP, and IS) that are common to both our study and the study by Adve *et al.*, our results show that variations in problem size have a significant impact on the difference between page-based and region-based data management. In SOR, for example, for the problem size used by Adve *et al.* (1000x1000 matrices), there is no significant difference between LRC and EC in their study and no significant difference in performance between LRC and MEC in our study. However, larger problem sizes in SOR favor MEC over LRC in our study.

The use of larger virtual memory pages for obtaining data aggregating effects in LRC has been previously considered by Amze *et al.* [3]. While larger virtual memory pages improves LRC performance for many applications, its effectiveness is limited by the increase in false sharing in others. On the other hand, MEC is capable of simultaneously eliminating false sharing along page boundaries and achieving much larger data aggregation, on the order of megabytes in some of the MEC applications we examine, in contrast with the 16 KB pages used in the study by Amze *et al.*.

Neves *et al.* [16] conduct a comparison of TreadMarks (LRC) and their system, called DiSOM, which implements EC. Their results show that EC can send significantly fewer messages and less data and thus obtain substantial reductions in execution times compared to LRC. The study by Neves *et al.* differs from our own in several respects, aside from the differences between MEC and EC already noted. The DiSOM system uses an object-oriented framework to avoid write trapping and exercise fine-grain control over communication, and their comparison between LRC in Treadmarks and EC in DiSOM is between two different DSM implementations that may differ in other respects as well. In contrast, our study compares MEC and LRC, both implemented within the Treadmarks framework.

Monnerat and Bianchini [15] introduce a protocol (ADSM) that dynamically and automatically associates locks with specific shared pages, in effect achieving part of the behaviour of entry consistency without the need for annotations, but still managing data at page granularity. Brecht and Sandhu [6] and Itzkovitz and Schuster [10] introduce two different techniques for managing data at region granularity without the need for annotations, using a novel pointer swizzling and page fault handling strategy in the former case, and conventional virtual memory fault handling in the latter. Both of these techniques improve the value of the MEC protocol described in this paper. Finally, Keleher [12] examined the performance impact of single versus multiple-writer protocols in a page-based release consistency context and found that multiple-writer protocols provide small improvements but considerably increase complexity. In MEC, using a multiple-writer protocol is intended primarily to allow a simpler programming style (since objects can be modified concurrently by different processors) than the single-writer EC protocol, and to allow applications to mix page and object based protocols without changing the synchronization model.

6. Conclusions. In this paper, we have presented a new model called Multiple-Writer Entry Consistency (MEC). The value of MEC is in its use of an RC-based synchronization structure while managing data at a granularity defined by the user. Thus, MEC permits the efficient integration of both page-based and region-based coherence protocols within the same RC framework. In this integrated environment, a program can be written initially for the RC model using page-based data management, and then MEC annotations added for those data structures which may obtain a performance advantage from region-based data management. MEC also presents a significant amount of flexibility in the way shared regions are defined by the user, by allowing a single region to be modified concurrently by different processors.

Our experimental evaluation of the performance of MEC and LRC shows that MEC improves execution times in five of the six applications that we study, by margins ranging from 5% to 46% for the default problem sizes, while leading to a degradation in performance of 48% in one case. These results, the first to compare page-based and region-based data management in an environment in which all other aspects of the system and the programs in the two models are nearly identical, suggests that integrating both page-based and region-based coherence protocols into one DSM framework is both practical and necessary.

7. Acknowledgements. We thank Ken Sevcik and the other members of the SIGPOW project at the University of Toronto for providing us with access to their cluster of workstations, which were used to perform our experiments. Also thanks to Paul Lu for providing us with the information needed to utilize the cluster.

REFERENCES

[1] S.V. Adve, A.L. Cox, S. Dwarkadas, R. Rajamony and W. Zwaenepoel, "A Comparison of Entry Consistency and Lazy Release Consistency Implementations", Proceedings of the 2nd International Symposium on High-Performance Computer Architecture, pp. 26-37, February, 1996.

[2] S.V. Adve and M.D. Hill, "Weak Ordering – A New Definition", Proceedings of the 17th Annual International Symposium on Computer Architecture, pp. 2-14, May 1990.

[3] C. Amza, A.L. Cox, K. Rajamani, and W. Zwaenepoel, "Tradeoffs between False Sharing and Aggregation in Software Distributed Shared Memory", Proceedings of the Sixth Conference on Principles and Practice of Parallel Programming, pp. 90-99, June 1997.

[4] E. Arjomandi, W. O'Farrell, I. Kalas, G. Koblents, F. Eigler and G. Gao, "ABC++: Concurrency by Inheritance in C++", IBM Systems Journal, Vol. 34, No. 1, pp. 120-137, 1995.

[5] B. Bershad, M. Zekauskas and W. Sawdon, "The Midway Distributed Shared Memory System", Proceedings of COMPCOM '93, pp. 528-537, February, 1993.

[6] T. Brecht, H. Sandhu "The Region Trap Library: Handling Traps on Application-Defined Regions of Memory", Proceedings of the 1999 USENIX Technical Conference, to appear.

[7] J. Carter, J. Bennett and W. Zwaenepoel, "Implementation and Performance of Munin", Proceedings of the 13th Symposium on Operating Systems Principles, pp. 152-164, October, 1991.

[8] M. Feeley and H. Levy, "Distributed Shared Memory with Versioned Objects", Proceedings of the Conference on Object-Oriented Programming Systems Languages, and Applications, October, 1992.

[9] K. Gharachorloo, D. Lenoski, J. Laudon, P. Gibbons, A. Gupta, J. Hennessy, "Memory Consistency and Event Ordering in Scalable Shared Memory Multiprocessors", Proceedings of the 17th Annual Symposium on Computer Architecture, pp. 15-26, May, 1990.

[10] A. Itzkovitz and A. Schuster, "MultiView and Millipage – Fine-Grain Sharing in Page-Based DSMs", Proceedings of the 3rd Symposium on Operating Systems Design and Implementation (OSDI '99), February, 1999.

[11] K. Johnson, F. Kaashoek and D. Wallach, "CRL: High-Performance All Software Distributed Shared Memory", Proceedings of the 15th Symposium on Operating Systems Principles, pp. 213-228, December, 1995.

[12] P. Keleher, "The Relative Importance of Concurrent Writers and Weak Consistency Models", Proceedings of the 16th International Conference on Distributed Computing Systems, May 28, 1996.

[13] P. Keleher, A. Cox, S. Dwarkadas and W. Zwaenepoel, "TreadMarks: Distributed Shared Memory on Standard Workstations and Operating Systems", Proceedings of the Winter 1995 USENIX Conference, pp. 115-131, 1994.

[14] H. Lu, S. Dwarkadas, A.L. Cox, and W. Zwaenepoel, "Message Passing Versus Distributed Shared Memory on Networks of Workstations", Proceedings of Supercomputing '95, December, 1995.

[15] L.R. Monnerat and R. Bianchini, "ADSM: A Hybrid DSM Protocol that Efficiently Adapts to Sharing Patterns", Federal University of Rio de Janerio, COPPE Systems Engineering Computer Science Department, Technical Report ES-425/97, March, 1997..

[16] N. Neves, M. Castro, and P. Guedes, "A Checkpoint Protocol for an Entry Consistent Shared Memory System", Proceedings of the 13th Annual ACM Symposium on Principles of Distributed Computing August, 1994.

[17] H. Sandhu, B. Gamsa and S. Zhou, "The Shared Regions Approach to Software Cache Coherence on Multiprocessors", Proceedings of the Fourth ACM SIGPLAN Symposium on Principles and Practice of Parallel Programming, pp. 229-238, May, 1993.

[18] J.P. Singh, W.-D. Weber and A. Gupta, "SPLASH: Stanford Parallel Applications for Shared-Memory", Computer Architecture News, Vol. 20, No. 1, pp. 5-44, March, 1992.

ON USING RELIABLE NETWORK RAM IN NETWORKS OF WORKSTATIONS

SOTIRIS IOANNIDIS†§ ATHANASIOS E. PAPATHANASIOU†‡ GRIGORIOS I. MAGKLIS†§ EVANGELOS P. MARKATOS†‡ DIONISIOS N. PNEVMATIKATOS†‡ AND JULIA SEVASLIDOU†

Abstract. File systems and databases usually make several *synchronous* disk write accesses in order to make sure that the disk always has a consistent view of their data, and that data can be recovered in the case of a system crash. Since synchronous disk operations are slow, some systems choose to employ *asynchronous* disk write operations, at the cost of low reliability: in case of a system crash all data that have not yet been written to disk are lost.

In this paper we describe a software-based approach into using the network memory in a workstation cluster as a layer of Non-Volatile memory (NVRAM). Our approach takes a set of volatile main memories residing in independent workstations and transforms it into a fault-tolerant memory - much like RAIDS do with magnetic disks. This layer of NVRAM allows us to create systems that combine the reliability of synchronous disk accesses with the cost of asynchronous disk accesses. We demonstrate the applicability of our approach by integrating it into existing database systems, and by developing novel systems from the ground up.

We use experimental evaluation using well-known database benchmarks and detailed simulation to characterize the performance of our systems. Our experiments suggest that our approach may improve performance by as much as two orders of magnitude.

Key words. cluster computing, networks of workstations, remote memory, distributed systems, transactional systems.

1. Introduction.

To speedup up I/O accesses, most file systems use large caches that keep disk data in main memory as much as possible. Published performance results suggest that large caches improve the performance of read access significantly, but do not improve the performance of write accesses by more than a mere 10% [4]. This is not due to insufficient cache size, but mostly due to the fact that data need to be written to disk to protect them from system crashes and power failures. Databases require that their data be written to disk even more often: usually at each transaction commit time. To decouple the application performance from the high disk latency, fast Non-Volatile RAM (NVRAM) has been proposed as a mean of speeding up synchronous write operations. Applications that want to write their data to disk, first write their data to NVRAM (at main memory speed). The main disadvantage of these products is their high price - they cost four to ten times as much as volatile DRAM memory of the same size [3].

The thrust of this paper is on exploring the use of remote main memory in a workstation cluster in order to speed up synchronous disk write operations frequently performed by file systems and databases. Our approach uses replication

†Institute of Computer Science (ICS), Foundation for Research & Technology - Hellas (FORTH), Crete, P.O.Box 1385, Heraklion, Crete, GR-711-10, GREECE, (markatos@ics.forth.gr).

‡Authors are also with the University of Crete.

§Authors are also with the University of Rochester.

to develop an NVRAM system, which does not require specialized hardware. To provide a non-volatile storage space, we use several independent, but *volatile* data repositories. Data that need to be written to non-volatile storage are written to *more than one* volatile storage repository. Data loss would occur, if *all* volatile storage repositories lose their data, an event with very low probability for all practical purposes. Our system uses the main memories of the workstations in a workstation cluster, as the independent storage repositories. Thus, if an application wants to write some data to non-volatile memory, it writes the data to its own memory and the memory of another workstation in the same cluster. As soon as the data are written in the main memory of another workstation, the application is free to proceed. If the workstation on which the application runs crashes before the data are completely transferred to disk, the data are not lost, and can be recovered from the remote memory where they also reside. Both local and remote workstations are connected to independent power supplies, so that a power outage will not result in data loss for *both* workstations.

2. Reliable Remote Memory Transaction Systems. The performance of transaction-based systems and file systems is usually limited by slow disk accesses. During its lifetime, a transaction makes a number of disk accesses to read its data (if the data have not been cached in main memory), makes a few calculations on the data, writes its results back (via a Log file), and then, if all goes well, it commits. Although disk read operations may be reduced with the help of large main memory caches (or even network main memory caches [2, 13]), disk write operations at transaction commit time are difficult to avoid, since the transaction's modified data and meta-data have to reach stable storage, before the transaction is able to commit. Two are the main sources of system crashes that may lead to data loss: (i) software failures and (ii) power loss.

Software failures are the result of events like software malfunctions and operating system crashes. After a crash, the contents of the main memory are lost, as well as all data that have not been written to stable storage. Data that must survive software failures are replicated to the main memories of (at least) two independent workstations. Since different workstations run different copies of the operating system, they will probably crash independently of each other and replicated data will survive software failures with high probability. [1]

Power losses are the result of malfunctions in the power supply system. To cope with power losses, we assume the existence of *two* power supplies: one could be the main power supply, and the second could be provided by an uninterrupted power supply (UPS). [2]

After studying the performance of RVM [25], a lightweight transaction-based system, and the EXODUS storage manager [7], we concluded that they spend

[1]Simple math calculations suggest that if each workstation crashes once every few months and stays crashed for several minutes, two workstations will crash within the same time interval once every several years, which leads to higher reliability than current disks provide. If, however, this level of reliability is not enough, data can be replicated to three or more main memories.

[2]Alternatively, both power supplies may be provided by two different UPSs.

a significant amount of their time, synchronously writing transaction data to their log file, which is used to implement the Write-Ahead Logging (or two-phase commit) Protocol. Specifically, the Write-Ahead Logging Protocol involves three copy operations: one memory-to-memory copy, one synchronous disk write to the log file and one asynchronous disk write to the database.

To illustrate our approach we have modified EXODUS and RVM to keep a copy of their log file in remote main memory. Essentially, we substitute a *synchronous disk write* operation with a *synchronous network write* operation plus an *asynchronous disk write* operation, without compromising data reliability. At transaction commit time, the transaction's sensitive data are synchronously written to the log in remote main memory and asynchronously to the local magnetic disk. The modified versions of RVM and EXODUS are called RRVM (Remote RVM) and REX (Remote EXODUS) respectively. [3]

2.1. Recovery. In the event of a workstation/network crash, our system needs to recover data and continue its operation. If the *local* workstation crashes, and reboots, it will read all its "seemingly lost" data from the remote memory, store them safely on the disk and continue its operation normally. It seems that there is a "window of vulnerability" during the period, that the data have been safely written to remote memory, but have not been saved to the magnetic disk. If the local system crashes during this interval, then the data that are still in the local main memory buffer cache will be lost during the crash, but may be recovered from the remote memory. Data loss may happen only if both local and remote systems crash during this interval, an occasion with a probability comparable (or even lower) to that of a magnetic disk malfunction. If the *remote* workstation crashes, the local transaction manager will realize it after a timeout period. After the timeout, it may either search for another remote memory server (if the network is operational), or just stop using remote memory and commit transactions to disk as usual. In all circumstances, the system can recover within a few seconds, because two copies of the log data always exist: if one copy is lost, the system can easily switch to the other copy quickly.

2.2. Experimental Evaluation.

2.2.1. RVM. We have implemented our RRVM system on top of Digital UNIX on a network of workstations. In this section we will describe some of our experiments to measure its usability and performance. Our experimental environment consists of a network of eight DEC Alpha 2000 workstations running at 233 MHz, equipped with 128 MBytes of main memory and 6GBytes of local disk each. The workstations are connected through an Ethernet interconnection network, a 100 Mbps FDDI, and a Memory Channel Interconnection Network. These three interconnection networks represent three different generations of LANs: Ethernet is a traditional low-bandwidth network that provides low-cost

[3]Our modification were rather small. Out of about 30,000 lines of RVM code, we modified (or added) less than 600 lines (2%). Out of 200,000 lines of EXODUS code, we modified (or added) less than 700 lines (a 0.3% change).

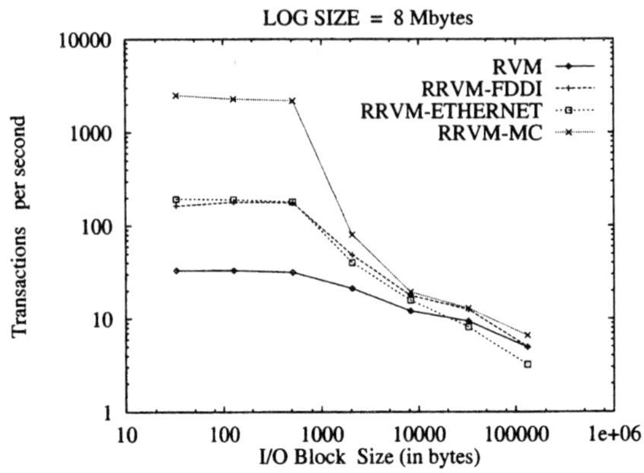

FIG. 2.1. *Performance of various versions of RVM as a function of the I/O block size - Random Accesses. Data File = 100 Mbytes, Log File = 8 Mbytes.*

connectivity without ambitious performance goals. FDDI is a high-bandwidth network that provides higher speed at a slightly increased cost. Memory Channel is a very high-bandwidth network that was designed to make possible a wide range of high performance applications in Networks of Workstations.

In our experiments we measured the performance of RRVM and compared it with its predecessor RVM [25]. We have experimented with four configurations:

(i) *RVM:* The unmodified RVM system [25]. It makes no use of the interconnection network, since all its data are stored in a local disk.

(ii) *RRVM-ETHERNET:* RRVM running on top of Ethernet.

(iii) *RRVM-FDDI:* RRVM system running on top of FDDI.

(iv) *RRVM-MC:* RRVM running on top of Memory Channel.

In order to find out the transaction throughput of our RRVM system and compare it to that of the unmodified RVM system the following experiment has been used: a sequence of 10000 transactions is executed over a 100 MBytes long file. Transactions modify file segments of various sizes.

Figure 2.1 plots the results. The unmodified *RVM* system is able to sustain up to about 40 transactions per second for small transactions. As the I/O block size gets larger, the number of transactions per second successfully executed gets even lower. All *RRVM-MC*, *RRVM-FDDI*, and *RRVM-ETHERNET* perform much better than *RVM*. For small transaction sizes both *RRVM-FDDI* and *RRVM-ETHERNET* systems are able to sustain close to 200 transactions per second, an order of magnitude improvement over unmodified *RVM*. *RRVM-MC* manages to sustain close to 2,500 transactions per second: a two orders of magnitude improvement.

To place our RRVM system in the right perspective w run the widely used TPC-A database benchmark on top of it (figure 2.1). In the results reported for the unmodified RVM system, the log file and the data file were stored on *different* local disks, so as to eliminate any interference between the accesses

TABLE 2.1
TPCA-A: Random Accesses

Accounts (×1024)	Unmodified RVM	RRVM-ETHERNET	RRVM-FDDI
32	43.2	182	230
128	40.4	144	171
512	41.6	89	96
1024	21.6	53	67

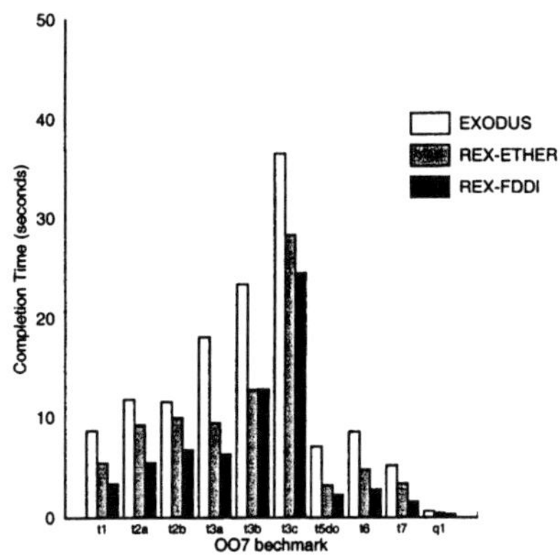

FIG. 2.2. *Performance of OO7 running on top of EXODUS.*

to the different files. The original RVM system barely achieves more than 40 transactions per second. Both RRVM systems are significantly better than the unmodified RVM. Their performance improvements range from a factor of 2.6 to 6.

2.2.2. EXODUS. Our experimental environment for EXODUS consists of a network of Supersparc-20 workstations. The workstations are connected through a 100 Mbps FDDI and a 10Mbps Ethernet interconnection network.

A common database benchmark called OO7 [6] is used to evaluate EXODUS. Three versions of EXODUS have been used:

(i) *EXODUS:* The unmodified EXODUS system [7].
(ii) *REX-FDDI:* Our modified EXODUS (REX) system on top of a FDDI.
(iii) *REX-ETHERNET:* REX running on top of Ethernet.

Figure 2.2 plots the completion time of various parts of the OO7 benchmark on top of EXODUS. REX has superior performance compared to the unmodified EXODUS systems. REX-FDDI is sometimes more than 3 times faster than EXODUS (t5do and t6 bars).

3. Main Memory Databases. So far we have demonstrated that using remote main memory to (reliably) store the log of a database system results in significant performance improvements. However, even higher performance improvements may be achieved for main memory databases, by completely eliminating the log file and by storing the entire database in reliable (main) memory.

We have designed a new transaction library for main memory databases called PERSEAS [24],[4] that eliminates the redo log file, used in the Write-Ahead Logging Protocol, as well as synchronous disk accesses by using network memory as reliable memory. A reliable network memory layer may be developed over a high-throughput, low-latency network interface, like Myrinet, U-net, Memory Channel, SCI, and ATM. Some Network interfaces, like Telegraphos [17] and SHRIMP [1], have transparent hardware support for mirroring, which makes PERSEAS easier to implement.

As described in [24], PERSEAS uses a layer of reliable network RAM to support atomic and recoverable transactions without the need for a *redo log file*. Applications can make persistent stores and atomic updates by accessing PERSEAS' simple interface. The main advantages of PERSEAS are the elimination of the redo log file and the availability of data. Data in network memory are always available and accessible by every node. In any case of single node failures, the database may be reconstructed quickly in any workstation of the network and normal operation of the database system can be restarted immediately.

3.1. Experimental Evaluation. To evaluate the performance of PERSEAS and compare it to previous systems, we conducted a series of performance measurements using a number of benchmarks, including TPC-B and TPC-C. We draw on the benchmarks used by Lowell and Chen [20] to measure the performance of RVM [25], and Vista [20]. [5] The benchmarks used include:

(i) *Synthetic*: a benchmark that measures the transaction overhead as a function of the transaction size (i.e. the size of the data that the transaction modifies). Each transaction modifies a random location of the database. We vary the amount of data changed by each transaction from 4 bytes to 1 MByte.

(ii) *debit-credit:* processes banking transactions very similar to TPC-B.

(iii) *order-entry:* follows TPC-C and models the activities of a wholesale supplier.

All our experiments were run on two PCs connected with an SCI interconnection network. Each PC was equipped with a 133 MHz processor.

3.1.1. Performance Results. The experiments conducted using the synthetic benchmark showed that, for very small transactions, the latency that PERSEAS imposes is less than 14 μs, which implies that our system is able to complete more than 70,000 (short synthetic) transactions per second. Even

[4] Perseus was one of the famous heroes of the ancient Greek mythology. Among the several achievements he accomplished the most important one was the elimination of Medusa, a woman-like beast with snakes instead of hair and the ability to turn into stone everyone, who looked at her gaze. Perseus managed to outcome her by using his shield as a mirror. When Medusa tried to petrify him, her gaze fell upon her reflection on Perseus' shield, while Perseus got the chance to approach her and cut her head. In the same way Perseus killed Medusa, the PERSEAS transactional library uses mirroring to support reliable and atomic transactions while at the same time eliminating its own opponent, the overhead imposed to transactions due to synchronous accesses to stable storage (usually magnetic disks).

[5] Sources available at `http://www.eecs.umich.edu/Rio/`.

large transactions (1 MByte) can be completed in less than a tenth of a second. Previously reported results for main memory databases [25], suggest that the original implementation of the RVM main memory database can sustain at most 50 (short) transactions per second - a 3-orders of magnitude performance difference. When RVM is implemented on top of the Rio file cache (Rio-RVM), it can sustain about 1,000 (short) transactions per second [20]. Comparing to Rio-RVM, our implementation achieves two orders of magnitude better performance. Rio-Vista, which is the fastest main memory database known to us, is able to achieve latency for small transactions compatable to PERSEAS [20].

As far as the order-entry and debit-credit benchmarks are concerned, we have used various-sized databases, and in all cases the performance of PERSEAS was almost constant, as long as the database was smaller than the main memory size. PERSEAS manages to execute more than 23,000 transactions per second for debit-credit. RVM barely achieves 100 transactions per second, RVM-Rio achieves little more than 1,000 transactions per second, and Vista achieves close to 50,000 transactions per second. For order-entry, PERSEAS manages to execute about 8,500 transactions per second. RVM achieves less than 90 transactions per second, and Vista achieves a bit more than 10,000 transactions per second.

4. Operating System Support for Reliable Remote Memory. Although our reported results demonstrate the performance advantages of our approach, they are applied only to user-level databases and transaction-based systems that are explicitly coded to cooperate with our libraries. Fortunately, our approach can be coded inside the operating system, in which case all applications will be able to reap its performance benefits. As in the previous systems we build the equivalent of an NVRAM using two volatile main memories residing in two different workstations: the client and the server. The purpose of the NVRAM servers is to accept data from clients, so that data reside in at least two workstations. A client that wants to store its data into stable storage, before being able to proceed, sends its data to the NVRAM server and *asynchronously* to the local disk. As soon as the NVRAM server acknowledges the receipt of the data, the client may proceed with each own work.

An NVRAM server continually reads data sent by the clients and stores them in its own memory. If its NVRAM segment fills up, the server sends a message back to the client telling it to synchronously write to the disk all its data that correspond to the NVRAM segment. [6] After the client flushes its data to the disk, it sends a message to the server to recycle the space used by them. Effectively, the server acts as a fast non-volatile buffer between the client and its disk.

4.1. Experimental Evaluation. The workload that drives our simulations consists of traces taken from database processing benchmarks. We use the

---

[6]Most probably all these data would already reside in the disk, since they were *asynchronously* written to the disk when they were initially sent to the NVRAM server.

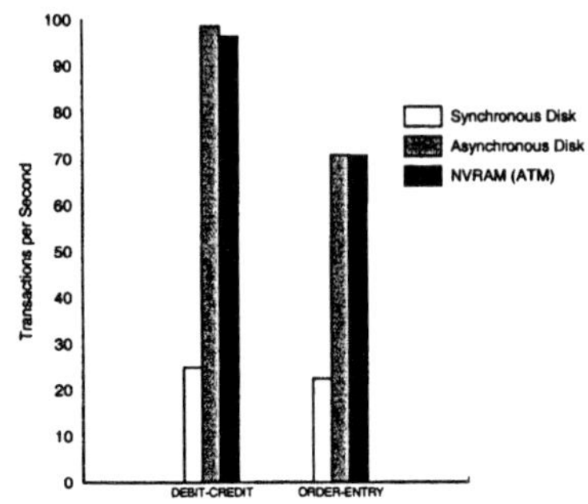

FIG. 4.1. *Performance (in transactions per second) of the three system configurations for our two applications. The disk simulated is a Seagate ST41601N.*

same benchmarks we used for the evaluation of PERSEAS, namely *debit-credit* and *order-entry*. We simulate three system configurations:

(i) *DISK:* At each transaction-commit time all operating system pages, modified by the transaction, are synchronously sent to the magnetic disk. The disk simulated is a Seagate ST41601N (modified to include a cache of 320 KBytes). [7]

(ii) *DISK-ASYNC:* This is the same system as *DISK* with the difference that the write operations to disk proceed *asynchronously*. Though not reliable, this configuration provides an upper bound to the performance of any system that would use a layer of non-volatile memory between the file system and the disk.

(iii) *NVRAM:* This is our proposed system, which at transaction-commit writes data to remote memory synchronously and to the magnetic disk asynchronously.

Our simulations were run on a cluster of SUN ULTRA II workstations connected with an ATM switch. The disk access times are simulated times provided by the disk simulator, while the data that should be sent to remote memory are *actually* sent to the remote server's memory using TCP/IP on top of ATM. Figure 4.1 shows the performance of our system as compared to traditional disk-based systems for a block size of 8Kbytes. A synchronous disk suffers a significant penalty compared to an asynchronous one (roughly 1/3rd to 1/4th of the performance); this result is of course expected and represents the cost of a simple implementation of reliability. Furthermore, our NVRAM system achieves same throughput comparable to that of the asynchronous disk (within 3%). Compared to the synchronous disk, the NVRAM system performance is between 3 to 4 times better.

5. Related Work. Using Remote Main Memory to improve the performance and reliability of I/O in a Network of Workstations (NOW) has been pre-

[7] The disk simulator has been provided by Greg Ganger, Bruce Worthington, and Yale Patt from `http://www.ece.cmu.edu/~ganger/disksim/`.

viously explored in the literature. For example, several file systems [2, 9, 15, 19] use the collective main memory of several clients and servers as a large file system cache. Paging systems may also use remote main memory in a workstation cluster to improve application performance [16, 18, 21]. Even Distributed Shared Memory systems can exploit the remote main memory in a NOW [12] for increased performance and reliability. For example, Feeley *et. al* describe a *log-based coherent* system that integrates coherency support with recoverability of persistent data [12]. Their objective is to allow several clients share a persistent storage through network accesses. Our approach is significantly simpler than [12], in that we do not provide recoverable support for shared-memory applications, but for traditional sequential applications. The simplicity in our approach leads to significant performance improvements. For example, [12] reports at most a factor of 9 improvement over unmodified traditional recoverable systems (i.e. RVM), while our performance results suggest that PERSEAS results in four orders of magnitude performance improvement compared to unmodified RVM.

Persistent storage systems provide a layer of virtual memory (navigated through pointers), which may outlive the process that accesses the persistent store [5, 22]. Our approach complements persistent stores in that it provides a high-speed front-end transaction library that can be used in conjunction with the persistent store.

The Harp file system uses replicated file servers to tolerate single server failures [19] and speedups write operations as follows: each file server is equipped with a UPS to tolerate power failures and disk accesses are removed from the critical path, by being replaced with communication between the primary and backup servers. Although our work and Harp use similar approaches (redundant power supplies and information replication) to survive both hardware and software failures, there are several differences, the most important being that we view network memory as a temporary non-volatile buffer space, while Harp uses full file system mirroring to survive server crashes. Thus, Harp requires at least twice as much disk space and puts significant pressure to the disk system, since each file is written at least twice.

The Rio file system uses virtual-memory protection mechanisms to avoid destroying its main memory contents in case of a crash [8]. Thus, if a workstation is equipped with a UPS and the Rio file system, it can survive all failures: power failures do not happen (due to the UPS), and software failures do not destroy the contents of the main memory. However, even Rio may lead to data loss in case of UPS malfunction. In these cases, our approach that keeps two copies of sensitive data in two workstations connected to two different power supplies, will be able to avoid data loss. Vista [20] is a recoverable memory library being implemented on top of Rio. Although Vista achieves impressive performance, it can provide recoverability only if run on top of Rio, which, by being a file system is not available in commercial operating systems. On the contrary, our approach provides performance comparable to Vista, while at the same time, it can be used on top of any operating system. We have run our approach on top of DEC's Digital UNIX, SUN's SUNOS, and Microsoft's Windows NT. In case of long crashes (e.g. due to hardware malfunction) data, although safe in Vista's cache, are not accessible, until the crashed machine is up and running again. In our approach, even during long crashes, data are always available, since data exist in the main memories of (at least) two different workstations: if one of them crashes, the data can still be accessed through the other workstation.

Network file systems like Sprite [23] and xfs [2, 11], can also be used to store replicated data and build a reliable network main memory. However, our approach would still result in better performance due to the minimum (block) size transfers that all file systems are forced to have. Moreover, our approach would result in wider portability, since being user-level, it can run on top of any operating system, while several file systems are usually implemented inside the operating system kernel.

Franklin *et. al.* have proposed the use of remote main memory in a NOW, as a large database cache [13]. They validate their approach using simulation and report very encouraging results. Griffioen *et. al* proposed the DERBY storage manager, that exploits remote memory and UPSs to reliably store a transaction's data [14]. They simulate the performance of their system and provide encouraging results.

Summarizing, network main memory can be used to implement reliable storage systems both in user-level and in kernel-level, without requiring any special hardware. Our experimental result suggests that our approach can result in significant performance improvements (compared to magnetic disks).

6. Conclusions. In this paper, we describe how to use the main memory of several workstations in a cluster to construct a layer of fast and reliable main memory. This layer can be exploited by file systems and databases both at user-level and at kernel-level. We demonstrate the applicability of our approach by integrating it into existing database systems and by developing novel systems from the ground up. We use experimental evaluation using well-known database benchmarks (like TPC-A, TPC-B, TPC-C, and OO7) and detailed simulation to characterize the performance of our systems. Our experiments suggest that our approach may improve performance by as much as two orders of magnitude. Based on our performance results we conclude:

(i) *Our approach decouples transaction performance from magnetic disk speed.* Redundant power supplies, mirroring, networks and fast main memories are used to provide a layer of recoverable memory.

(ii) *Our approach results in significant performance improvements.* The exact amount of performance improvement varies depending on the system measured with the highest being realized in main memory databases (up to 3 orders of magnitude).

(iii) *Our approach provides efficient and simple recovery.* Mirrored data are accessible from any node in the network. In traditional reliable RAM systems (solid-state disks and FLASH memory), recovery may take a long time, if the reliable RAM device is fixed on a single workstation that remains out-of-order for a long time.

(iv) *The performance benefits of our approach will increase with time.* According to current architecture trends, magnetic disk speed improves 10-20% per year, while interconnection network speed improves at the rate of 20-45% per year [10].

Acknowledgments. This work was supported in part by PENED project "Exploitation of idle memory in a workstation cluster" (2041 2270/1-2-95), and in part by the ESPRIT/OMI project "ARCHES" (ESPIRIT 20693), funded by the European Union. We deeply appreciate this financial support.

Dolphin Inc. donated two PCI-SCI network interfaces. Some of the experiments were run at the Parallab Supercomputing Center and at the Center for High-Performance Computing of the University of Crete (http://www.csd.uch.gr /hpcc/).

Greg Ganger provided the sources of the magnetic disk simulator. David E. Lowell and Peter M. Chen provided the sources for TPC-B and TPC-C. M. Satyanarayanan, Henry H Mashburn, Puneet Kumar, David C. Steere, and James J. Kistler provided the sources of RVM and TPC-A. We thank them all.

REFERENCES

[1] R. D. Alpert, A. Bilas, M. A. Blumrich, D. W. Clark, S. Damianakis, C. Dubnicki, W. F. E, L. Iftode, and K. Li, *Early experience with message-passing on the SHRIMP multicomputer*, in Proc. 23-th International Symposium on Comp. Arch., Philadelphia, PA, May 1996.

[2] T. E. Anderson, M. D. Dahlin, J. M. Neefe, D. A. Patterson, D. S. Roselli, and R. Y. Wang, *Serverless Network File Systems*, ACM Trans. Comput. Syst., 14 (1996), pp. 41–79.

[3] M. Baker, S. Asami, E. Deprit, J. Ousterhout, and M. Seltzer, *Non-volatile memory for fast, reliable file systems*, in Proc. of the 5-th International Conference on Architectural Support for Programming Languages and Operating Systems, Boston, MA, October 1992, pp. 10–22.

[4] M. G. Baker, J. H. Hartman, M. D. Kupfer, K. W. Shirriff, and J. K. Ousterhout, *Measurements of a distributed file system*, in Proc. 13-th Symposium on Operating Systems Principles, October 1991, pp. 198–212.

[5] M. Carey, D. Dewitt, and M. Franklin, *Shoring up persistent applications*, in Proc. of the 1994 ACM SIGMOD Conf. on Management of Data, 1994.

[6] M. Carey, D. DeWitt, and J. Naughton, *The OO7 bechmark*, in Proceedings of the 1993 ACM SIGMOD Conference, 1993, pp. 12–21.

[7] M. Carey and D. D. et. al., *The EXODUS extensible DBMS project: An overview*, in Readings in Object-Oriented Database Systems, S.Zdonik and D.Maie, eds., Morgan Kaufman, 1990.

[8] P. M. Chen, W. T. Ng, S. Chandra, C. Aycock, G. Rajamani, and D. Lowell, *The Rio file cache: Surviving operating system crashes*, in Proc. of the 7-th International Conference on Architectural Support for Programming Languages and Operating Systems, 1996, pp. 74–83.

[9] T. Cortes, S. Girona, and J. Labarta, *Design issues of a cooperative cache with no coherence problems*, in Proceedings of the 5th workshop on I/O in Parallel and Distributed Systems (IOPADS'97), 1997.

[10] M. Dahlin, *Serverless Network File Systems*, PhD thesis, UC Berkeley, December 1995.

[11] M. Dahlin, R. Wang, T. Anderson, and D. Patterson, *Cooperative cahing: Using remote client memory to improve file system performance*, in First Symposium on Operating System Design and Implementation, 1994, pp. 267–280.

[12] M. J. Feeley, J. S. Chase, V. R. Narasayya, and H. M. Levy, *Integrating coherency and recovery in distributed systems*, First Symposium on Operating System Design and Implementation, (November 1994), pp. 215–227.

[13] M. Franklin, M. Carey, and M. Livny, *Global memory management in client-server DBMS architectures*, in Proceedings of the 18th VLDB Conference, August 1992, pp. 596–609.

[14] J. Griffioen, R. Vingralek, T. Anderson, and Y. Breitbart, *Derby: A Memory Management System for Distributed Main Memory Databases*, in Proceedings of the 6th Internations Workshop on Research Issues in Data Engineering (RIDE '96), February 1996, pp. 150–159.

[15] J. Hartman and J. Ousterhout, *The Zebra striped network file system*, Proc. 14-th Symposium on Operating Systems Principles, (December 1993), pp. 29–43.

[16] L. Iftode, K. Li, and K. Petersen, *Memory servers for multicomputers*, in Proceedings of COMPCON 93, 1993, pp. 538–547.

[17] M. G. Katevenis, E. P. Markatos, G. Kalokairinos, and A. Dollas, *Telegraphos: A substrate for high performance computing on workstation clusters*, Journal of Parallel and Distributed Computing, 43 (1997), pp. 94–108.

[18] K. Li and K. Petersen, *Evaluation of memory system extensions*, in Proc. 18-th International Symposium on Comp. Arch., 1991, pp. 84–93.

[19] B. Liskov, S. Ghemawat, R. Gruber, P. Johnson, L. Shrira, and M. Williams, *Replication in the Harp file system*, Proc. 13-th Symposium on Operating Systems Principles, (October 1991), pp. 226–238.

[20] D. E. Lowell and P. M. Chen, *Free transactions with Rio Vista*, in Proc. 16-th Symposium on Operating Systems Principles, October 1997, pp. 92–101.

[21] E. Markatos and G. Dramitinos, *Implementation of a reliable remote memory pager*, in Proceedings of the 1996 Usenix Technical Conference, Jan. 1996, pp. 177–190.

[22] J. E. B. Moss, *Design of the Mneme persistent storage*, ACM Transactions on Office Information Systems, 8 (1990), pp. 103–139.

[23] M. Nelson, B. Welch, and J. Ousterhout, *Caching in the Sprite network file system*, ACM Trans. Comput. Syst., 6 (February 1988), pp. 134–154.

[24] A. Papathanasiou and E. P. Markatos, *Lightweight transactions on Networks of Workstations*, in Proc. 18-th Int. Conf. on Distr. Comp. Syst., 1998, pp. 544–553.

[25] M. Satyanarayanan, H. H. Mashburn, P. Kumar, D. C. Steere, and J. J. Kistler, *Lightweight recoverable virtual memory*, ACM Trans. Comput. Syst., 12 (1994), pp. 33–57.

FILE DECLUSTERING FOR EFFICIENT PARALLEL I/O ON NETWORKS OF WORKSTATIONS

HAU-YANG CHENG AND CHUNG-TA KING *

Abstract. This paper presents the issues involved in selecting an appropriate file declustering method to serve various access patterns on distributed parallel computing environments. A good file declustering method for multiple access patterns must (1) maximize the overall local access ratio, (2) minimize the performance variance between the access patterns, and (3) balance disk loads. The *variable striping file declustering* (VSFD) method is proposed for optimizing the file allocation in the I/O nodes with multiple access patterns and can increase the local access ratio. In addition, VSFD can provide uniform and consistent performance across different access patterns, because it is able to induce the smallest variance in local disk access ratios for different access patterns.

1. Introduction. The I/O system in a network of workstations (NOW) can take advantages of the multiple disks spread across the nodes by storing different parts of a file in different disks [2, 6, 9, 10]. Then applications can access files in parallel. If during a computation every node only has to access those data stored in its local hard disks, then there will be no communication over the network and the total data bandwidth available to the application will be only bounded by the throughput of the disk system. On the other hand if data are allocated improperly, then certain nodes may have to access remote hard disks, which incur communications over the network. This not only induces communication overhead, which is very high in NOWs, but also adds an extra bound to the I/O bandwidth. The resultant communication overhead depends on the data locality of the application file access, which is in turn determined by the relation between file declustering and access patterns. File declustering, which dictates how different parts of a file are distributed to the disks of different nodes in a (NOW) thus has significant effects on the performance of a parallel I/O system. It is very important to decluster files in an adequate way in order to reduce the communication overhead.

If a file is accessed by only one program with a single unchanged data access pattern, then it is easy to select a proper declustering method. Files however may often be accessed in more than one way, e.g. when a program accesses the file in different ways at differ phases or to pass data between each other. A typical example of latter is in designing an aircraft. A number of discipline codes are needed to analyze aerodynamics, structural designs, and performance. These discipline codes interact with each other by exchanging their data through files. In such a *multidisciplinary optimization* problem [5], different discipline codes may have different data access patterns. It becomes a nontrivial problem to find an appropriate file declustering method that allows high parallelism and high data locality for all the programs to access the files [9].

*Department of Computer Science, National Tsing Hua University, Hsinchu, Taiwan. Email: king@cs.nthu.edu.tw

In this paper, we study the issues involved in selecting an appropriate declustering method for a given file that is accessed by multiple block-cyclic data access patterns on a NOW. The data access patterns will be supplied by the users, and they will occur with an equal probability. Our goal is to find a proper declustering method for distributing the file into specific nodes. A good file declustering method for multiple block-cyclic access patterns must:

1. maximize the proportion of local accesses in all the disk accesses by all the patterns for reducing communication overhead (**locality**),
2. satisfy the majority of data access patterns, i.e., induce similar amount of remote accesses to obtain consistent performance (**uniformity**), and
3. distribute proportionate portions of data to each I/O node for balanced disk load (**evenness**).

To meet the above criteria, we propose a file declustering method, called *variable striping file declustering* (VSFD). By using VSFD, we can maintain the same average locality for each access pattern as using other simple-minded methods, but at the same time induce the smallest variance in local disk access ratios and balance the disks loads. The *common-stride descriptor(CSD)* [7] will be used to describe the block-cyclic access patterns, and to represent striping-based file declustering patterns. Because the *CSD* is closed under intersection, it can help the calculation of data locality of different block-cyclic access patterns with different file declustering methods.

The remainder of the paper is organized as follows. The system model and issues in designing the file declustering method for multiple access patterns are discussed in Section 2. Traditional file declustering methods and our proposed method are presented in Section 3. Performance results and analysis are given in Section 4. Finally Section 5 concludes the paper.

2. Preliminaries.

2.1. System Model. FIG. 2.1 shows a model of the NOW upon which our study of the file declustering problem is based. In our model each node is a complete computer system, running a full operating system with a shared-nothing disk configuration. Such a system architecture is very popular in high performance computing and has been a cost-effective alternative to expensive supercomputers.

With hard disks attached to the individual nodes, a file I/O request in such a system may be satisfied locally or remotely, depending on the location of the requested data. It is essential to distribute the data properly across the disks so as to increase the local disk access ratio, or data locality, and to reduce the communication overhead. File declustering thus has significant effects on the performance of a parallel I/O system.

2.2. The Mapping Problem. Scientific programs usually access their data with some patterns. Such a characteristic is captured by parallel programming languages such as HPF, which provide intrinsics to allow users to specify their data access patterns. On the other hand, when files are distributed to hard disks in a parallel I/O system, they also need a specific declustering pattern. In

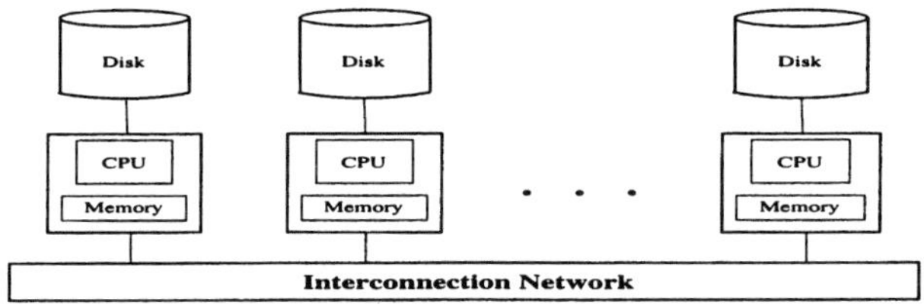

FIG. 2.1. *The system model*

a system such as that shown in FIG. 2.1, if the data access pattern matches the file declustering pattern well, then a majority of file accesses can be satisfied locally as shown in FIG. 2.2(b). Otherwise we will see a lot of remote file accesses, see FIG. 2.2(a), which increase the communication overhead and degrade the performance of the computation. Obviously, different file declustering patterns result in very different performance. Therefore, file declustering is critical to the performance of parallel I/O systems.

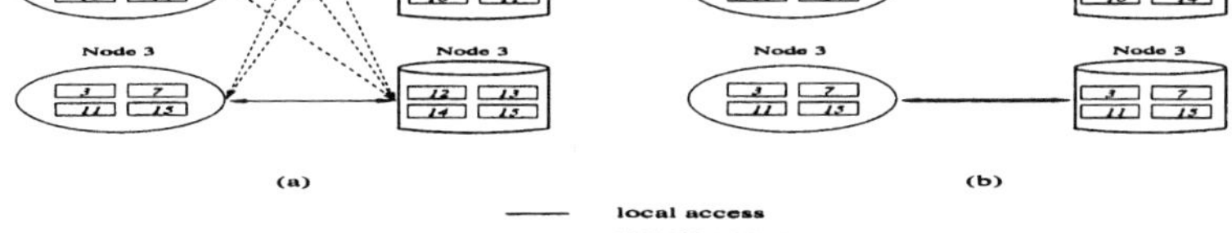

FIG. 2.2. *The mapping between file declustering and data access*

2.3. Multiple Access Patterns. When a file is accessed by only one application with a single access pattern, its declustering is very simple — using the data access pattern as the file declustering pattern. However, if the application has several different access patterns or the file is accessed by several different applications with different patterns, e.g., in multidisciplinary optimization codes, then it is very difficult to come up with a single file declustering pattern that can match all data access patterns.

For example, with the file declustering pattern shown in FIG. 2.2(b), if there is another program which needs to access array A in a block fashion, then no matter how the file is declustered one program (or even both) will have to access its data from remote hard disks. In either case, 75% of data accesses in one of the programs will have to go through the network. Although this results in a 62.5% local data access ratio in average, all communication loads are come from one of the access patterns. Obviously, the I/O performance of different access patterns will be very different. In other words, the I/O processing time will not be consistent between applications with different access patterns to a file. Note that a balanced communication load allows more opportunities for latency tolerating with overlapped communications and disk accesses. Therefore, keeping the variance of remote access ratios of different access patterns low is an important factor in file declustering.

3. File Declustering. File declustering is the spreading of a file across multiple disks. A proper file declustering method increases the ratio of local disk accesses and satisfies a majority of common data access requests. Moreover, it also balances the loads of the disks.

3.1. Constant Striping for File Declustering. Most parallel file systems employ a linear model to decluster files. Under the linear file model, the given file is declustered using a fixed and constant *striping unit* [3, 12]. The striping unit is the sequence of logically contiguous data (records) that are also physically contiguous within a disk. File data are distributed in striping units to the disks in a round-robin manner. A *stripe* consists of the data distributed in one round. Suppose the given file contains N records, numbered from 0 to $N-1$. Let s be the striping unit used to decluster the file. Then the data allocated in each node by using constant-stripe file declustering method can be represented by a *CSD* [7]:

$$\varphi(p) = ((l_1, l_2, \ldots, l_s) : (u_1, u_2, \ldots, u_s) : S),$$

where $0 < i \leq s$, $l_i = p \times s + i$, $u_i = N$, and $S = s \times P$. In the expression, P is the total number of nodes and S is the stride of applying the striping unit s on the P nodes. The notations $l_1, \ldots, l_s$, and $u_1, \ldots, u_s$ denote the lower bounds and uper bounds of the allocated records. Thus, $l_1, \ldots, l_s$ are the first block of records assigned to node P, $l_1 + S, \ldots, l_s + S$ are the second block of records, and so on. The set $\varphi(p)$ contains all records which are distributed to node p according to the striping unit s.

Now suppose the file is accessed by applications using several different block-cyclic access patterns. Let M be the total number of such access patterns, each having a block size of b_k, $0 \leq k < M$. These access patterns can again be described using *CSDs*:

$$\psi(k, p) = ((l_1, l_2, \ldots, l_{b_k}) : (u_1, u2, \ldots, u_{b_k}) : S_m),$$

where $(0 < j \leq b_k)$, $l_j = p \times b_k + j$, $u_j = N$, and $S_m = b_k \times P$. From these representations, the amount of local disk accesses, denoted as Γ, can be obtained as

$$(3.1)\ \Gamma = \sum_{p=0}^{P-1} (\|\psi(1,p) \cap \varphi(p)\| + \|\psi(2,p) \cap \varphi(p)\| + \ldots + \|\psi(i,p) \cap \varphi(p)\|).$$

Given a file and the patterns to access the file, the file declustering problem now becomes that of determining the constant striping unit s which maximizes Γ. This problem has been solved in [9].

Consider the example in which the given file contains 24 records and is to be spread among four nodes. The file will be referenced by three access patterns, A, B and C, which access the file data in block-cyclic fashion with block sizes 1, 4 and 6 respectively. Fig. 3.1 shows the total hits to local disks by A, B and C under declustering with a stripping unit of 1, 4, and 6. As is shown in fig. 3.1,

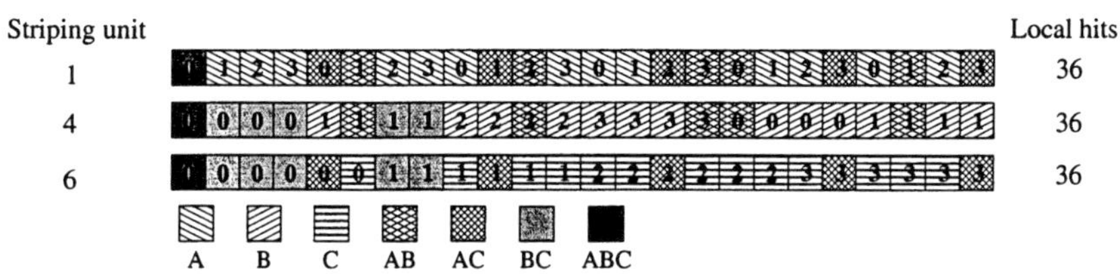

FIG. 3.1. *Local disk hits by three access patterns under constant striping*

we can get the same number of hits to local disks when the file is declustered using the striping unit of one of the three access patterns. The total number of local disk hits by the three access patterns under striping unit 1 is 36, giving an overall local access ratio of 50%. However, if we look at the accesses by the patterns individually, we can see that their local hits vary very much. When the striping unit is 1, the declustering method matches the access pattern of A perfectly and A hits a local disk for every file access, giving a local access hits of 24. But patterns B and C both have only 6 local hits. In other words, the I/O access requests from patterns B and C introduce extensive communication loads.

Basically, when an access pattern has a block size equal to the striping unit of the file, there is a perfect match and all file accesses are local accesses. However other access patterns, which have a block size different from the file striping unit, may have a very low local hit ratio and the ratio is inversely proportional to the number of nodes. This in turn causes applications using these patterns to run poorly.

From the above discussion, we can see that a good file declustering method must not only achieve the maximum local hit ratio, but also maintain consistent performance across different applications and access patterns. Apparently, a constant-striping file declustering method is not sufficient when a file is referenced by several access patterns.

3.2. Variable Striping for File Declustering. From the discussion in the previous subsection, we can see that a single constant striping unit is not sufficient to serve multiple access patterns. In this subsection we propose a new file declustering method, which uses a variable striping unit.

The basic idea of our method is to partition a file into several chunks. Each chunk is declustered with a particular striping unit. Suppose there are M different patterns to access a given file, each having a block size. Those block sizes are used as the striping units of file declustering, and the striping units are sorted in a decreasing order. The variable-striping file declustering method partitions the file into M equal-sized chunks. The i-th chunk is spread to the multiple hard disks with a striping unit of s_i. The assignment of the records in chunk i to the nodes is calculated as follows. Suppose the j-th record of the file is in chunk i. Then the node which contains this record is:

$$p(j) = \lfloor j/s_i \rfloor \mod P. \tag{3.2}$$

Note that this expression uses the global address of record j in the file. Note also that the assignment is fixed whenever the striping unit to be applied to the chunk is known.

Using this declustering method, each access pattern has at least one chunk whose declustering pattern matches the access pattern perfectly. This in turn results in at least $1/M$ file accesses to the local disks. In other words, the local access ratio must be greater than $1/M$ for each access pattern, no matter how nodes are scaled in the system. The result is that the communication overhead generated by the I/O operations will not vary much from access patterns to access patterns, and the performance of different applications can be maintained.

Suppose a file is equally partitioned into nc chunks and the global address of the first record in each chunk is divisible by every striping unit. The data distributed to node p according to the striping unit s_i in the i-th chunk can be represented by a *CSD*:

$$\varphi_i(p) = ((l_1, l_2, \ldots, l_{s_i}) : (u_1, u_2, \ldots, u_{s_i}) : S),$$

where

$$\begin{aligned} l_k &= p_i(p) \times s_i + c_i + k, & u_k &= c_i + N/nc & \forall k, 0 < k \le s_i, \\ S &= s_i \times P, & c_i &= i \times N/nc, \\ p_i(p) &= (P + p - p(c_i)) \bmod P. \end{aligned}$$

The c_i is the address of the first record in chunk i. The $p_i(p)$ is the sequence number of node p in the i-th chunk, i.e., if the first stripe in chunk i is allocated to the node $p(c_i)$, the first stripe to be allocated to node p is the $p_i(p)$-th stripe in the chunk. The data allocated in each node by using the variable-striping file declustering method can be represented by a union of *CSDs*:

$$\varphi_v(p) = \bigcup_{i=0}^{nc-1} \varphi_i(p).$$

The amount of local disk accesses can be obtained as

$$L_v = \sum_{p=0}^{P-1} (\|\psi(1,p) \cap \varphi_v(p)\| + \|\psi(2,p) \cap \varphi_v(p)\| + \ldots + \|\psi(i,p) \cap \varphi_v(p)\|). \tag{3.3}$$

Consider the example shown in Fig. 3.1 again. Since there are three access patterns, A, B and C, we can divide the file into three chunks. Each chunk has 8 records. The first, second and third chunks are declustered according to the block size of C, B and A, i.e., 6, 4 and 1, respectively. The result of using the variable-striping file declustering method is shown in Fig. 3.2. Using this declustering method, we can obtain 38 local hits with an average local access ratio of 38/72 = 52.8%. If we look at the patterns individually, we can see that A hits local disks 12 times, and B and C both have 13 local hits. The difference in local access hits is very small between those three patterns. This implies that they have similar communication performance in file I/O. One drawback of the

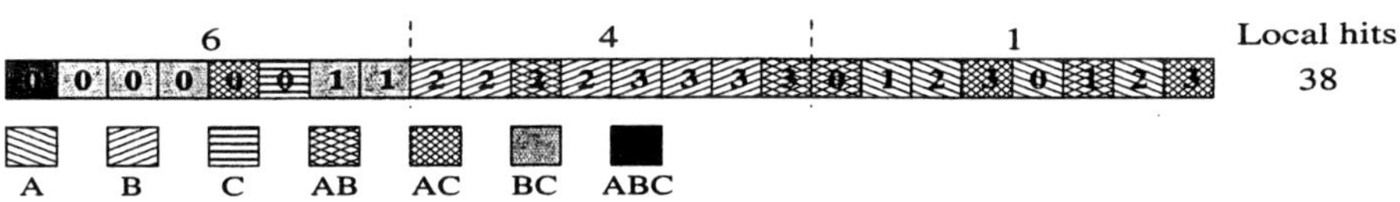

FIG. 3.2. *Local disk hits by three access patterns using variable striping*

simple variable-striping file declustering method discussed above is that it may cause disk loads imbalance. As shown in Fig. 3.2, 83% of the file data are placed in nodes 0, 2 and 3, and node 1 is allocated only 1/6 of the data. In other words, 83% of the disk I/O operations go to nodes 0, 2 and 3 and increase their workload. To solve this problem, we must distribute the file evenly to the nodes.

Note that if the size of the striping unit times the number of nodes is not a factor of the number of records within a chunk, the chunk cannot be evenly distributed. In the previous example, data in the third chunk are equally allocated among the four nodes, but data in the first chunk are only spread over nodes 1 and 2, and in the second chunk spread over nodes 2 and 3. This is because the first and second chunk have a very large striping unit. In the following we will give a heuristic method to solve the unevenness problem.

This heuristic first partitions the file into $M \times P$ chunks and then selects P chunks for each access pattern. The problem is how these P chunks are selected?

Let cn be the number of records in a chunk. First, we classify the striping units of the access patterns into the following categories: (1) $cn \bmod (s_i \times P) = 0$, (2) $cn \bmod s_i = 0$, (3) $s_i > cn$, and (4) the others. If a striping unit s_i satisfies condition (1), data can be equally distributed to every node no matter which chunk the access pattern is applied to. Next, consider a striping unit s_i which satisfies condition (2), where $cn = k \times s_i$. We can partition all chunks in the file into k groups. The j-th chunk belongs to the group ($j \bmod k$). Now if we apply the striping unit s_i to any chunk j in the first group, then according to Eq.(3.2) the first s_i records of the chunk will be assigned to node 0, the second s_i records to node 1, ..., the last s_i records to node $(k-1) \bmod P$. Similarly, if we pick any chunk in the second group and apply the striping unit s_i, then the first s_i records will be assigned to node ($k \bmod P$) according to Eq.(3.2), ..., and the last s_i records to node ($2k - 1 \bmod P$). We can see that the node assignments are in a sequential order across chunks of successive groups. Thus if we pick any P/k chunks from every group, then data in these chunks can be evenly spread into every node with the striping unit of s_i. For s_i satisfying (3), if there exists P chunks in each chunk that all records are allocated to the same node, and the nodes assigned to different chunks are different, then these chunks also can be equally distributed by using s_i as a striping unit. The heuristic declustering procedure then consists of the following steps:

- For each s_i satisfying condition (3), find out a set of P chunks that each can be allocated to one distinct node. If no such a set exists, then put the striping unit into the fourth category.
- For each s_i in category two, partition the chunks into k groups and select (P/k) chunks from each group. If it is not possible to select such P chunks, then put the striping unit into the fourth category.
- For each s_i in the fourth category, apply a greedy method to allocate P chunks, starting with the largest striping unit until the smallest. Given a striping unit, the greedy method first selects a chunk at random. It then calculates the distribution of the records to the nodes according to Eq.(3.2), and notes the node which is allocated the least number of records. It then searches a second chunk, whose distribution according to Eq.(3.2) would allocate the most number of records to the node recorded in the first chunk. This process continues until P chunks are selected.
- For each s_i satisfying condition (1), pick any P chunks from the remaining chunk.

The file declustering by applying the heuristic method to the previous example is shown in Fig. 3.3. Using this declustering method, the three patterns can obtain the same amount of local hits as in the previous simple method. Moreover, every node is allocated the same number of records. Thus, **evenness** is achieved in this example with the heuristic VSFD method. Note that however there is no guarantee that data will be distributed uniformly all the time.

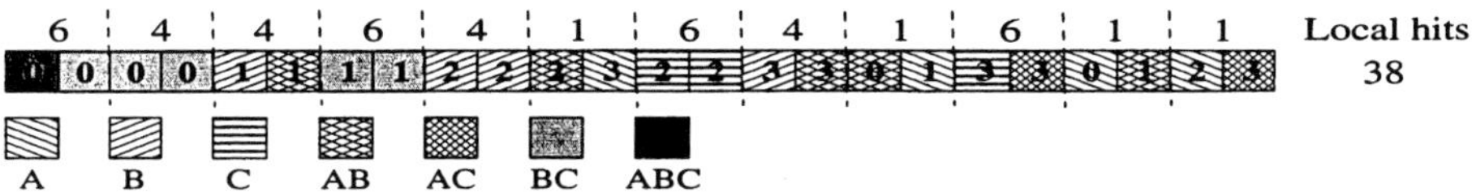

FIG. 3.3. *Local disk hits using variable striping with even data distribution*

4. Performance Evaluation. In this section we evaluate the performance of the proposed VSFD method. We first use an analytical model to evaluate the performance and then verify the results with experiments.

4.1. Performance by Analysis. In a NOW, the performance bound of a parallel I/O system is determined primarily by the disk bandwidth and the communication bandwidth. Let D_b be the total disk bandwidth available on each node. In the ideal case in which all disks are operating in their full speed and all I/O operations can be overlapped fully with the communication operations, the maximum bandwidth for an I/O operation is given by

$$\min\{B_d, \frac{B_c}{\gamma}\},$$

where $B_d (= P \times D_b)$ is the total disk bandwidth, B_c is the communication bandwidth, and γ is the proportion of remote disk accesses. In this case the average time to perform an I/O operation, which reads every element in the file using the M possible access patterns, is given by

$$T_{avg} = \frac{\sum_{i=1}^{M} \max\{\frac{N}{B_d}, \frac{\gamma \times N}{B_c}\}}{M}. \tag{4.1}$$

The average bandwidth of the given declustering scheme can be obtained as follows.

$$B_m = \frac{N}{T_{avg}}. \tag{4.2}$$

The fraction of the peak bandwidth that this declustering scheme results in is determined as

$$F_p = \frac{B_m}{B_d}. \tag{4.3}$$

From the above equations, we can see that if the rate at which remote disks are accessed per access pattern is smaller than B_c/B_d, then the disks can be operated at their full speed in the ideal case. Apparently, to stay within this bound the file must be declustered in such a way that the local access ratio is large and the variance of different access patterns is small. Furthermore, when the remote access proportions of the access patterns are small, the same network bandwidth can also serve more disks.

In the following we apply the above analytic model to two cases and see how VSFD performs. In the first case, two applications, A and B, need to access a file with each node accessing 6 Mbyte data. Let P be the number of nodes. Then, the file size is equal to $6 \times P$ Mbytes. The two applications access the file with data access patterns of *block_cyclic(1M)* and block_cyclic(6M) respectively. We use the notation CSFD to denote the constant striping file declustering method, and VSFD the variable striping file declustering method. In the second case, another application, C, also accesses the same file with the *block_cyclic(4M)* data access pattern. Again each node in C needs to access 6 Mbyte of data.

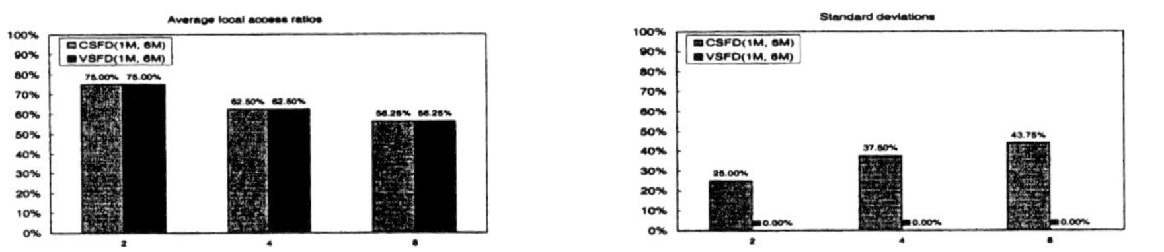

(*a*)

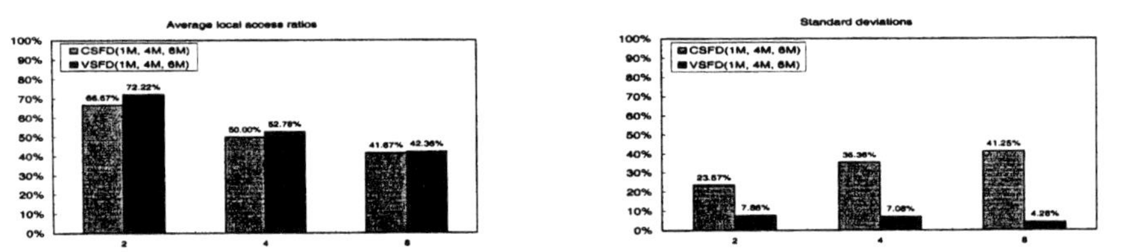

(*b*)

FIG. 4.1. *Average local access ratios and their standard deviations from the analytical model for (a) case 1 and (b) case 2.*

Fig. 4.1(a) shows the average local access ratios and the corresponding standard deviations of applications A and B in case 1. The standard deviation represents the variance of different access patterns. Note that the total amount of local accesses using the best declustering schemes from CSFD and VSFD are the same in this case. However the standard deviation of local accesses ratios of different access patterns in VSFD is zero. The average local access ratios and standard deviations of A, B and C are shown in Fig. 4.1(b).

In the figure, we can see that VSFD results in a very uniform local disk access ratio while local accesses in CSFD vary dramatically from one access pattern to another. In fact, only when the access pattern matches the declustering pattern perfectly can we get the highest local access ratio (100%). In all other cases, the local access ratios are very poor. This implies that some applications may perform well due to fast I/O operations, while others do not.

Moreover, from the standard deviation figures we can see that using CSFD the variance of local access ratios of different access patterns increases as the number of nodes increases. This implies that the performance gap between the pattern which matches the declustering pattern and others becomes even larger. On the other hand, the variance in VSFD is not affected much with different numbers of nodes. Furthermore, in the second case, if we want to get the peak disk bandwidth on two nodes for every access pattern, the communication bandwidth B_c must be greater than D_b using CSFD and $(2/3 \times D_b)$ using VSFD. When the number of nodes is 8, B_c must be greater than $(7 \times D_b)$ with CSFD and $(5 \times D_b)$ with VSFD to achieve the disk bandwidth for all access patterns. Thus, the VSFD provides better scalability than CSFD.

4.2. Performance by Experiments. Our experiments were conducted on an 8-node DEC Alpha Farm. Each node had 256 MB main memory, 3GB hard disk and ran DEC OSF1 4.0 operating system. The experimental system was built on top of the UNIX file system. There was a sever process running on each node and programs used a set of libraries to perform parallel I/O operations. Disk accesses and communications between nodes were implemented using UNIX system file functions and sockets on top of TCP/IP. Currently, the experimental system dose not provide collective I/O functions. Thus all file accesses were performed individually and each node accessed its parts of the data simultaneously.

We executed the two cases in the previous subsection. The striping unit used by CSFD was 1M. The performance results and their corresponding standard deviations are shown in Fig. 4.2.

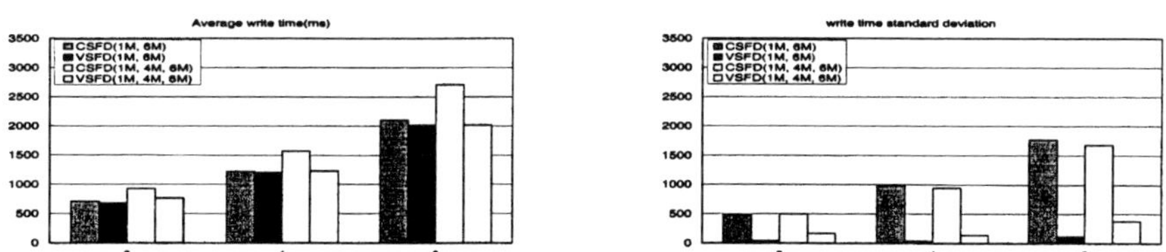

(a)

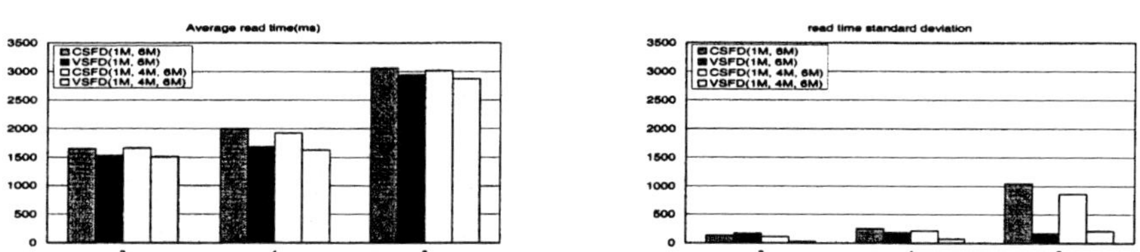

(b)

FIG. 4.2. *Average access time and their standard deviation from the experiments for (a) writes and (b) reads*

The figure shows that writes ran faster than reads. This is because the write operation returns before data are actually written to the hard disks. From the figure we can also see the performance trend is very similar to that obtained from the analytical model. This thus verifies the correctness of the analytic model and confirms the superior of VSFD.

5. Conclusions. File declustering has significant effects on the performance of a parallel I/O system, especially in systems that have high communication latencies and limited bandwidth. It is essential to distribute the data properly across the disks so as to increase the local disk access ratio, or data locality, and to reduce the communication overhead. This paper described the issues involved in selecting an appropriate declustering method for a given file, which is accessed by multiple parallel scientific applications running in shared-nothing NOWs. The *variable striping file declustering* method proposed in this paper can increase the overall local access ratios and induce the smallest variance in the ratios for different access patterns. The evaluation results confirm that VSFD can provide uniform and consistent performance across different access patterns.

REFERENCES

[1] R. Bordawekar, J. M. del Rosario, and A. Choudhary, *Design and evaluation of primitives for parallel I/O*, Proc. Supercomputing '93, Oregon, Nov. 1993, pp. 452–461.

[2] L. F. Cabrera and D. D. E. Long, *Using data striping in a local area network*, Technical Report UCSC-CRL-92-09, Univ. California at Santa Cruz, March 1992.

[3] P. M. Chen and D. A. Patterson, *Maximizing performance in a striped disk array*, Proc. the 17th Int'l. Symp. on Computer Architecture, May 1990, pp. 52–63.

[4] P. F. Corbett and D. G. Feitelson, *The Vesta parallel file system*, ACM Trans. on Comput. Syst., Vol. 14, No. 3, Aug. 1996, pp. 225–264.

[5] M. Haines, B. Hess, and P. Mehrotra, *Exploiting parallelism in multidisciplinary application using Opus*, Proc. Seventh SIAM Conference on Parallel Processing for Scientific Computing, San Francisco, Feb. 1995, pp. 710–715.

[6] J. H. Hartman and J. K. Ousterhout, *The Zebra striped network file system*, ACM Trans. on Comput. Syst., Vol. 13, No. 3, Aug. 1995, pp. 274–310.

[7] G. H. Hwang and J. K. Lee, *An Expression-Rewriting Framework to Generate Communication Sets for HPF Programs with Block-Cyclic Distribution*, Proc. the 12th International Parallel Processing Symposium, Orlando, Florida, Mar. 1998, pp. 62–68.

[8] D. Kotz and N. Nieuwejaar, *Flexibility and performance of parallel file systems*, ACM Operating Systems Review, Vol. 30, No. 2, Apr. 1996, pp. 63–73.

[9] J. K. Lee, I. K. Tsaur, and S. Y. Hwang, *Parallel Array Object I/O Support on Distributed Environments*, J. Parallel Distrib. Comput., 40, 1997, pp. 227–241.

[10] S. A. Moyer and V.S. Sunderam *Characterizing Concurrency Control Performance for the PIOUS Parallel File System*, J. Parallel Distrib. Comput., 38, 1996, pp. 81–91.

[11] A. L. N. Reddy and P. Banerjee, *An evaluation of multiple-disk I/O systems*, IEEE Trans. Comput., Vol. 38, No. 12, Dec. 1989, pp. 1680–1690.

[12] K. Salem and H. Garcia-Molina, *Disk striping*, Proc. the Second Data Engineering Conference, 1986, pp. 336–342.

A SURVEY OF MESSAGING SOFTWARE ISSUES AND SYSTEMS FOR MYRINET-BASED CLUSTERS*

RODRIGO WEBER DOS SANTOS, RICARDO BIANCHINI, AND CLAUDIO L. AMORIM †

Abstract. Several messaging software architectures (MSAs) have been proposed that entirely remove the operating system from the critical communication path, providing direct user-level access to the network interface and avoiding excessive data copying. In this paper we discuss the most important design issues and tradeoffs related to the functionality and performance of MSAs: the communication model, DMA versus programmed I/O transfers, data copying and protection, message pipelining, message arrival notification, and reliability. In order to illustrate how these issues and tradeoffs are tackled in modern systems, we survey a large number of recently proposed MSAs for the Myrinet interconnection network, including AM, FM, U-Net, VMMC, BIP, PM, and Trapeze.

Key words. Cluster computing, Messaging software, Myrinet network

1. Introduction. Historically, the operating system has been responsible for all tasks related to the communication between processes in message-passing systems. As a result, the critical path of a message from its source to destination has traditionally included expensive operations, such as several crossings of the operating system boundary, plenty of data copying at both ends, and protection checking. Needless to say, operating system overhead has always accounted for a non-negligible fraction of the messaging overhead. Nevertheless, this overhead was never the most important concern for high-performance message-passing system designers, since local-area networks (LANs) were themselves pretty inefficient.

This scenario has changed significantly in the last few years with the advent of high-performance (Gbit/s) LANs, such as ATM and Myricom's Myrinet. Initial experience with these networks showed that overall communication performance did not improve significantly; the messaging software of those days simply overwhelmed most of the gains in network performance. Careful analysis showed that the operating system involvement was the main contributor to the messaging software overhead.

Recently, several messaging software architectures (MSAs) have been proposed that entirely remove the operating system from the critical communication path, providing direct user-level access to the network interface and avoiding excessive data copying. In some MSAs protection checks are still performed by the operating system however, but protection is only enforced once, instead of every time a message is sent. These features reduce the software overhead significantly, bringing communication latency and bandwidth close to the hardware limits. Efficient messaging software layers are the reason why cluster computing

*This work was supported by Brazilian CNPq, CAPES, and FINEP.

†COPPE Systems Engineering, Federal University of Rio de Janeiro, Rio de Janeiro, Brazil 21945-970, {rodrigo,ricardo,amorim}@cos.ufrj.br

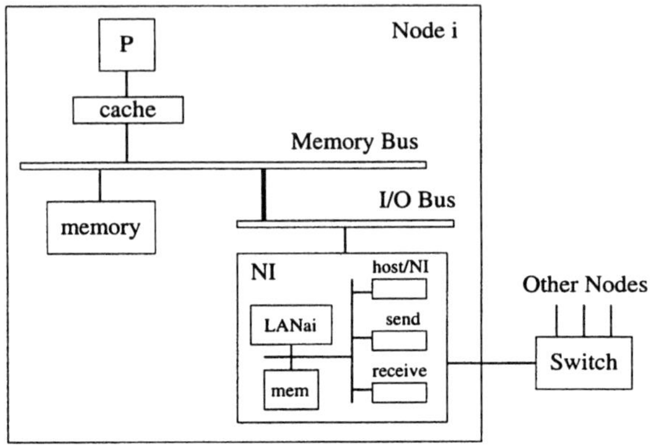

FIG. 1. *Organization of Myrinet-Based Cluster.*

is currently gaining wide acceptance.

In this paper we discuss the most important design issues and tradeoffs related to the functionality and performance provided by MSAs: the communication model, direct memory access (DMA) versus programmed I/O transfers, data copying and protection, message pipelining, message arrival notification, and reliability. These issues and tradeoffs become particularly interesting for sophisticated I/O bus-based network interfaces (NIs) such as the Myrinet NI [3], which includes a programmable processor and multiple DMA engines. Given this type of hardware configuration, the MSA involves three software components: the operating system-network interface, the (high-level) routines that define the programmer interface and run on the workstation processor, and the (low-level) code that controls the different components of the network interface and runs on the NI processor.

A large number of MSAs have recently been proposed and implemented for the Myrinet. We overview 9 of these MSAs and their various versions for a total of 13 systems: AM [7] and AM-II [15], FM [13] and FM 2.x [11], U-Net [1], BIP [14], PM [17] and PM 1.2 [18], VMMC [6] and VMMC-2 [5], BDM [9], MyriAPI [10], and Trapeze [21]. These MSAs differ substantially in terms of performance, allowing us to illustrate the impact of their design choices.

The remainder of this paper is organized as follows. The next section describes the Myrinet hardware. Section 3 discusses the main issues involved in MSAs. Section 4 overviews the most important MSAs that have been proposed for the Myrinet. Finally, section 5 presents our conclusions.

2. The Myrinet Interconnection Technology. The Myrinet is a high-speed interconnection technology for cluster computing. Figure 1 illustrates the architecture of a Myrinet-based cluster of workstations. The Myrinet consists of three basic components: a switch, an NI card per workstation (host), and the cables that connect each card to the switch. The switch transfers variable-length packets using wormhole routing. Many packets can be transferred concurrently, each traversing the network at 1.28 Gbit/s. The switch ensures hardware flow control via back-pressure, in-order delivery, and extremely low bit error rates.

The NI card connects to the I/O bus of the host and contains three DMA engines, a custom programmable network controller called LANai, and up to 1 Mbyte of fast SRAM. One of the DMA engines takes care of extracting incoming messages from the network link to the SRAM, another moves data in the opposite direction, and a third engine moves data from NI SRAM to host memory and vice-versa. The LANai processor runs at 33 MHz, controls the DMA operations, and runs the low-level layer of an MSA. The LANai cannot access host memory directly; all host memory accesses must be performed by the host/NI DMA engine. The NI memory stores the code that implements the low-level layer of the MSA and must stage all communicated data. The NI memory can be mapped into the host's virtual address space.

A complete MSA for the Myrinet could work as follows: (1) The user starts a send operation by using the high-level API to copy the data to a buffer (in host memory) accessible by the host/NI DMA engine. The send operation includes placing the address of the buffer at a position (in NI memory) that is constantly polled by the low-level layer of the MSA; (2) The LANai sets the host/NI DMA engine to copy the data from host memory to NI memory and later sets the send DMA engine to transfer the data from NI memory to the network; (3) On the receiving side, the LANai sets the receive DMA engine to copy the data to NI memory and later sets the host/NI DMA engine to copy the data to an address in host memory that was previously specified by a message receive call to the high-level layer of the MSA; and (4) After both copies are performed, the receiver LANai notifies the host of the arrival of a message by setting a flag in host memory that is polled by the host.

3. Messaging Software Architecture Issues and Tradeoffs. While avoiding operating system calls has proven extremely beneficial to high-performance networking, there are other important issues related to the functionality and performance of MSAs: the communication model supported by the MSA; whether data transfers are implemented via DMA or programmed I/O operations;
whether it is possible to transfer data without making intermediate copies; how multiplexing and protection are implemented; whether the NI implements any pipelining of messages; how the destination is notified of a message arrival; and whether communication is reliable. In the next few subsections, we discuss these issues in turn.

3.1. The Communication Model. The communication model or API defines how the higher-level software must interface with the MSA. Ideally, the communication model supported by the MSA should match the communication model of higher-level layers and applications. The most common communication models are:

Standard Message Passing. In this communication model, a message send operation involves specifying the destination and a pointer to the data to be transferred. The receiver is responsible for determining where in memory the data should be stored via rendezvous-style data transfers, queues of buffers, or redirection. Under a rendezvous-style implementation, a data transfer only takes place when the message receive operation is executed, forcing send and receive primitives to synchronize. The message receive operation specifies where the data should be placed in memory.

Under a queue of buffers implementation, each communicating node defines a set of free buffers where incoming data should be placed. Each entry in the queue comprises a buffer descriptor (address and length) that is used when a message arrives. After transferring the message to the specified buffer, the descriptor is moved to the reception queue, which the user can check for received messages. Another queue of descriptors is used for sending messages. The sender simply provides the descriptors for where the data to be transferred has been placed.

The redirection mechanism sits between the other two approaches. Under this mechanism, the receiver transfers the data directly to its final destination, if the message receive operation has been executed when the data arrives. Otherwise, the data is transferred to a temporary staging area and later moved to its final destination when the message receive operation is executed.

Remote Memory Write. In this model, a communication setup phase creates a mapping between virtual memory addresses at the sender and at the receiver. During this setup phase, nodes "export" the virtual pages that they intend to use as receive buffers. A message send operation specifies the virtual address where to store the data at the destination. Messages are usually sent explicitly and received implicitly.

Handler-Carrying Message. In this model, the message send operation specifies the address of a handler that should be executed on the receiver side upon message arrival. The handler task is then used to extract the message from the network and integrate it into the on-going computation.

3.2. Data Movement via DMA vs. Programmed I/O. During communication, messages must be transferred from the host memory to the NI and vice-versa. There are two strategies for effecting these transfers: via a DMA device or via programmed I/O by the host itself. DMA operations are usually more efficient than programmed I/O and free the host processor from spending time on data movement. For short messages however, the DMA setup time may be as long as the data transfer itself, making programmed I/O more appropriate. In addition, given that the DMA device only deals with physical addresses while user processes deal with virtual addresses, the user cannot configure the DMA to transfer data straight to the NI. The usual approach is then to copy data to a buffer inside the operating system kernel or to a pinned-down buffer (a region of memory in user space but with a well-known physical address and with pages marked as unswappable) before initiating the DMA operation. This memory copy generates extra overhead. Using the host itself to transfer data can eliminate the copy, achieving the so-called zero-copy data transfers.

3.3. Zero-Copy Data Transfers. The downside of letting the host processor itself move the data to the NI is that the processor is kept involved in the network operation for too long when transferring long messages. To avoid this and yet achieve zero-copy transfers, several MSAs have proposed that a TLB-like data structure should store the virtual-to-physical address translations of communication buffers. This data structure can then be used whenever the DMA must be programmed to transfer data to/from buffers that are specified by virtual addresses. Managing this TLB structure normally involves the operating system for two operations: assigning physical pages to represent virtual ones and marking all pages with translations in the TLB unswappable. The user process can manage the TLBs assisted by the NI device driver.

Based on the communication model used by the MSA, a TLB can be placed and managed at the NI memory, the host memory, or both. Zero-copy can be achieved via remote memory write with a TLB placed and managed at the host memory for send operations, if messages carry the physical address of the destination buffer. For ensuring protection however, each message usually carries the virtual address of the buffer. Under this scheme, the TLB is placed at the host memory for sending and at the NI memory for receiving.

In the rendezvous and redirection models, a single TLB can be maintained by the host processor using its own memory for storage. During rendezvous-style communication, the receive primitive can do the address translation and provide the NI with the correct physical address of the destination buffer for the incoming message, given that a receive operation must have been executed before a message arrives at the NI. Under redirection, the message receive operation can perform these same actions when executed, but the physical addresses of temporary buffers must also have been made available (at communication setup time) for when messages are received before their corresponding receive operations are executed.

In the queue of buffers model, each receive queue entry can point to physical addresses or virtual addresses. When using virtual addresses, translations are handled by a TLB at the NI. The NI must then interface with the device driver to manage the TLB on a miss or a replacement event. When using physical addresses, the TLB management should be performed by the host processor.

Sometimes the zero-copy techniques described above are not enough to really eliminate extra copies. We point out three common cases where this can actually happen. First, applications running under the queue of buffers model may be unable to determine the order in which messages will be received, making zero-copy virtually impossible. Second, if a message should contain data spread over the user space, the user may have to pack the data into a contiguous buffer before issuing the network operation. To avoid this extra copy, the MSA should provide scatter/gather operations. Extra copies may also be necessary when implementing techniques for ensuring reliable message delivery (discussed later). For instance, when retransmissions may be required for reliability, message data must be copied to special buffers in a way that the data is kept unmodified by the user process until the delivery is guaranteed.

3.4. Multiplexing and Protection. Protection is most important when multiple processes must multiplex the NI. When using programmed I/O data transfers, protection is simply an extension of the traditional virtual memory addressing implemented by operating systems. On the other hand, when using DMA-based transfers, protection becomes more complex, as mentioned in the previous subsection.

Regardless of the type of data transfer, the operating system is usually involved in setting up the communication system. For instance, in a remote memory write-based MSA, the operating system is called to create the mapping between addresses in the sender and receiver memories. After the mapping phase, all message transfers can be effected directly from user space. In the queue of buffers model, multiprogramming is achieved by creating multiple endpoint entities. Each endpoint comprises all the queues and buffer areas used by a process. Communication can then be seen as occurring between endpoints. Protection is guaranteed by using the operating system to create two endpoints and to establish a connection between them.

3.5. Message Pipelining. There can be up to four DMA operations involved during a message transfer: from host memory to NI memory (host-send), from NI memory to network (NI-send), from network to NI memory (NI-recv), and from NI memory to host memory (host-recv). One way of increasing throughput is to overlap multiple message transfers by pipelining DMA operations on the sender and/or receiver side. On the sender side of a transmission, for instance, a host-send operation may start a new message transfer even before the NI-send operation of previous message finishes. We refer to this technique as inter-message pipelining.

Another technique extends this idea by overlapping different DMA operations belonging to a single message transfer. This strategy not only increases throughput but also reduces per message latency in the same way as wormhole routing does. On the sender side, for instance, the NI-send operation for a message may start even before the host-send operation has finished. We refer to this technique as intra-message pipelining.

3.6. Message Arrival Notification. The host processor may be notified of message arrival by polling flags in the NI or by receiving interrupts triggered by the NI. The tradeoff between these two mechanisms is one of messaging latency and overhead. Using interrupts, the host processor does not need to check for message arrival, but servicing an interrupt is usually expensive. To avoid this overhead, the host processor may check for message arrival by polling a status flag maintained by the NI. The question here is how often the host processor should poll. If it polls too frequently, it may waste time on unnecessary checks. If it pools too seldomly, it may end up increasing the messaging latency significantly.

3.7. Reliable Message Delivery. Many distributed applications require that reliable message delivery be guaranteed for proper execution. Message transfers may be unreliable however, due to unreliable network hardware and/or flow control (buffer overflow) problems. In the presence of unreliable hardware, the usual approach is to use timeouts, acknowledgement (ACK/NACK) messages, and retransmission. When the hardware is extremely reliable, as in the case of the Myrinet, hardware failures can be treated as catastrophic events; the MSA may focus solely on preventing buffer overflow problems by using window-based or return-to-sender flow control techniques [2]. These techniques obviate the need for timeouts, but still require ACK/NACK messages and occasional retransmissions.

4. Overview of MSAs for Myrinet. Several MSAs have been developed for the Myrinet. In the following subsections we present the main characteristics of the most important of these MSAs.

4.1. Active Messages. Active Messages (AM) [7] introduced the handler-carrying message communication model to efficiently integrate communication and computation in parallel machines. Communication in AM is always effected in request-reply fashion. AM was first implemented on the Thinking Machines CM-5, but today the General Active Messages (GAM) specification has been implemented on several different platforms, such as FDDI, ATM and Myrinet. GAM 1.1 [16] is a specification of primitives that implement AM for SPMD-like programs. GAM ensures reliable message delivery, appropriate buffering for messages, and uses polling for message arrival notification and handler dispatching.

AM-II [15] is a new specification that also involves multi-user and protection features. These features are implemented by virtualizing the network interface through multiple communication endpoints. The NI multiplexes and schedules the endpoints. In order to overcome the lack of memory space in the NI and yet allow an unlimited number of processes to use the network, AM-II treats the NI memory as a cache of endpoints. Whenever an endpoint miss occurs, the NI handshakes with a kernel module in order to fetch the endpoint from the host memory.

AM-II supports three message types: short, medium and bulk. Short messages use programmed I/O to move data directly to the NI endpoint and vice-versa, while medium and bulk messages use the DMA. AM-II uses retransmission and timeouts managed by the NI in order to provide reliable message delivery, instead of a pure flow-control technique like the window-based reliability of GAM.

4.2. Fast Messages. Fast Messages (FM) [13] implements a messaging layer optimized for short messages. FM is similar to AM in the sense both MSAs use the handler-carrying message concept and polling for message arrival notification and handler dispatching. However, FM differs from AM in that communication in FM does not have to follow the request-reply model.

The first version of FM, FM 1.0, uses programmed I/O when sending messages, while using DMA transfers when receiving messages. This policy reduces latency for small messages, but increases software overhead for large messages. FM 1.0 ensures reliable message delivery using return-to-sender flow-control, while FM 1.1 uses window-based flow control and hence guarantees in-order delivery.

Recently, FM 2.x [11] was introduced. The changes to the earlier version of the software were driven by the need for a better interface to higher-level messaging layers written atop FM, such as MPI. The new interface includes features such as: scatter/gather support, layer interleaving, and reception flow control. The most recent version of FM, FM 2.1, also permits multiple processes per node by allowing multiple network contexts to co-exist.

4.3. U-Net. U-Net [1] is a communication architecture that completely bypasses the operating system to enable user-level access to the network, but still allows multiple user-level processes to share the NI safely. In order to accomplish this, protection is guaranteed through the communication channel abstraction, which is equivalent to a TCP connection and is setup by the operating system. To provide multiplexing, the system uses the endpoint abstraction. Each process creates its own endpoints, each of which contains a communication segment (for holding the message data) and descriptor queues (free, send, and receive).

U-Net does not implement any buffer management, i.e. the user is responsible for managing the descriptor queues and the communication segment. The communication segment has limited size since it must be pinned-down to memory by the kernel, in such a way that DMA transfers can take place.

U-Net does not provide any flow control either, so reliable message delivery must be implemented by a higher-level layer when necessary. Notification of message arrival can be implemented either via polling or interrupts. In fact, U-Net also provides a watermark mechanism, where polling is the default notification scheme but an interrupt is generated when the free queue is almost empty.

4.4. BIP. The Basic Interface for Parallelism (BIP) [14] was designed to fully expose the network performance of Myrinet to parallel applications based on the message-passing paradigm. BIP's send and receive primitives follow the rendezvous model (except for small messages which are allowed to be buffered) and can be blocking or non-blocking. For small messages, the host moves the data itself while for large messages the DMA does it.

BIP ensures in-order delivery and detects transmission errors, but error recovery is not provided. Furthermore, BIP does not allow multiple processes to share the NI and does not consider protection issues.

BIP hides packetization from the user and implements zero-copy data transfers. Zero-copy is done by pinning pages to memory on demand and maintaining a TLB in user space. The distinguishing feature of BIP is that packet size is not fixed across messages; the packet size depends on the message length and is determined according to an analytical model of message latency. The goal is to reduce latency of individual messages by pipelining all four DMA operations involved in message transmission.

4.5. PM. PM communication library [17] was proposed with Score, an Unix-like operating system, to provide a multi-user parallel environment on clusters of workstations. PM provides multiple channels so a user process can share the NI with the Score kernel communication tasks. Due to Myrinet's on board SRAM size limitation, the number of channels cannot track the number of processes running on a workstation. Therefore, PM also time-multiplexes each channel among different processes, using primitives to save and restore a channel's state.

PM uses a new flow control algorithm called Modified ACK/NACK to achieve reliable in-order delivery and yet be scalable with respect to the number of workstations (something that window-based mechanisms cannot offer). PM provides intra-message pipelining during a message send operation and inter-message pipelining on both send and receive operations.

PM adopts polling for message arrival notification but also permits interrupts. PM 1.2 [18] enables zero-copy transfers via remote memory write operations and a TLB placed in NI memory. Only 1024 pages can be pinned to memory with PM. This memory is dynamically treated as a cache by user processes, the pin-down cache. The user keeps a list of pages previously pinned-down, so as to avoid trying to pin pages that are already pinned-down.

4.6. VMMC. The Virtual Memory-Mapped Communication (VMMC) MSA [6] achieves zero-copy using the remote memory write communication model. VMMC uses notification notices to notify receiving processes. A sending process can attach a notification notice to a message that will cause a user-level handler to be executed upon message arrival. VMMC moves data from send buffers to NI memory using DMA for long messages and programmed I/O for small messages. VMMC also uses a limited form of intra-message pipelining to increase throughput.

The VMMC-2 MSA [5] extends VMMC by providing zero-copy transfers for connection-oriented messaging mechanisms, such as Unix sockets. Since this kind of communication cannot predict the correct address for message delivery, VMMC-2 also implements the transfer redirection mechanism. In addition, VMMC-2 provides reliable communication using retransmission and sender-side buffering on the NI.

VMMC-2 avoids the overhead of interrupts and NI-kernel handshakes during a LANai TLB miss event by using User-TLBs (UTLBs). Each process maintains a UTLB in host memory. Address translation and page pinning are performed by the kernel when a send or redirect command is posted and the buffer is not present in the UTLB. Since the UTLB is placed in host memory and transfers are effected by the NI DMA, the NI keeps a cache of each UTLB in its memory to speed up the UTLB lookup task.

4.7. Trapeze. Trapeze [21] was designed to support low-latency transfer of virtual memory pages by the operating system kernel. Each Trapeze message is composed by a 128-byte control message and an optional payload of up to 8 Kbytes (the page size). The control data is transferred by the host processor itself. The payload data is transferred to or from the NI by the DMA. To achieve best per-message latency results, Trapeze pipelines the DMA operations both for outgoing and incoming packets using intra-message pipelining. The DMA is done as a series of shorter DMA pulses. Short pulses achieve greater pipelining but also increase the number of I/O bus acquire operations. To resolve this tradeoff, the pulse length was chosen by running many experiments with different pulse lengths and comparing the latency results.

Trapeze does not provide any form of flow control, so reliable message delivery is left to upper layers. Arrival notification can be done by either polling or interrupts.

4.8. BDM. The distinguishing feature of BDM [9] is its ability to provide five different levels of service to the user: (1) unreliable service, where packets may be lost because of software or hardware errors; (2) bounce/unordered service, where packets may be lost because of hardware errors, return-to-sender flow control is used to cope with software errors, and packets may be delivered out-of-order; (3) bounce/ordered service, where packets may be lost because of hardware errors and return-to-sender flow control together with a sequence number is used to cope with software errors and to preserve in-order delivery; (4) reliable/unordered service, which implements ACK/NACK flow control and CRC checks to guarantee reliable out-of-order delivery; and (5) reliable/ordered service, which implements ACK/NACK flow control, CRC checks, and sequence numbers to guarantee reliable in-order delivery.

The best performance is achieved by the unreliable service. The reliable protocols are not as efficient, but can recover from hardware and software errors. Hardware errors include transmission bit errors, unplugged cables or a network switch turned off, while software errors are due to lack of buffer space on the receiving side.

BDM is implemented through descriptor queues that manage buffers allocated in the NI memory. It is up to the host to move data to and from the NI, i.e. BDM does not use the NI DMA to move data to the network. Notification of message arrival is done by polling.

4.9. MyriAPI. MyriAPI [10] is Myricom's MSA for the Myrinet. MyriAPI supports multi-channel communication, scatter-gather operations, and dynamic network configuration. It does not provide reliable message delivery. Buffers are located in a statically pinned region at the host memory. MyriAPI uses three descriptor queues (free, send, and receive) of scatter-gather message pointers that are shared by the host and the NI. Data are always transferred to and from the NI via DMA operations. Notification is done by polling.

4.10. Features and Performance. We conclude this section by summarizing the main features of the most important MSAs we discussed in table 1 and by presenting a collection of reported performance results for these MSAs in table 2. (Entries marked with "*" represent information that is missing in the original references.) These tables allow us to make several general and performance-related observations:

Communication Model. The different MSAs implement many different communication models, each of which is intended to support the system's ex-

TABLE 1
Summary of MSA Features

MSA	Comm Model	Xfer Send	Xfer Rec	0-copy Send	0-copy Rec	Prot	Pipe	Notif	Rely
AM-II	Handler	hybrid	hybrid	no	no	yes	no	both	yes
FM 2.1	Handler	I/O	DMA	I/O	no	yes	no	poll	yes
U-Net	Queue	DMA	DMA	no	no	yes	no	both	no
BIP	Rendez	hybrid	hybrid	TLB	TLB	no	yes	poll	no
PM 1.2	Queue + RMW	DMA	DMA	TLB	TLB	yes	yes	both	yes
VMMC-2	RMW + Redir	hybrid	DMA	TLB	TLB	yes	yes	both	yes
Trapeze	Queue	hybrid	hybrid	yes	yes	no	yes	both	no
BDM	Queue	I/O	I/O	I/O	I/O	no	no	poll	yes
MyriAPI	Queue	DMA	DMA	no	no	no	no	poll	no

TABLE 2
MSA Performance Results

MSA	One-way Latency in us (message size)	Max Bandwidth in Mbytes/s (message size)	Configuration
AM-II [4]	21 (16bytes)	31 (8Kbytes)	167MHz UltraSPARC, SBUS
FM 2.1 [12]	11 (4bytes)	77 (64Kbytes)	200MHz PentiumPro, PCI
U-Net [20]	13 (*)	35 (4Kbytes)	167MHz UltraSPARC, SBUS
BIP [8]	5 (4bytes)	126 (8Mbytes)	200MHz PentiumPro, PCI
PM 1.2 [18]	8 (4bytes)	114 (256Kbytes)	166MHz Pentium, PCI
VMMC-2 [5]	20 (4bytes)	93 (16Kbytes)	166MHz Pentium, PCI
Trapeze [19]	30 (128bytes)	120 (16Kbytes)	200MHz PentiumPro, PCI
BDM [9]	20 (*)	42 (8Kbytes)	167MHz UltraSPARC, SBUS
MyriAPI [10]	35 (*)	70 (8Kbytes)	* Pentium, PCI

pected applications more naturally. Given the need to support traditional message passing applications, the most common communication model has become the standard message passing model in its queue of buffers (Queue) variation. Although most MSAs implement this variation, the implementations differ in terms of their buffer management. For instance, while in U-Net the user is responsible for managing all buffer queues explicitly, in PM 1.2 buffer management is handled transparently by the MSA. Clearly the tradeoff here is one of simplicity and flexibility. In U-Net the user is burdened with the task of buffer management, but can manage buffers in a way that best matches its application needs.

Even though queue of buffers is the most popular communication model, some MSAs offer combined or extended models and hence can support a larger class of applications. This is the case of PM 1.2, which combines standard queue of buffers primitives with remote memory write (RMW) ones. As another example, VMMC-2 extends the remote memory write model with redirection in order to cope with socket-like communication. No model has been proven more efficient than the others in terms of performance.

DMA vs. Programmed I/O. All MSAs exploit DMA operations, except for FM and BDM for sending messages and BDM for receiving messages. DMA operations produce higher bandwidth data transfers, while allowing the computation and the communication to overlap. However, using programmed I/O for sending messages is required for optimizing short message transfers. As a result, many MSAs adopt a hybrid approach when sending messages to achieve low latency for short messages (I/O) and high bandwidth (DMA) for long messages. On the receiving side, transferring data from NI to host memory is usually implemented with DMA, since the I/O reads are inefficient even for relatively short messages. Furthermore, the NI memory is limited in size, leading most MSAs to DMA messages to host memory almost immediately upon reception.

Zero-Copy Transfers and Message Pipelining. The MSAs that implement message pipelining and zero-copy transfers via DMA operations (BIP, PM 1.2, VMMC-2, and Trapeze) achieve very good performance results. However, the actual implementation of these features differs somewhat across the MSAs. BIP implements intra-message pipelining by dividing a long message into multiple packets of equal size. VMMC-2 implements a similar yet limited form of intra-message pipelining where the packet size is equal to the page size (4 Kbytes), except for the first packet which is only as long as necessary to reach the next page boundary. Intra-message pipelining is also implemented by Trapeze and PM 1.2, but in these MSAs messages are not actually split; the MSAs control the operation of each DMA engine and dynamically start DMA transfers according to their progress. The tradeoffs between these intra-message pipelining strategies are yet to be addressed.

The implementation of zero-copy transfers is usually a function of the communication model adopted by the MSA. In redirection (VMMC-2) and rendezvous (BIP), the TLB data structure can be placed in host memory and managed entirely by the host. In contrast, in the queue of buffers and remote memory write models, due to their intrinsic communication asynchrony, the NI has to perform TLB lookups when receiving messages, which leads the MSAs to place the TLB or part of it in NI memory. For instance, PM 1.2 maintains the whole TLB in NI memory. Since the NI memory is limited in size, the TLB has to be fairly small. VMMC-2 overcomes this limitation by treating the NI TLB as a cache of the complete translation table in host memory. Upon a TLB cache miss event, VMMC-2 issues DMA operations to fetch the desired data from host memory.

Arrival Notification. Notification via polling is invariably provided by the MSAs, as interrupts are usually much too expensive. However, the MSAs differ in the way they implement polling. For instance, BIP and PM 1.2 poll a message arrival flag allocated in NI memory, while U-Net polls a message arrival flag allocated in host memory. Polling host memory avoids creating I/O bus traffic, but may entail greater communication latency, since the LANai must program the host/NI DMA engine to set the arrival flag. Even though polling is usually more efficient, interrupt-based notification is also implemented in some MSAs. U-Net is an interesting example of hybrid system, where polling and interrupts are combined via the watermark mechanism.

Reliability and Protection. The majority of the MSAs surveyed offer reliable message delivery and multi-user features. The support for multiple concurrent users is not always extensive, however. MSAs such as U-Net and FM 2.1, for instance, allow only a small number of concurrent users as a result of NI memory size limitations. Other MSAs overcome this problem by treating the NI memory as a cache of user information, such as the context cache of PM 1.2 and the endpoint cache of AM-II. Regarding reliability, the most robust MSAs are VMMC-2 and AM-II, which do not assume that the Myrinet hardware is completely reliable.

Traditionally, reliability and protection have hindered performance, but modern user-level MSAs can cope with these requirements without sacrificing performance.

5. Conclusions. In this paper we have discussed the most important issues and tradeoffs related to MSAs, including the communication model, data transfer and notification mechanisms, and reliability. In addition, we have surveyed several of these MSAs for the Myrinet network, including AM, FM, U-Net, VMMC, BIP, PM, and Trapeze. The MSAs differ sometimes significantly in terms of their features and performance. However, the best MSA can only be determined in face of the communication requirements imposed by higher-level software layers and applications.

Acknowledgements. We would like to thank Carla Barros, Silvio Canola, Vinicio Carrera, Eduardo Pinheiro, Raquel Pinto, Cristiana Seidel, and Lauro Whately for their comments on an earlier version of this paper. We would also like to thank Wagner Meira Jr. for suggestions and discussions on the topic of the paper. Finally, we would like to thank the referee for having suggested several extensions to the paper.

REFERENCES

[1] A. Basu, V. Buch, W. Vogels, and T. von Eicken. U-Net: A User-Level Network Interface for Parallel and Distributed Computing. In *Proceedings of 15th ACM Symposium on Operating Systems Principles*, December 1995.

[2] D. Bertsekas and R. Gallager. *Data Networks.* Prentice-Hall International, 1992.

[3] N. Boden, D. Cohen, R. Felderman, A. Kulawik, C. Seitz, J. Seizovic, and W. Su. Myrinet: A Gigabit-per-Second Local Area Network. *IEEE MICRO*, 15(1), February 1995.

[4] B. Chun, A. Mainwaring, and D. Culler. Virtual Network Transport Protocols for Myrinet. In *Proceedings of Hot Interconnects '97*, April 1997.

[5] C. Dubnicki, A. Bilas, Y. Chen, S. Damianakis, and K. Li. VMMC-2: Efficient Support for Reliable, Connection-Oriented Communication. In *Proceedings of Hot Interconnects V.* IEEE, August 1997.

[6] C. Dubnicki, A. Bilas, K. Li, and J. Philbin. Design and Implementation of Virtual Memory-Mapped Communication on Myrinet. In *Proceedings of the International Parallel Processing Symposium '97*, April 1997.

[7] T. Eicken, D. Culler, S. Goldstein, and K. Schauser. Active Messages: A Mechanism for Integrated Communication and Computation. In *Proceedings of the 19th International Symposium on Computer Architecture*, May 1992.

[8] Laboratory for High Performance Computing. BIP Home Page. http://lhpca.univ-lyon1.fr.

[9] G. Henley, N. Doss, T. McMahon, and A. Skjellum. BDM: A Multiprotocol Myrinet Control Program and Host Application Programmer Interface. Technical Report MSSU-EIRS-ERC-97-3, Mississippi State University, May 1997.

[10] Myricom Inc. Myrinet Home Page. http://www.myri.com.

[11] M. Lauria, S. Pakin, and A. Chien. Efficient Layering for High Speed Communication: Fast Messages 2.x. In *Proceedings of the 7th High Performance Distributed Computing Conference*, July 1998.

[12] University of Illinois at Urbana-Champaign. Fast Messages Home Page. http://www-csag.cs.uiuc.edu/projects/comm/fm.htm.

[13] S. Pakin, M. Lauria, and A. Chien. High Performance Messaging on Workstations: Illinois Fast Messages (FM) for Myrinet. In *Proceedings of Supercomputing '95*, December 1995.

[14] L. Prylli and B. Tourancheau. BIP: A New Protocol Designed for High-Performance Networking on Myrinet. In *Proceedings of International Parallel Processing Symposium '98*, March 1998.

[15] AM-II specification. Active Messages Release 2.0. http:// now.cs.berkeley.edu/ AM/ lamrelease.html.

[16] GAM specification. The Generic Active Message Interface Specification. http:// now.cs.berkeley.edu/ Papers/Papers/gamspec.ps, 1994.

[17] H. Tezuka, A. Hori, and Y. Ishikawa. PM: A High-Performance Communication Library for Multi-User Parallel Environments. Technical Report TR-96015, Real World Computing Partnership, November 1996.

[18] H. Tezuka, F. O'Carroll, A. Hori, and Y. Ishikawa. Pin-down Cache: A Virtual Memory Management Technique for Zero-copy Communication. In *Proceedings of the International Parallel Processing Symposium '98*, March 1998.

[19] Duke University. Trapeze Home Page. http://www.cs.duke.edu/ari/trapeze.

[20] M. Welsh, D. Oppenheimer, and D. Culler. U-Net/SLE: A Java-based User-Customizable Virtual Network Interface. In *Proceedings of EuroPar98*, September 1998.

[21] K. Yocum, J. Chase, A. Gallatin, and A. Lebeck. Cut-Through Delivery in Trapeze: An Exercise in Low Latency Messaging. In *Proceedings of the 6th High Performance Distributed Computing Conference*, August 1997.

INDEX

N

O

P

R

W

Z